Wakefield Press

In the Name of the Law

Amanda Nettelbeck lectures in the English Discipline at the University of Adelaide. She publishes and teaches in the areas of colonial and contemporary Australian writing and autobiography.

Robert Foster lectures in the History Discipline at the University of Adelaide. He publishes and teaches in the areas of South Australian Indigenous history, comparative Indigenous history, and the history of Aboriginal rights to land.

Their last book, *Fatal Collisions: The South Australian Frontier and the Violence of Memory*, written with Rick Hosking, won the John Tregenza Prize for South Australian History and was short-listed for the NSW Premiers Prize for Literature in 2002. They are presently collaborating on a third book exploring the history and memory of frontier conflict in South and Central Australia.

In the Name of the Law

William Willshire and the Policing of the Australian Frontier

Amanda Nettelbeck and Robert Foster

Wakefield Press

Wakefield Press
16 Rose Street
Mile End
South Australia 5031
www.wakefieldpress.com.au

First published 2007
Reprinted 2018

Designed by Liz Nicholson, designBITE
Typeset by Clinton Ellicott, Wakefield Press

National Library of Australia Cataloguing-in-publication entry

Nettelbeck, Amanda.
In the name of the law: William Willshire and the policing of the Australian frontier.

Bibliography.
Includes index.
ISBN 978 1 86254 748 3 (pbk.).

1. Willshire, William. 2. Northern Territory – Native Police
Corps – Biography. 3. Police, Rural – Northern Territory – Biography. 4. Australian
Aboriginal police – Northern Territory – Biography. 5. Aboriginal
Australians – Australia, Central – Government relations – 1851–1901. 6. Aboriginal
Australians – Northern Territory – Government relations – 1851–1901. 7. Trials
(Murder) – Northern Territory – Alice Springs. I. Foster, Robert. II. Title.

363.2809942

CORIOLE
McLAREN VALE

Wakefield Press thanks
Coriole Vineyards for
continued support

For Dorothy and Esme

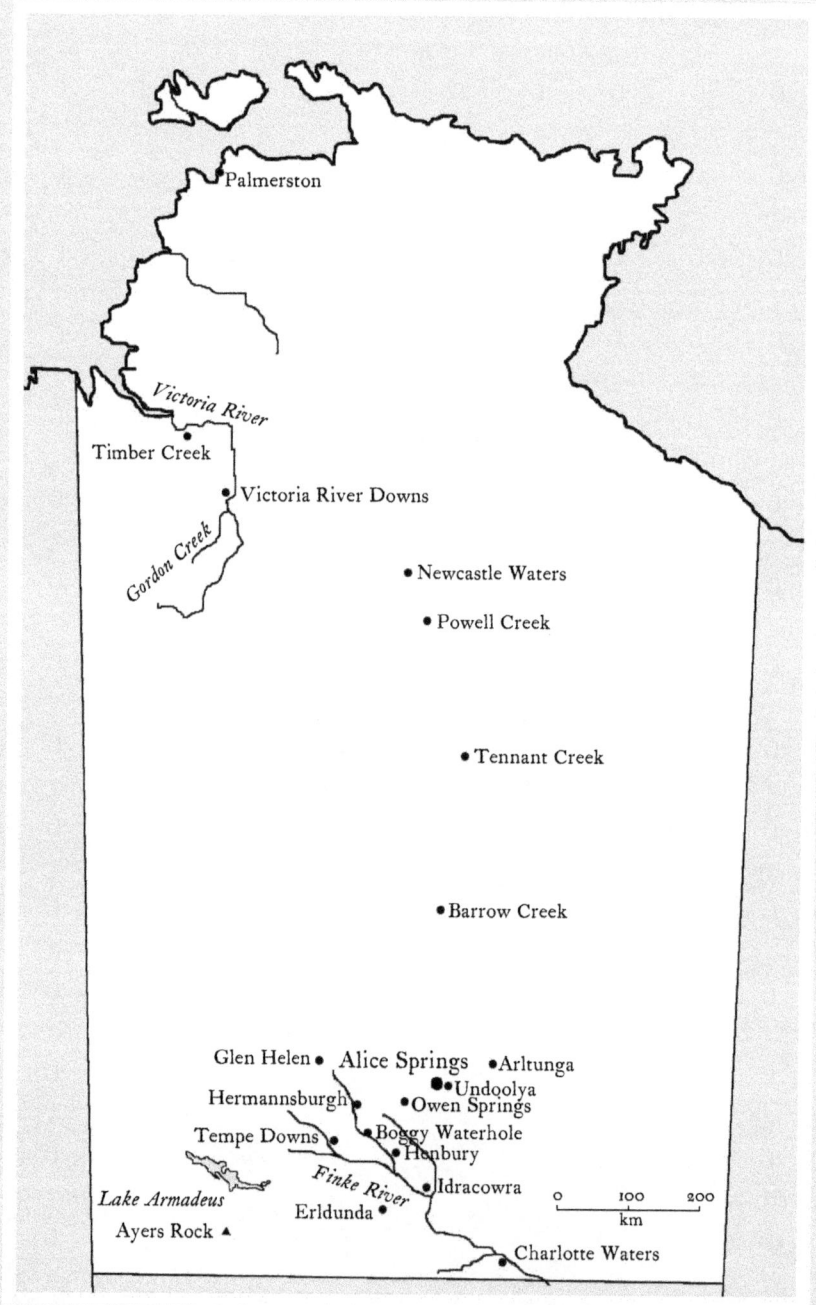

Palmerston

Victoria River

Timber Creek

Victoria River Downs

Gordon Creek

Newcastle Waters

Powell Creek

Tennant Creek

Barrow Creek

Glen Helen • Alice Springs • Arltunga
Undoolya
Hermannsburgh • Owen Springs
Tempe Downs • Boggy Waterhole
Henbury

Lake Armadeus *Finke River* Idracowra

Ayers Rock ▲ Erldunda

Charlotte Waters

0   100   200
         km

Northern Territory, Australia

CONTENTS

PREFACE

On the evening of 27 April 1891, an unusual drama was unfolding at the Alice Springs police station in Central Australia. Mounted Constable William Willshire, the Officer in Charge of the Native Police, was arrested for the murder of two Aboriginal men. Mounted Constable William South, who had spent the past decade patrolling the region as his colleague, was the arresting officer. Francis Gillen, a Justice of the Peace who in 1884 had been among petitioners for the establishment of a Native Police force under Willshire's command, was the magistrate who committed him for trial.

Willshire's career was primarily played out in the Northern Territory during the 1880s and 1890s, at a time when it was administered by South Australia. He commanded the Central Australian corps of Native Police, initially under South Australian and later under the Northern Territory administration, from its establishment in November 1884 until his arrest for murder in April 1891. During this period, when Aboriginal resistance to European incursions upon their land was at its height, Willshire's task was to patrol the pastoral districts and protect the station owners, their stock and property. His activities on this, one of the last of Australia's pastoral frontiers, fed the material for his modest literary output of three slim books. His books are unsophisticated and, from a contemporary view, deeply offensive; but they are a telling representation of the spirit of the age in the way that a caricature, through exaggeration, captures the essence of its subject.

Willshire was alert to the spirit of his time, the hardening racial attitudes and national sentiment; it shaped his sense of himself and of his role on this late colonial frontier. In his literary accounts of his frontier experiences he represents himself as an explorer in the service of his country, pulling back the veil on the remotest regions of the continent, at a time when an earlier age of exploration is gaining a mythic status in popular culture. He is the servant of science, contributing anthropological knowledge of the Aborigines of Australia, at a time when anthropological interest in the 'uncontaminated' indigenous peoples of the Empire is burgeoning. He is the representative of the law, working to make the country safe for the 'brave pioneers who push out the frontier, and are exposed to the full force of the naked barbarians'.[1] He is the hero of nascent national sentiment – the white Australian bushman – at a time when the bushman legend is still in its genesis and the nation is yet to be. By his own pen, Willshire represents himself as the hero of a frontier adventure narrative – and after his trial in 1891, he is its martyr. From his own story, he emerges as a larger-than-life character: self-aggrandising, autocratic, contemptuous of bureaucratic form but devoted to duty, romantic and violent. By his own admission, Willshire shot dead innumerable Aboriginal people in the course of his patrols in the Interior. He was also an amateur ethnographer who compiled Aboriginal vocabularies, wrote with reasonable familiarity about Aboriginal cultural life, and regarded himself as a guardian, even at times a spiritual brother, of Aboriginal people. The two aspects of his history – his policing activities and his literary representations of them – are mutually reinforcing. Each serves to justify the other.

Throughout the 1880s, Willshire and his colleagues enjoyed an extraordinary autonomy on this isolated and fragile frontier. For some years missionaries at the Hermannsburg mission west of Alice Springs had been reporting police violence against Aboriginal people but, in an atmosphere of knowing complicity between police and pastoralists, their concerns were easily dismissed. But by the turn of the next decade in 1890, pastoral settlement was spreading, mining interests were expanding, and so was the administrative reach of government. The autonomy that came with isolation was diminishing. It is perhaps appropriate that, when he had outlived his usefulness as a frontier officer, Willshire's superiors relegated him to the life of an obscure country policeman, the posterity he coveted surviving only as a form of notoriety attached to an age that had passed. Willshire became marginal to the very story he presumes to tell, subsumed within a larger story that his policing helped to shape, that his writings clumsily prefigure, but in which he eventually has no role.

What were the forces that led to Willshire's rise to the power he held, and then to its decline? It is difficult not to regard him as an aberrant personality who, through circumstance, came to hold an extraordinary measure of authority at a time in which frontier law was its own business, in an arena of several hundred kilometres' radius that was beyond the range of metropolitan surveillance. But to analyse his story solely in terms of an aberrant and paradoxical personality would be a mistake. His personality is more important in understanding the record of his actions than it is in explaining them. Willshire's history is important, not only for what he did and what he wrote, but also for his place within a late nineteenth-century culture that worked, knowingly and systematically, towards the service of white nationhood.

At the time of Willshire's arrival there, Central Australia was perceived as being both the middle of nowhere and the heart of colonial endeavour. It was also the metaphorical heartland for an emerging national figure in colonial fiction and popular culture more generally: the explorer/bushman. In his three books, published between 1888 and 1896, Willshire justified the brutality of his policing activities in terms of this evolving national myth. What his story illuminates is the paradoxical logic of a late settler colonial culture, a logic that seamlessly combines the recognition and the elimination of indigeneity.[2]

The most potent site of this paradoxical logic is the frontier. As Deborah Bird Rose identifies it, the Australian frontier is a site of antici-pated nationhood, the place that dismantles the Aboriginal past and casts the shape for the nation's future. The frontier, writes Rose, 'is a cauldron of modernity, a time and place where modern culture simultaneously reveals its capacity for destruction and reinvents its own myth of creation.'[3] In this sense 'the frontier is quite explicitly not the nation, but rather a site for the making of the nation'.[4] This is a story that takes place in such a site for the making of the nation. It is a story of contradictions, and those contradictions provide a vivid insight into the construction of race and nationalism disguised under the rule of the law.

OPENING THE CENTRE

Several years before William Willshire's arrival in Central Australia, on 22 February 1874, seven white men and an Aboriginal employee, outside of his own country, sat talking in the dusk outside the northern wall of the Barrow Creek telegraph station. The Overland Telegraph Line had only recently been completed and it now linked the entire continent from south to north. It was a tool of empire that in the coming decade would provide a nodal point for pastoral and mining expansion, and mark the beginning of permanent European settlement.[1] At this stage, though, Barrow Creek was one of four isolated stations in the Centre – the others were Alice Springs, Charlotte Waters and Tennant Creek – that monitored the Overland Telegraph Line and provided a departure point for exploration.[2]

As the dusk settled, a large party of Kaytetye men approaching from the gully to the south attacked the station.[3] In the first volley of spears the stationmaster, James Stapleton, was struck in the chest. The eight Barrow Creek men rushed towards the building's only entrance gate, around the corner on the eastern side. Finding the gate blocked by the attackers, they circled the building but, with nowhere to go, they made another dash for the entrance. Linesman John Frank was struck by a spear before he reached it, and died instantly. Three others, including Stapleton and the Aboriginal employee Jemmy, had been wounded, but seven had now reached the safety of the station building and their Snider rifles. They had trouble taking aim at their attackers through the loop-holes strategically built into the fortified structure, but they managed to shoot dead at least two Kaytetye men. Outside, the attacking party retreated, but did not leave.

Overhead, the Line remained intact. The embattled men used it to wire to Adelaide with news of the attack. The closest reinforcements were a travelling line-repair party, 130 kilometres and two days' journey away. The Adelaide telegraph office buzzed with the need to organise reinforcements for Barrow Creek, and the Commissioner of Police wired the besieged station to tell the men to save their ammunition by only firing with effect.[4] Meanwhile the stationmaster, James Stapleton, lay mortally wounded. Before he died, he wired a message to his wife, who had been brought to the Adelaide telegraph office to receive it. A young Francis Gillen, the Adelaide operator, later recalled that it had been his 'painful duty' to conduct the 'telegraphic conversation between the dying man on the Barrow and his heart-broken-wife in Adelaide'.[5] Stapleton's last message is said to have read, 'God Bless you and the children.' The other wounded man, Ernest Flint, would recover; through the Line, a doctor in Adelaide, Dr Charles Gosse, was consulted each hour or so on the treatment of his injury. The fate of the injured Aboriginal station hand, Jemmy, was not recorded at the time. Four days later, and after another attack from the Kaytetye party outside, the Tennant Creek line-repair party arrived as reinforcements and relief.[6]

Contemporary speculations about why the attack had occurred considered that the Kaytetye were motivated by the presence of the station's rations, or purely by innate 'savagery'. That the actions of station employees might have caused offence, or that the Kaytetye might have been responding to the uninvited occupation of their country, were inconceivable possibilities.

Over the following six weeks, four punitive expeditions were organised. The Chief Secretary in Adelaide urged the importance of 'teach[ing] the blacks the consequences to themselves of such wanton and cruel acts of destruction lest worst disasters follow'.[7] The Commissioner of Police also sought quick punitive action for fear that Aboriginal attackers would pull down the telegraph and that 'communication with Australia and the world beyond' would be cut off,[8] and he advised that in affecting such action a strict 'adherence to legal forms should not be insisted on'.[9] The Adelaide press demanded a punitive response: 'We can hardly expect that many arrests will be made, but a punishment will doubtless be given to the bloodthirsty rascals, which will be remembered for some years to come,' wrote the Adelaide *Advertiser*'s editor. He hoped that police parties would not be 'hampered by too many instructions ... Retribution, to be useful, must be sharp, swift, and severe.'[10]

The punitive expeditions moved around the region of the Taylor Creek, led by the police officer posted at the Barrow Creek telegraph station, Mounted Constable Samuel Gason. Gason was an experienced officer who had served in the Lake Eyre region in the late 1860s, during the worst of the frontier violence there. His official reports of the Barrow Creek expeditions documented the deaths of 11 Aboriginal suspects. Other reports suggest that the number of Aboriginal lives taken in reprisal for the station attack was between 50 and 90, possibly higher.[11] This was the first large-scale clash between Aboriginal people and Europeans in the Territory.

This event is just one of many from the colonial period which would come to feed Australia's burgeoning pioneer mythology of hardships endured and overcome in the winning of the country, and of harsh reprisals against 'treacherous blacks'. Yet the episode resonates with some fascinating contradictions. An isolated telegraph station is attacked. Inside their small fortress, several whites, and one Aboriginal employee, are vulnerable in a vast and largely uncolonised territory. However, the Line provides them with the colonial infrastructure in various forms: the dying man 'speaks' to his wife in Adelaide via the wire; the injured man receives regular medical advice from a metropolitan doctor; and a telegraph party

130 kilometres north learns of the attack from an operator and provides reinforcement to the besieged station. The Line brought the entire interior of the continent under the control of the colonial administration in Adelaide, and open to imperial gaze. At the same time, Central Australia was, in that historical moment, a space on the threshold of a radical change that had not quite arrived. The drama of the Barrow Creek story lies in the contradictions of a belated frontier which was still in the making.

At about the same time that the Kaytetye were facing the wrath of police punitive expeditions in the aftermath of the Barrow Creek attack, another equally dramatic series of events was unfolding to the west of the Alice Springs telegraph station which would resonate for years to come. In *Journey to Horseshoe Bend*, a narrative of heroic missionary endeavour, anthropologist Ted Strehlow describes an almost Byzantine sub-plot of tribal retribution and revenge. In about 1875, as he records it, a number of highly respected elders committed a terrible sacrilege at Irbmangkara, an important ceremonial site about 190 kilometres west of Alice Springs, and about 30 kilometres south of where Willshire's last police camp in the Centre would be situated 14 years later. According to Strehlow, the sacrilege was of a kind 'always punished by death'.[12] An avenging party of 50 to 60 warriors, mainly Matuntara men, was formed under the leadership of Tjinawariti, who came from the country south of what Europeans would come to know as Tempe Downs. The party formed a *tnengka*, a body of men large enough to overcome their opponents in a daylight attack. Forming themselves into three groups they waited patiently until they believed all members of the Irbmangkara camp were present. When they attacked they did so without mercy, attempting to spear and club to death all who were there; survivors, it was feared, could incite further reprisals. The dead, writes Strehlow, 'could well have reached the high figure of eighty to a hundred men, women, and children'.[13] There were survivors, however, and others who arrived after the massacre had occurred.

One of these was Nameia. Returning late from a hunt with a companion, he came unexpectedly on the scene of the massacre and was immediately attacked. His companion was killed, but Nameia, although injured, escaped. Nameia's wife and two children died in the attack. Nameia, and his kin who had escaped the slaughter, began planning their people's revenge. Theirs would not be a *tnengka* expedition, designed for immediate and overpowering payback, but a *leltja* party – small, patient and stealthy – which could eliminate the enemy in ones and twos until the task was complete. And so it transpired. In the following years Namiea and his men picked off their targets, pursuing them as far south as Horseshoe Bend and beyond the South Australian border until Tjinawariti and Kapaluru, the leaders of the Irbmangkara massacre, were assassinated. On their return – 'it was 1878 by now' – Nameia and his party were welcomed by their clan as heroes, 'and no one ever forgot the amazing achievement of these warriors – an achievement that would bear comparison with that of any modern day guerrilla fighters in any other part of the world'.[14]

But the world they had returned to had changed. Ntaria, 65 kilometres north of Irbmangkara, was now the Hermannsburg mission station, while in the valleys of the Finke and Palmer rivers, Europeans were establishing pastoral stations, oblivious to the claims of the owners of that country and ignorant of their politics. Nameia's triumphant return was not the end of the story. The Matuntara, writes Strehlow,

> remained unhappy, for in Tjinawariti and Kapaluru they had lost two of
> their outstanding leader figures and ceremonial chiefs . . . In return for
> their deaths it was decided by their kinsmen that at least one Irbmangara
> man should lose his life. The man marked for the final killing that would
> close the whole grim episode was, naturally, Nameia.[15]

At the time of these events at Barrow Creek and Irbmangkara, the history of exploration in Central Australia was little more than a decade old, though the Interior's status as an inland mystery to be unveiled and as a resource to be utilised had a longer history. In 1844 the explorer Charles Sturt began his abortive expedition to discover an inland sea. Though unsuccessful in that endeavour, his published account of the expedition, *Narrative of an Expedition into Central Australia* (1849) has remained one of the best-known examples of Australian exploration literature. In 1860, John McDouall Stuart began his much publicised expedition across the continent, and in 1862 he successfully completed a crossing from south to north. For a colonial audience fascinated with exploration, his reports provided stimulating accounts of tribulations overcome, and also of the country's potential for settlement. The region around the Finke River was, he reported, 'as fine a country as any man would wish to see'. At the continent's heart – or as close to it as the nearest peak allowed, a peak that would eventually be named after him – Stuart built a cairn and on it raised the British flag. He and his party 'then gave three hearty cheers for the flag, the emblem of civil and religious liberty, and may it be a sign to the natives that the dawn of liberty, civilisation, and Christianity is about to break upon them'.[16]

The South Australian government was so impressed by Stuart's reports that it acquired control of the Northern Territory in 1863. Up to this point, Central Australian Aboriginal groups had had little contact with Europeans, other than sometimes hostile and sometimes conciliatory encounters with exploration parties. That situation would change with the building of the Overland Telegraph Line. The construction of the Line from Adelaide to Palmerston (Darwin) was undertaken in 1870 and completed in 1872. From south to north, there were nine repeater stations in the Territory: Alice Springs, Barrow Creek, Tennant Creek, Powell Creek, Frew's Pond, Daly Waters, Katherine, Yam Creek and Darwin. The Line was part of a larger technological network that tied the British empire together. By the turn of the new century, a line would be completed that would 'gird the globe with a cable passing only through British territories ... a cable network upon which the sun never set'.[17] In Australia, though, its effect was less esoteric and more material. The wire 'acted like a safety net in the wilderness', making possible exploration right along its length and outwards from its stretch.[18]

By the time of its completion, pastoralists and prospectors were using the Line as a departure point for entrepreneurial excursions in search of promising cattle country or precious minerals. Even before its completion, the waterholes along the Line were stocked with cattle and horses to service the repeater stations and exploration parties. The north-western expansion of South Australia's pastoral frontier had stalled in the late 1860s as the limits of good grazing land was reached, but new reports about the Territory indicated fresh grazing lands just beyond the border, and it would not be long before larger herds were driven overland from the south. One of the first to make the leap was Edward Meade Bagot. He had been awarded the contract to build the southern section of the Overland Telegraph Line from Port Augusta to near the South Australian/Northern Territory border, and was encouraged by the lushness of the country he had seen in the Centre during the wet years of 1871 and 1872.[19] This lushness would, in the next decade, prove to be elusive. But in 1873 he established the Centre's first two stations: Undoolya and Owen Springs. The Undoolya homestead was located 20 kilometres east of the Alice Springs telegraph station, and Owen Springs 65 kilometres to the south-west. Together the claims covered 2400 square kilometres, and within the following three years they would be fully stocked with cattle and horses. By 1878 more stations had been established in the region: Glen Helen, Indracowra, Henbury. During the first years of the 1880s, pastoral enterprise expanded with the establishment of Crown Point, Bond Springs, Erldunda, Tempe Downs and Anna's Reservoir.

European civilisation was spreading into the Centre in other ways. Accounts from explorers such as Stuart, Giles and Gosse had aroused the concern of the South Australian Lutheran community in Adelaide about the welfare, both material and spiritual, of Aboriginal people in the Centre. In 1874 the Lutherans, who already had a long tradition of mission-work among the Aboriginal people of South Australia, took their proposal to the government and were granted a 1450 square kilometres lease, 110 kilometres to the west of the Alice Springs telegraph station. The first missionaries, Pastors A H Kempe and W F Schwarz, were members of the Hermannsburg Mission Institute in Germany, and arrived together in Adelaide in September 1875, with the task of converting to Christianity the Aboriginal people of the Interior, 1600 kilometres to the north. Neither had any experience of the Australian environment or its colonial social forms.

A special service at the Hahndorf Lutheran church in the Adelaide Hills celebrated the departure of the missionaries' expedition to the Centre in October 1875. Kempe, Schwarz and the appointed mission super-intendent G A Heidenreich set off, with one assistant, on their journey. It proved to be a long and laborious trek of a year and a half slowed by drought and a physical environment unsuited to wagons. 'The Lord our God help us, for He alone can,' wrote Kempe.[20] It was not until June 1877 that they finally reached their destination: a country of grassed plains backed by the MacDonnell Ranges. Selecting a tall gum, Heidenreich scored out on its bark the sign of the cross.[21] Leaving his colleagues there, he left for the return journey south with the prayer for 'a blessed entry of the Holy Gospel into the hearts of the heathen sitting in darkness'.[22]

By the early 1880s, Australia's 'Centre' was more or less defined: it was 'a largish island of passable pastoral country surrounded by desert', con-nected to Adelaide in the south and Palmerston in the north by a narrow thread of copper wire.[23] European occupation was sparse and elemental. In 1881, the country stretching from the South Australian border to Barrow Creek – a country inhabited by about 4500 Aboriginal people – counted 82 Europeans, three of whom were women.[24] The pivot of white settlement was the Alice Springs telegraph station, managed by a stationmaster and a staff that included an assistant and four linesmen. The largest concen-tration of Europeans was at the Hermannsburg mission to the west. The Hermannsburg missionaries were just settling in, supported by a growing staff of lay workers and their families. The remaining Europeans were squatters, nervously depasturing their stock around the few permanent waters they were able to find. In the decade to follow their numbers would grow, but not significantly; by 1891 there were still only 392 Europeans in the Centre, and most of those were working modest mineral discoveries in the Arltunga district east of Alice Springs.[25] These early sites of European occupation were primarily on Arrernte land, which incorporated the grassed plains around the Alice and MacDonnell Ranges. To the south-west lay the country of the Luritja, who had many traditional affiliations with the southern Arrernte. The closest European settlement to the south of Alice Springs was the Charlotte Waters telegraph station, 374 kilometres distant; to the north, the nearest was the Barrow Creek telegraph station, 272 kilometres away.

The police were late arrivals in Alice Springs, relative to the speed with which the South Australian colony's economic interests had expanded there. But with signs that Aboriginal people were beginning to attack the settlers' stock, a permanent police presence had become established there by the beginning of 1879. At this time, William Henry Willshire was thousands of kilometres south of Alice Springs, having begun his career in the South Australian Police Force on 1 January 1878.

He had been born into a middle-class Adelaide family on 5 March 1852. His father James, the youngest son of a London architect, had immigrated to Australia in 1844 and built a successful life in South Australia as a journalist, teacher and civil servant. William, one of three sons and three daughters, received a middle-class education and had before him every prospect of a comfortable middle-class life. His education and background might have led him into one form of civil administration or another, but his attraction, it seems, was to bush life. Little is known of Willshire's early career beyond the fact that he worked as a drover.

Trooper 3rd Class William Willshire's first posting was to the Adelaide Hills town of Mount Barker where, in 1880, he received commendation for his arrest of an armed man.[26] With each new posting he was gradually working his way north. By 1881 he had been posted to Melrose, in the southern Flinders Ranges. Melrose was then the base of the Far Northern Police Division of the South Australian Police Force, and from here the vast southern region of the Territory – Central Australia – was administered. While at Melrose, Willshire was involved in a minor incident that hinted at the shape of what would become, in later years, a distaste for administrative formalities. In November 1881 he was called to account for the way in which he mediated a dispute between two local pastoralists. One of them, Mr Johnston, complained to Willshire's superiors that Willshire was dismissive, apparently telling him that he 'had too much to do to attend to ranger duties'. Willshire refuted this, replying that despite the gentleman's 'abrupt and domineering manner' he had remained courteous, and that on the request of '<u>this</u> Mr Johnston' he had despatched a Mounted Constable to resolve the matter. The Acting Commissioner of Police, William Peterswald, was not amused by what he regarded as Willshire's 'most offensive way of writing'. Willshire's immediate superior, Sub Inspector of Police Brian Besley, agreed that Willshire was endeavouring to be sarcastic but, as he would in future, he placated the Commissioner on Willshire's behalf.[27] It was a minor spat, but a telling one for the future: Willshire's practice of policing in his own way – a practice in which the satisfaction of ego was more important than the fulfilment of regulation – would gain the support of his superiors, but only so long as it was commensurate with the requirements of the administration.

On 4 August 1882 William Willshire was posted to the station at Alice Springs. The Alice and its surrounding region would be the base for his patrols for the next decade. He would come to know and admire the valleys of the Palmer and Finke. He would soon learn Arrernte politics and, in years to come, his chosen part in the longstanding history of Nameia's clan warfare would ultimately sabotage the regional control he believed he enjoyed.

'THE RULE OF LAW'

Rules of engagement

The promising lushness of the country that greeted the first settlers of the Centre in the early 1870s proved to be transitory – just another cycle of the Great Southern Oscillation. By the early 1880s the wheel had turned again. As drought set in, and access to waterholes and traditional resources were compromised, Aboriginal attacks on stock and property escalated. Pastoralists responded by demanding an increased police presence. By 1884, cattle killing on Anna's Reservoir, Glen Helen, Owen Springs and Undoolya stations was considered to be so prevalent that Mounted Constable Brooks was sent south from Barrow Creek to deal with the 'present emergencies'.[1] Through that year, petitions for greater police protection of pastoral interests reached the offices of the Chief Secretary and the Commissioner of Police in Adelaide, and they were stated in terms of an economic imperative that was relevant to the future of the whole colony.[2] 'The heavy expenses and risks of settling the northern Country are in themselves causes of anxiety,' wrote one petitioner, 'but this further danger . . . is one which seriously retards progress.'[3] In so far as 'benefit to the natives themselves' was considered in these petitions, it was within an understood frontier culture in which settlers, without such support, would be obliged to take matters into their own hands and 'the natives [would be] the greatest sufferers'.[4] A 'sufficient display' of 'the force of law' would 'transform them into peaceable assistants in the occupation of the country'.[5]

By the 1880s, the task of controlling the Central Australian frontier was in the hands of South Australia's Mounted Police. The role of Mounted Police – their 'rules of engagement' – had evolved over the years in response to the particular conditions of the Australian frontier. Although the military detachments had been employed in the early years of settlement, it was soon realised that regiments of foot soldiers did not suit the realities of frontier policing. Aboriginal resistance took the form of guerrilla warfare and experience suggested that it was best matched by small, mobile and well-armed detachments. Mounted Police, supported by Aboriginal trackers or, when circumstances required, armed and mounted Native Police, constituted a paramilitary force designed specifically for the realities of Australia's frontier.[6] These forces operated under a different set of rules to their comrades down-country: they were tacitly and sometimes openly licensed to go beyond 'the rule of law'. In the isolation of the frontier, the Mounted Police were the representatives of an expedient form of law. From a legal view, of course, Aboriginal people were British subjects against whom 'war' could not be waged, yet there is an undeniable language of warfare evident in many of the official reports of patrols in the Centre, and by the early 1880s the practise of 'dispersal' would characterise the Centre's policing policy for some years to come.[7] In 1884 two episodes, one in the Centre and the other in the Top End, would bear out that policy very powerfully. They were the attack on Anna's Reservoir station, and the murder of European miners on the Daly River.

Anna's Reservoir and Daly River attacks

In August 1884, the homestead at Anna's Reservoir station, 160 kilometres north of Alice Springs, was attacked by a large party of Unmatjera men. Present at the homestead were two station employees, Thomas Coombes and Harry Figg. Caught outside the building when attacked, Coombes was struck by multiple spears, but Figg was able to retreat to the cover of the homestead. While Figg fired from the doorway with his Colt .38, the attackers set fire to the roof. When it began to collapse he was forced outside, still firing. He reportedly killed one or two of his attackers before the others, perhaps as many as 150, retreated.[8] Figg placed his badly wounded mate on a spring cart and drove him 50 kilometres to where the other station hands were camped.

A strong party was formed to pursue the offenders. It was to be led by Mounted Constable Willshire and included Mounted Constable Brooks, several trackers, the station manager Mr Benstead, two special constables and some station hands. This was to be Willshire's first major punitive expedition in the Centre. He and his party left Alice Springs on 11 August for the 160 kilometre trip north. His official report of that patrol is characteristic of his later reports, both for what it reveals of the reality of frontier warfare, and for its assumed understanding that his lay outside the normal rule of law. It also reveals a strong literary taste for drama that would later become expanded in the published memoirs of his policing activities. Although the report begins with reference to the formal objective to 'try and arrest the principal offenders', it proceeds readily into a description of violent struggles waged and won. He describes how he and his party pursued tracks 'over range after range' without sufficient water for the horses, but fearing that to divert their course would be to fall too far behind. Eventually, 'on the 7th day out things began to look warm'. Finding a camp recently vacated, 'with five puppies and any amount of weapons', they 'burnt and smashed them all up and killed the dogs, watered our horses at a rockhole and proceeded on'. When that night they tracked to an occupied camp, their approach was planned around the best potential for unexpected attack:

> 3am saddled up quietly kept no fire that night and no talking but led the horses up to foot of range ready to attack camp at daylight we made a rush full gallop [up] some small hills and observed the natives running up with weapons in hand a bigger adjoining hill. Price and I to the front soon had

6 bailed up and our trackers telling them to drop their spears but they said
the[y] would not and sent about a dozen 10 foot spears whizzing at us . . .
I went straight for one who turned neatly and struck me with his boomerang
he . . . was escaping when a bullet from a snider rifle brought him to the
ground after the affray was over I called the men together and enquired
what each had done when one of the trackers told me he had shot Slim Jim
dead this was good news to me knowing that Slim Jim was the leader at the
burning of the Station and also the principle ringleader of cattle killers.[9]

The impression from this scene of waging a battle is belied by the next,
in which it is clear that the party's attack is not against a dangerous and
equal enemy, but against a whole (now ransacked) community: 'I believe
there were about 100 women and children around us when the fight was
over all yabbering away at the same time. I marched the whole lot down
off the range and made them show where the water was'. As the leader of
the conquering party, however, Willshire is mindful of chivalry, or at least
the impression thereof: 'all my party were manly fellows and treated the
Lubras and piccaninnies with kindness we then discharged them and
returned to water our horses.'

Even in an official report, Willshire shows a strikingly operatic taste
for the drama of battle and its success. On 5 September, reporting on the
pursuit of more 'cattle killers' during the same patrol, he writes: 'as soon as
they saw us they ran through the Mulga scrub towards the Reynolds Range
we took to them as fast as we could . . . on this occasion the notorious
cattle killer Jimmy Mullins was brought down by a Spencer rifle, the rest
narrowly escaped.' Two days later, on 7 September,

another batch of niggers was seen, amongst them was 'Boko' for whom I
held a warrant my tracker tried to take this fellow alive but I think 'Boko'
could handle his waddy too well . . . the tracker was in a terrible rage at
being got at by a wild nigger so he levelled his rifle and 'Boko' came
toppling down from rock to rock and landed at the trackers feet.[10]

That Willshire regarded himself as engaged in a frustratingly difficult form of warfare is suggested by his grudging respect for his enemy's courage and elusiveness: 'I may here state that the natives both at Anna's Reservoir and Owen Springs are getting worse instead of better in my opinion they don't care about death a bit then [take] refuge in the big high ranges and without a fellow [being] most particularly smart he wont even be able to get a shot at them'. He closes his report with the suggestion that he could work the same country with impunity if camels were provided.[11]

This first of Willshire's official reports of punitive expeditions in the Centre establishes some patterns that would recur in his subsequent reports, and throughout his literary works: he is always on familiar terms with his weapons, the Snider, the Spencer and the Martini-Henry rifles; each named Aboriginal victim is often identified as a notorious cattle killer, shot either resisting arrest or in self-defence; and if someone is credited with firing the fatal shot, it is usually an Aboriginal tracker, rather than Willshire himself.

While Willshire and his men were pursuing those considered responsible for the Anna's Reservoir attack, another crisis was unfolding at a copper mine on the Daly River, in the Territory's Top End. In early September three men working the Mount Haywood copper load were attacked outside their camp. John Landers, Henry Roberts and Johannes Noltenius were all speared as they ran for the safety of their camp. Roberts, who had passed out when wounded, regained consciousness after the attack and removed most of the spears from his companions' bodies. Returning to the camp, they found the dead body of the cook, Schollert. The three wounded men tried to make it to Glencoe, a cattle station on the Daly River, but Landers and Noltenius were so weak they had to be left along the way. Roberts alone arrived at the station and arranged for help to be sent back, but when the rescue party arrived, both Landers and Noltenius were dead, and the camp was plundered. When the police investigated, it appeared that both men had been not only speared but also shot, presumably with their own revolvers.[12]

Immediately the Northern Division of the Territory's police, under the direction of Inspector Paul Foelsche, organised a party to respond to the murders. Led by Corporal Montagu, the police were to capture 'any members of the tribe who committed the Daly River murders ... and hold them as hostages until the actual murderers are given up'.[13] Corporal Montagu's report documents 20–30 Aboriginal deaths, but other contemporary reports suggest between 70–150, and modern estimates are higher.[14] In his report of the expedition, Montagu admitted that 'what the other parties out have done I do not know, but I believe the natives have received such a lesson this time as will exercise a salutary effect over the survivors in time to come'. He concluded: 'One result of this expedition has been to convince me of the superiority of the Martini-Henry rifle, both for accuracy of aim and quickness of action.'[15]

If it was understood within the Territory administration that such cases required a degree of legal flexibility to achieve the sort of 'salutary effect' that Montagu desired, the NT Times & Gazette's editorial on the Daly River punitive expedition expressed this view with plain-speaking vitriol:

> Backward the natives must move before the tide of civilisation, or ... as every man will crush a snake under his heel, so must the hand of every man be raised against a tribe of inhuman monsters, whose cowardly and murderous nature renders them unfit to live ... [N]othing but the most severe punishment will have any lasting effect on them ... legal technicalities should be utterly dispensed with, and a sharp lesson administered ... we do not expect to hear many particulars of the chase; the less the better, in such cases as the present.[16]

The extremity of punitive action in this case did not go unprotested in Adelaide. After the publication of Corporal Montagu's report, the press recorded an outcry from South Australians whose own memories of the frontier were now more than a generation old.[17] Settlers in the Top End might well have felt that such reaction showed little understanding of the realities of frontier life, but in response to public pressure a Board of Inquiry was held into the punitive party's actions. Its Chairman was A P Baines, who had been a member of that very party, and the expedition members were cleared of any wrongdoing.[18]

After the events at Anna's Reservoir and Daly River, it was apparent that European occupation of this country would be opposed, as it had been on most other Australian frontiers. In his end-of-year report, the Territory's Government Resident acknowledged this reality, and its origins in incommensurate expectations of the land: 'how, while facilitating the settlement and stocking of the country by Europeans, at the same time to atone for what is an undoubted loss of food supply in consequence to the natives, is a problem much easier to state than to resolve. That settlement and stocking must and will go on is certain – that outrages will be committed by both sides is probable'.[19] His speculation was an accurate picture of things to come over the decade.

The Native Police

On 22 September 1884, having just returned from his Anna's Reservoir expedition, William Willshire received a letter from Mr Ross, the manager of Undoolya station, stating that 'the natives were killing cattle indiscriminately' on the run and asking him 'to come at once and do what I could'. Willshire left for Undoolya that afternoon, taking with him his rifles and one tracker.[20] They arrived at Undoolya the following day, and immediately set out along the Trepeena Creek in search of tracks. Finding two dead beasts along the river, they picked up tracks and moved on. They camped overnight and the next day rode until in the afternoon they came upon 'natives close to a big range'. Finding themselves under a volley of stones, spears and boomerangs, Willshire and his tracker 'got behind big rocks and now and again got a shot at them'. Three Aboriginal men were shot dead and four others wounded, according to Willshire's report, while the rest 'got away from us'.

Willshire then offers the Sub Inspector his view of the pressing need to 'get' more natives than has hitherto been achieved. Strikingly, having just described the deaths of three men, he comments on the lack of fatalities in encounters with cattle killers: 'I desire to draw the Inspectors attention to this that there have been cattle stations up here this last 8-9-&10 years and the natives have killed hundreds of cattle, very few natives have been got at and I doubt if any have been shot.' Drawing attention to his own success in such encounters, he writes: 'I take full charge of the party and have always got at the natives I wanted even in their pet ranges ... this seems surprising to men who have been up here for years ... nothing stops me but the want of water and that seldom occurs for when in hot pursuit after niggers you are bound to fetch water. I have been successful I know but I had to work hard for it.'[21]

By the time Willshire wrote this report, discussions were already under way in Adelaide between the Police Commissioner and the Chief Secretary about establishing a Native Police force in the Territory. Pastoralists' petitions urged the establishment of such a force, and suggested Willshire as the man to lead it.

Willshire, based at the heart of the pastoral frontier, shared this aspiration. His report of the Undoolya patrol concludes with an unofficial application to be appointed Officer in Charge of a Native Police force, should one be established. He assures the Sub Inspector of the personal support he enjoys from pastoralists in the Centre, and lists the 'letters congratulating me [which] have come from all directions'. He anticipates campaigns yet to come: 'now the next thing is the Owen Springs country, the natives are now killing valuable horses, this I deem unbearable and for it they shall be punished.'[22] He offers to supply all necessary information regarding a Native Police force's organisation and outfitting, and outlines its potential success under his command:

6 trackers and one smart man who knows how to work them and knows
the country ... would soon give satisfaction to all. Why even now with my

assistance it appears that I can do good in stopping outrages by natives . . .
should a native force be organised I trust that the Inspect. will consider
what I have done and my experience amongst the natives, though
I have only been here 2 years I know more about them than any man in
the district.[23]

Careful not to overstep Sub Inspector Besley's authority, though, he
concludes on a modest note:

Three gentlemen have asked me if they could do anything for me by
speaking to the Commissioner or Mr Tennant MP. I told them no and that
I did not care about it & said that Sub Inspector Besley was in charge of
this division . . . I feel confident that I have pursued the proper course and
should the Inspt recommend me to have charge of the trackers I will be
able to work them properly.

Besley forwarded Willshire's letter to the Commissioner of Police
with a comment that Willshire's 'perseverance and courage well deserves
our commendation.[24]

Over the following weeks, discussions continued about the role a
Native Police force could play and the form it could take. Not everyone
involved in the Territory's administration was comfortable with the
prospect.[25] The reputation for uncontrolled violence that the Native Police
forces in New South Wales and Queensland had generated during the
1850s and 1860s was a legitimate cause for caution. Initially established in
New South Wales in the 1840s as a settler-financed initiative, Native Police
corps continued to be supported by colonial governments elsewhere around
Australia – although with some unease.[26] In Queensland the Native Police
corps had been conceived as a protection against Aboriginal oppression as
well as Aboriginal outrage, but it soon became apparent that they served
only the one function: to 'disperse' Aboriginal people, as a paramilitary
force, in the aid of pastoralist protection and expansion.[27] A Select

Committee inquiry that had been established in Queensland in 1861 to investigate charges of atrocities by the Native Police produced plenty of evidence to suggest, as one witness put it, that when it came to 'the destruction of the aborigines, [the Native Police] are the most efficient force for that purpose'.[28] By the time the South Australian government was contemplating the establishment of Native Police corps in the Territory, it had become the orthodox experience on earlier pastoral frontiers that despite the technical requirements of treating Aboriginal offenders as British subjects under the law, the conditions of 'unsettled' regions and the assumption of a policing mentality of collective guilt meant that Aboriginal prisoners rarely reached trial. It was routinely reported that they were shot in self-defence, resisting arrest, or attempting escape.[29]

The 'unfavourable comment' that Native Police forces had generated elsewhere, did not pass un-noticed by the Territory administration. Sub Inspector Besley's counterpart in the Top End, Inspector Foelsche, was uncomfortable with the idea of a Native Police corps, and when one was eventually established, he framed careful guidelines for the Officer in Charge with the caution, 'it is to be borne in mind that the system termed "dispersing the natives" which simply means shooting them is not to be practised and for this the officer in charge will be held strictly responsible.'[30]

Despite such precedents – indeed, perhaps informed by them – station owners' desire for such a force in the expanding Territory was strong. As they saw it, a Native Police force – as opposed to a purely European one – would yield the benefit of combining European leadership and weaponry with Aboriginal bush skills. On 2 October 1884, three days after Willshire wrote his unofficial application for the position of Officer in Charge of a Native Police force, 18 pastoral lessees and managers wrote to the Chief Secretary:

> The hostile and unsettled state of natives ... prove that the assistance of
> Native Police, or Black Trackers, should be called in to assist the Police

Constables in this district . . . A great area of said country is composed of ranges, hills, and rough ground quite inaccessible to mounted men, and to dislodge or capture native offenders from these fastnesses – to which they retreat after they have committed any depredations – they require to be met with equal cunning and strategy, and this would obtain by employing Native trackers . . . MC Willshire being stationed in the Centre of the district [has] been especially energetic and successful, and in our opinion would be a fit and proper person to be connected with the charge of such a body as we propose to be organised.[31]

Three weeks later, Mr D Murray, of the Barrow Creek Pastoral Company, wrote to the Chief Secretary with the same proposal. A Native Police force, he wrote, would prove to be 'the most efficient, as well as the most economical mode of keeping the natives in check'. On the question of an Officer in Charge, he submitted that as

a position in which the Commanding trooper will have to exercise discretionary power – there being but few opportunities of cooperation such as are possible nearer civilisation southwards – I would strongly recommend Willshire – now stationed at Alice Springs – from his ability, knowledge of the country as well as from his possessing the confidence of all the settlers in the vicinity, as being the most suitable man.[32]

The Chief Secretary forwarded these petitions to William Peterswald, the Commissioner of Police, who acknowledged the need 'for the protection of the Stations in the interior against the outrages of the Blacks'.[33] That he regarded Willshire less highly than Besley was signalled early by his dry comment, in reply to Besley's commendation, that Willshire's unofficial application 'would have been a much more interesting narrative if the writer had not put himself so prominently forward'. Nonetheless, he wrote to the Chief Secretary that Willshire 'is very well qualified to be the leader of a party for this purpose'.[34]

Two weeks later, on 14 November 1884, Peterswald wrote to Besley authorising him to 'engage six Blacks @ 1- per diem and rations, and call them Native Police'. Willshire was to be the Officer in Charge.[35] When the authorisation came through, Willshire was away, escorting six Native Police to Palmerston in the Top End. When he returned to the Centre, he recruited another six Native Constables, with whom he would patrol the districts around Alice Springs.

At the same time as settlers in the Centre were petitioning the Chief Secretary for the formation of a Native Police force to protect their pastoral interests, the missionaries at Hermannsburg were expressing their unease about settlers' abuses against Aboriginal people in the region. In October, the Adelaide-based Protector of Aborigines, Edward Hamilton, requested information from the mission about the degree to which local Aboriginal people might have 'suffered injury from whites'. Reverend Schwarz replied with a cautionary letter, expressing the view that if Aboriginal people were showing hostility to the whites, 'most decidedly has [their] treatment much to do with it'. Drawing on 'what I myself have seen', he asks: when 'treated in the most unjust manner, who can wonder that the Natives at last exasperated try to avenge themselves?' Settlers' punishment of native outrages, he continued, was fatal rather than legal, and made no differentiation between the innocent and the guilty, 'for instance an old woman was brought here who was looking indeed miserable, shot by whites and died here. Most certainly she had not killed any cattle. There could be written much more over this matter'.[36]

Hamilton forwarded Schwarz's letter to the Commissioner of Crown Lands, with a reminder of the economic as well as the moral benefits to be gained by preserving Aboriginal goodwill in the Centre. He urged:

the desirability of some steps being taken to protect these Aborigines from arbitrary and oppressive ill treatment at the hands of European settlers and their employees. There is little doubt but acts of this nature frequently occur and they tend to establish ill feeling, and lead to outrages on both sides involving the Government in a costly and inglorious struggle with the Blacks, who if they were treated with a little more justice and forbearance would doubtless live amicably with and prove of much use to the pioneer settlers of these remote localities.[37]

Acknowledging the recent expansion of the police force with Native Constables, he argued that the police be resourced such that, with 'more frequent Police patrols', Aboriginal people as well as settlers would be assured of the law's protection.[38] Sub Inspector Besley, who was also Sub Protector of Aborigines, concurred. Responding to Hamilton's recommendation, Besley stated that 'when the Native Police have been fairly established at the Alice Springs a continual patrol shall be kept up ... This patrol will have the effect I am sure of keeping the Europeans, as well as the Blacks in check'.[39]

In the three years between the end of 1884 and the end of 1887, a system of patrolling emerged in which the two Mounted Constables based at Alice Springs – Willshire and Erwin Wurmbrand – would alternate in leading the Native Police in response to specific complaints of cattle killing. Several regulatory checks provided theoretical controls over the force. It was not free to patrol at will but was responsible for responding to particular requests for police assistance. Occasionally there was trouble in two locations at once, and when this occurred Mounted Constable Daer, at Charlotte Waters, was called in to take charge of the police station. Sometimes a trusted Native Constable was sent out ahead, or very infrequently, was left in charge at Alice Springs. The patrol party usually consisted of the Officer in Charge and three or four Native Constables. In making arrests, shots were not to be fired except in self-defence, or when absolutely necessary when offenders resisted arrest. For the maintenance of all these regulations, the Officer in Charge was responsible for the entire party.

It was a police requirement that the Officer in Charge keep a daily memo book and complete, on his return to Alice Springs, a full report of the patrol for the benefit of the Sub Inspector. Of course, warrants were to be sought and issued for particular suspects who, on their arrest, were to be escorted south to Port Augusta for trial. Port Augusta, the administrative headquarters of the Far Northern Police Division and the location of the nearest local court, was a very long way from Alice Springs. Aboriginal prisoners were rarely taken down for trial. It soon became apparent that the officers who commanded the Native Police could with impunity ignore administrative rhetoric about monitoring European as well as Aboriginal 'outrages'. Reports emanating from the Alice Springs police station soon made it clear that the police had one role: Aboriginal pacification.

Patrolling

On 13 November 1884, the day before the Commissioner of Police formally established the Native Police force, Mounted Constable Erwin Wurmbrand left the Alice Springs police station with a patrolling party, bound for the Glen Helen station. Wurmbrand's task was to capture Aboriginal offenders implicated in a recent murder attempt on three of the station's employees, Messrs McDonald, Schleicher and Miller, in a gorge on the Glen Helen run. Willshire was away from Alice Springs, travelling north to Palmerston with the six Native Police recruited for the Top End, and Wurmbrand was the Officer in Charge of this patrol, which was to last three weeks. His party included the trackers (soon to be Native Constables) Dick, Jemmy, Tommy and Charley, and two settlers, William Craigie and James Norman. Taking their rifles, packs and 11 horses, they travelled south-westwards from Alice Springs along the Jay Creek to Owen Springs, then to the Hermannsburg mission station, and finally to Glen Helen.

Wurmbrand's report of their patrol proceeds as follows. Hearing at Glen Helen that men involved in the attack had taken refuge nearby at Hermannsburg, the police party surrounded the mission station's Aboriginal camps and, moving just before daybreak, followed Wurmbrand's instructions 'to close circle gradually and clear all the wurleys of their inmates regardless of age or sex'.[40] Three men suspected of involvement in the

Glen Helen attack were arrested and chained together by the neck, and a march with the prisoners was begun back to Glen Helen.

The party followed the Finke River to a point where several gullies intercepted a chain of hills, and there, according to Wurmbrand's report, the prisoners 'made a sudden rush for the rocks'. Recognising 'the futility of my attempt at recapture' Wurmbrand ordered the party to fire. 'Prisoners are dead', he reported.

The police party continued its search for more offenders north-west, around Mount Sonder. On the fourth day, they tracked them to an Aboriginal camp. 'A cloudy sky and a slight breeze favoured my further approach to reconnoitre and I found the camp situated in a rough gully inaccessible on horseback, the wurleys as usual widely scattered. It was nigh on day break when we cautiously facing the wind crept on the camp.' The police party had prepared for a silent approach by dismounting and removing their boots but, despite their caution, the camp was alarmed: 'the trackers instantly called on them in their own language to surrender but a flight of spears was the savages reply.' In the resulting volley of bullets, four Aboriginal men were shot dead, while 'the rest seeing their leaders fall immediately made for rocks, – our bare feet, sorely tried by sharp stones & Spinifex, favoured the fugitives, who were soon out of reach & sight'. The police party burned the camp's huts and goods, and would have continued the search for further offenders, but abandoned the action 'on a/c of our scanty supply of very inferior rations having completely run out'.

The party returned to Alice Springs with a tally of seven Aboriginal deaths and no successful arrests. Wurmbrand concluded his report with the view that if more police were available to continually patrol the MacDonnell and neighbouring ranges, the blacks 'would soon be pacified. At the present they are well aware that a white man is no match for them in their rocky haunts'.[41] Two days after he had concurred in writing with the Protector of Aborigines' suggestion for more police patrols in the interests of Aboriginal, as well as European, protection, Besley forwarded Wurmbrand's report of seven Aboriginal fatalities to the Commissioner of

Police, who perused and returned it without comment. It was filed in the first days of 1885.[42]

Within a month of Wurmbrand's patrol to Glen Helen, William Willshire had completed his first patrol in the formal role of Officer in Charge of the newly established Native Police. He was still away from Alice Springs, escorting the six Native Constables to Palmerston from where they were to be deployed. While he was in the district of Powell's Creek, the Territory's Government Resident issued him with warrants for the arrest of four Aboriginal men for 'killing a steer and carrying away the meat'. On 10 December, Willshire wired a report of his search for them to Sub Inspector Besley. The previous day, Willshire reports, he and his party of four Native Constables and one settler had followed tracks until they came upon a large camp, in which two of the offenders were recognised. He warned the Native Constables, he continues, to 'take them alive and on no account to shoot them, until I gave instructions'. At this moment, however, the suspects and 'one name unknown' set up a fight: 'spears boomerangs & stones were thrown in all directions – and the offenders were fast getting away into a thick Lance wood Scrub.' Compelled to 'use the last resource', he ordered his party to fire and the three men were shot dead. The remaining people in the camp attempted to flee; the police 'kept rounding them up with our horses' but eventually allowed them 'to go unmolested'. Willshire concludes his first report in his official capacity as Officer in Charge of the Native Police with the comment that 'the trackers worked well, and their obedience to instructions was conspicuously observed'.[43]

Besley forwarded Willshire's report to the Commissioner of Police on the day the telegram arrived. A fortnight later, he forwarded the same report (this time in his capacity not as Sub Inspector of Police but as Sub Protector of Aborigines) to the Protector of Aborigines, Edward Hamilton. The likelihood that Hamilton had raised concerns about the actions of the police and sought an alternative source of information is suggested by Besley's note that the incident had 'occurred a long way beyond the boundary of any district'; that he considered it 'impossible for you to obtain the information from any other source [than Mounted Constable Willshire] for sometime to come'; and that these considerations would 'probably justify what would otherwise be considered irregular'.[44] With these observations Besley acknowledged a crucial reality of the Central Australian frontier at this time: the Officers in Charge of the Native Police could work more or less unchecked.

The rule of law and the culture of terror

Aboriginal people were British subjects and, in theory, equally protected by the law as all other subjects. This was the official rhetoric. When the Native Police force was established Willshire's superior, Sub Inspector Besley, made the observation that this 'patrol will have the effect I am sure of keeping the Europeans, as well as the Blacks in check'.[45] Willshire and his compatriot Wurmbrand understood the rhetoric, but they also understood the reality: their role was to protect the pastoralists by 'pacifying' the Aboriginal people whose lands were being usurped. As Willshire put it on one occasion, his 'duty was to see that the wild natives do not interfere with the white settlers'.[46] To achieve this end they knew they needed – and were expected – to go beyond the rule of law. Their reports were usually scripted to indicate that due process was being observed: the intention of a raid is to identify and arrest suspects; identified suspects are duly called upon to surrender; handcuffs are at the ready; if the suspects are shot it is described as a 'last resource' of self-defence. Despite this almost formulaic acknowledgement of judicial process, these same reports nonetheless reveal the implicit purpose of patrols.

In his September 1884 report of a patrol to Undoolya station in which three Aboriginal people were shot dead and four others wounded, Willshire wrote, 'now the next thing is the Owen Springs country, the natives are now killing valuable horses. This I deem unbearable and for it they shall be punished'.[47] The nature of that anticipated punishment is not elaborated. In a report by Wurmbrand defending the actions of the Native

Police, he admits that at times 'stringent measures had to be adopted, measures which may seem harsh to people who do not know what the savages up here are capable of doing'.[48] When police, or settlers, or both in combination, followed up attacks on themselves, their stock or property, their intentions were invariably punitive. This is as evident in the aftermath of a raid as in the raid itself; the Mounted Police frequently report burning wurleys, burning or smashing any weapons left behind, shooting the dogs, and rounding up the women and children, before later releasing them.[49] The clear purpose was intimidation.

If their task had been simple 'policing', they would have arrested suspects, yet they rarely report doing so. On two of the rare occasions when suspects were arrested they were later shot while reportedly trying to escape.[50] Arrests entailed a long and tedious journey south to the local court at Port Augusta. One of the very few times Willshire and Wurmbrand undertook this journey with a prisoner happened to coincide with the publication of Willshire's first book – a book he arranged to have printed at Port Augusta.[51] Willshire and Wurmbrand understood that their primary task was not to arrest offenders, but to subdue Aboriginal resistance. The small community they served most directly, the pastoralists, also understood this. In 1890 Robert Warburton, manager of Erldunda station, wrote a letter to the Minister controlling the Territory defending the actions of the police. After reflecting on the violence of earlier Australian frontiers, he indicated that what was happening at this time in the Centre was an inevitable phase of frontier settlement:

> of course things are difficult and will be until the blacks knuckle under, but not before, when you have subdued them you can be as kind as you like to them, its only the same old story of pioneer settlement over and over again ever since Australia was first settled . . .[52]

It was a well-established frontier tradition, adhered to by government, settlers and police, that Aboriginal aggressions had to be countered by exemplary shows of force. As the anthropologist Barry Morris put it, a 'culture of terror' prevailed:

> The retaliatory raid provided the means for acts of redemptive violence.
> For Europeans, the acts of violence by Aborigines could only be
> extinguished by the exercise of greater terror through violence.[53]

This was a late frontier; the phase that followed Aboriginal subjugation had by the 1880s become well established elsewhere around Australia. A 'sufficient display' of 'the force of law' would 'transform' Aboriginal people 'into peaceable assistants in the occupation of the country'.[54]

Given the task that the police were implicitly given, and the rhetoric they were obliged to observe, how true a record of events were the reports of officers like Willshire and Wurmbrand? In this period when most of the killings took place beyond the reach of any official inquests, how many reports underestimated the number of deaths, and how many deaths went unreported? What other sources of information are there? The pastoralists had a vested interest in the Native Police. The force was established at their request and they regarded its role as one of 'dispersing' Aboriginal cattle killers. Station managers and their employees were frequently members of Willshire's and Wurmbrand's patrol parties. The missionaries were advocates of Aboriginal people and they frequently complained about the actions of the settlers and police. However, most of their reports of violence were based on what Aboriginal people had told them rather than on what they had seen. It is hardly surprising that Willshire, in his reports as well as in his published writings, vilified both Aboriginal people and missionaries as liars.

Sometimes Willsire's own pen provides unexpected glimpses of activities that he would normally have been more circumspect in reporting. He is usually careful to convey the impression that the Native Constables are always under his command, operating at his direction – but sometimes this clearly was not so. Early in January 1891, Willshire reported an extended patrol in search of cattle killers in the Tempe Downs region. While on remote patrol, he writes, 'on many occasions my boys are away for two or three days, whilst I remain alone looking after the camp'.[55] Clearly, there were times when the Native Constables enjoyed considerable autonomy. What happened on these independent patrols are rarely reported, except in the most veiled terms. In *Land of the Dawning*, he mentions how 'some of my lads came home . . . with a fine collection of spears and boomerangs – they had evidently been amongst them'.[56] On another occasion Willshire, writing with a degree of panic after his camp has just been attacked, remarks on the daring of the cattle killers: 'they think nothing if one or two of their clique are shot dead, they come again.'[57] How figurative is Willshire being in his reference to 'one or two' deaths; who are those deaths' witnesses; and where are they reported?

In June 1885, Wurmbrand reported that while on patrol in April– May, a clash had occurred that resulted in the death of one Aboriginal man among a party of over 20. The Hermannsburg missionaries, however, heard from another member of the patrol party, a Glen Helen station stockman, that 17 Aboriginal people had been killed. Asked for an explanation by his superiors, Wurmbrand reiterated his original report, and there the matter rested.[58] William Benstead, one-time manager of Glen Helen station, had accompanied Wurmbrand on this patrol and wrote about it years later in his memoir. Warrants were held for the arrest of those they were tracking, he wrote, 'so on this occasion we ran no risks as far as our necks were concerned; but all the same, caution was used, and whatever happened, it was usually reported as having successfully dispersed the natives; it read better.' 'What happened that day,' he continues, 'it is a thing of the past, and of little use writing up now; but I am sure that seventeen out of this lot never killed or troubled anyone else.'[59] Benstead's account not only is in keeping with the missionaries' account, but captures a grass-roots understanding of the nature and purpose of punitive violence. Of the consequence of this raid, Benstead wrote: 'It was a lesson they never forgot. It instilled fear into their tribe for 200 miles around, and was the means of putting an end to their murderous attempts.'[60]

Covert violence was a characteristic of the Australian frontier. Often we get hints of it in coded euphemisms, sometimes we get evidence of it in private accounts made public by the passage of time, but all too often we are left with no choice but to speculate. Contemporary official records, writes Northern Territory historian Dick Kimber, report the killings of about 44 Aboriginal people in the Centre by Europeans between 1860 and 1895, but his analysis of a broader range of evidence suggests a figure closer to 650. Whatever the exact number of fatalities during this period, there is little doubt that it far exceeds the 'official' record.

THE NATIVE POLICE

By the end of 1884, the missionaries' concerns about the behaviour of the settlers had extended to the actions of the police. In December Reverend Schwarz complained to Hamilton that Aboriginal people had been coming onto the mission station 'for fear of the police, who had shot a number of Natives around the neighbouring cattle stations'.[1] Within months, Reverend Kempe was writing to the Protector with the same concerns. Responding to Hamilton's assurance that violence against Aboriginal people would be kept in check by the expansion of the police force at Alice Springs, Kempe wrote: 'Whether from this measure shall arise any good for the natives is rather doubtful as long as there is nobody to control the actions of the police troopers. The only difference will be that the natives are now shot down by policemen whilst before the other whites did it.'[2] In his letter he raises the case of the three Aboriginal prisoners taken from the mission station by Wurmbrand's party five months previously who, bound 'with a strong trace chain fastened together round their necks', had been shot dead en route to Glen Helen. Kempe visited the site where the bodies still lay and expressed disbelief at Wurmbrand's report of events:

> the natives informed us the 3 natives were shot down by the whites.
> We went there & convinced ourselves [of] the truth of this statement.

Now we expected directly the whites would say they tried to escape & so they did when we asked them. But who can believe it? Who can believe that they broke the strong chain? Who can further believe that escaping they kept together? One should think, if it happened that they got unfastened the chain, they would run away in every direction, but the bodies were lying on one heap & exactly as they were tied together.[3]

Kempe's letter was forwarded by Protector Hamilton to the Commissioner of Police, who sent it to Besley for explanation. Besley sought further information from Mounted Constable Daer, who was stationed at Charlotte Waters and had spent some time patrolling with Wurmbrand. Daer's comments cast no new light on the matter: 'I know nothing of the alleged shooting of blacks by a police trooper, during my residence in the Interior when my duties have brought one in to collision with the natives I have always tried to avoid taking violent measures.'[4] The correspondence was forwarded to Wurmbrand, still at Alice Springs police station, who respectfully referred the Inspector back to his original report, which stated that the prisoners had been shot escaping arrest, only after attempts at recapture proved futile.[5]

Kempe pursued the incident further during a meeting in Adelaide in November 1885, attended by Chief Secretary Bray, Commissioner of Police Peterswald and the Protector of Aborigines. The Chief Secretary asked Kempe if he wished criminal proceedings to be instigated, but the missionary declined to pursue that course. He was satisfied with an undertaking from the Commissioner that instructions would be issued to the police not to use firearms except in self-defence. Given that the Commissioner could have taken that rule for granted, it was a curious undertaking to give.[6]

Although repeated complaints about police violence emerged from Hermannsburg through the 1880s, the missionaries' most regular complaint concerned a different, apparently less covert issue: the alleged sexual exploitation of Aboriginal women. In the same letter to the Protector of

Aborigines in which he queried the official fate of the three chained prisoners, Kempe complained about white men 'whoring' with Aboriginal women and girls. In this matter it was not only, or even primarily, Aboriginal women's welfare that was at stake. The possibility of sexual coercion was less significant in the missionary's eyes, it seems, than the perceived evil of unsettling the racial hierarchy: 'It is indeed shameful, that the whites degrade themselves so much as they do, whoring with the native females who are nothing better than wild dogs, as they say, and doing this not secretly but quite publicly, they boast about doing so, and for this mean purpose they use not only full grown females but even mere children.' Settlers, Kempe implied, would lure away the mission station's women, who were then lost to Christian care. Mounted Constable Daer's response to this aspect of Kempe's complaint – 'I have no knowledge of females being decoyed from the mission station by white men' – again provided no further information, and the matter, in this instance, was not pursued further by the authorities. But protests from the mission station, both about the abuse of Aboriginal women and unrestrained police violence, were far from over, and in the coming years would prove to be a thorn in the side of the police at Alice Springs.

By the end of 1885, the climate of economic restraint brought on by recession in South Australia caused the Commissioner of Police to wonder whether the Native Police force in the Centre could be retrenched. After a year of its operation, Peterswald believed that it constituted a 'heavy expense' that could be cut from the colony's purse.[7] Although persuaded that the force's presence had so far 'prevented many outrages from being committed', he noted that its contingent expenses were not included in his office's annual provisions and he was 'saddled with expenses which should be borne by the Northern Territory'. For a sense of the force's continuing value he consulted Besley, who replied that 'it would be a most unwise step to retrench the Native Police, as the more uncivilised Blacks know they cannot escape from them'.[8] The Mounted Constables at Alice Springs were also keen to see the Native Police force maintained. At the same time as Peterswald was considering the force's retrenchment, Wurmbrand wrote to Besley requisitioning Native Police supplies for the year to follow, and justifying the force's critical role:

> Hitherto the native Police has done their work to the advantage of the settlers, having checked the outrages by Natives to a great extent . . . I also trust that my commanding officers are satisfied as to the efficiency of the Native Police Force, although they may have experienced annoyance by unfounded & unjustified reports charging us with unnecessary severity. I acknowledge now, as I have done in my previous reports, that sometimes stringent measures had to be adopted, measures which may seem even harsh to people, who do not know what the savages up here of capable of doing.[9]

Aware of the call for economies, he confined his requisition to 'the absolute necessaries indispensable for the working of the Native Police to the satisfaction of my commanding Officers and the advantage of the General public'. Included in the request for billycans, iron, kegs, kerosene, tents and 'coats of blue serge with SA buttons, for the Native Constables' was the 'absolute' requirement of revolvers, 'as a rifle in a mêlée . . . is a great hindrance'. Although he drew attention to the unusual form of the requisition, the Commissioner of Police approved it in the new year.[10]

Through the following two years, Willshire and Wurmbrand patrolled with the Native Police through large regions of the Centre. On 21 April 1886, they shifted their camp from Alice Springs to Heavitree Gap, eight kilometres south of Alice Springs, and it was from here that their patrols moved out in a radius of hundreds of kilometres, for weeks and sometimes for months at a time. Between May and September of 1886, for instance, Wurmbrand undertook an extensive patrol that incorporated visits to most of the pastoral stations south of Alice Springs, lasted over three months, and covered well in excess of 2500 kilometres. Sometimes their reports record no incidents of conflict, sometimes they record the loss of Aboriginal offenders, who had fled into the ranges, and sometimes they record the deaths of offenders who, so they say, have been killed either resisting or escaping arrest.[11] Their range was extensive, and despite requirements on them to keep full records of their activities, they did not always do so, particularly when on remote patrol.

By October 1886, Reverend Kempe was again writing to the Protector of Aborigines in Adelaide with complaints against the police and settlers. Is it permissible, he asked, for a settler or a trooper to come onto the mission station and persuade an Aboriginal person to go with them? Is it permissible for the whites to have girls with them to use as concubines? Are whites allowed to drive Aborigines away from waterholes and shoot them if they don't go? Can young Aboriginal women from the mission be brought back from surrounding stations, where they are being prostituted? In response, Hamilton pointed out that there existed no special legislation to address these complaints.[12]

Others besides the missionaries were raising concerns about the activities of the police in the Territory. A Mr Warland from the Roper River district had earlier the same year written to the Commissioner of Police, complaining about the Northern Division of the Native Police force that had been patrolling that district since 1884 under the administration of Inspector Paul Foelsche. Writing as 'a private gentleman', Warland lodged a protest about the fact that the bodies of four Aboriginal men, shot by the Native Police during a patrol under the direction of Mounted Constable Power, remained unburied, and he urged Peterswald to monitor the force's activities:

> As head of the South Australian police I must think it my duty to give you
> an alarming note of what is as certain to happen here . . . that is great
> Trouble with the blacks and the whites unless great tact is observed and the
> greatest precaution taken, and that at once. [Don't] neglect the signs now
> observable to one as well used to all sorts, both black and white on the
> Back Country as myself. You may ask what is there to fear. Late events of

shooting and spearing in this district of which you are well informed. Also that the bodies are still unburied. The men on this establishment are asking me if men and dogs are equal in the light of govt. that no inquest or enquiries is or has been held. And that the bodies of men are to rot above ground like knocked up cattle. This terrible affair has a terribly demoralising effect on all classes here out of which trouble will come, especially to your police force . . . I am gauging events as they arise and . . . events cast their shadow . . .[13]

When Warland's letter was forwarded for comment to Foelsche, the Inspector returned it to the Minister of Education with an angry memo which noted: 'when up country in May last, I heard a gentleman say – "If you tell people you believe what Warland tells you, people will not believe you".' An inquiry could not be held, he argued, because a coroner's jury 'could not have been obtained within a radius of two hundred miles'.[14] When Foelsche wrote his memo, the bodies had been buried.

Meanwhile, the police in the Centre were in their turn feeling resentment towards the administrative economies that kept them on the frontier with minimal resources. In early 1887, Willshire wrote to Besley requesting a more permanent camp at Heavitree Gap. Situated on a large plain between two ranges, he observed that the police horses were thriving, and that the country suited him equally: the plain was covered with cotton, salt bush and various native grasses, and Willshire seemed to enjoy having 'it all to myself'. The accommodation, though, left much to be desired. The police buildings consisted of one bough wurley, one log hut with a thatched roof, and two tents. 'But still the bough wurley and the log hut are dangerous as they are low, and would easy catch fire, more especially in my absence, as it is not safe to be weeks away & only a blackboy in charge of so many valuable things such as our rations firearms & store goods & my private things'. When, could the Inspector kindly inform him, would it be likely that the building of a more solid police station be commenced?[15] He was aware 'that curtailment of expenses is the order of the day, but still I notice in the Govt Gazette that other buildings & works are going on all the same down country', and his own application for a building 'is just as much absolutely necessary as buildings in townships below'.[16]

The conditions of frontier policing were a regular and simmering subtext in reports from the Centre, and undoubtedly did little to develop officers' respect for authorities who were more comfortably housed 'down country'. Wurmbrand's December 1884 report to Besley on the Glen Helen patrol had closed with a lengthy reminder that frontier conditions were more difficult than town-based police would appreciate, and that frontier officers were heroic in their endurance of them: 'in spite of hard times we had caused by want of food, continual travelling by day and watching by night and other difficulties, all members of the party kept up their spirits and energetically and minutely carried out all instructions issued . . . As for rations, one remark will be sufficient to explain the state of affairs 105 lbs of borrowed flour containing of 50 per cent weevils and maggots had to be shared out amongst 13 men for 3 weeks.'

Hard as conditions were for the Officers in Charge, they were undoubtedly worse for the Native Constables. When in 1889 the South Australian government revised the terms of payment for Native Police from a daily remuneration to an annual lump sum, considerable correspondence was generated on what that figure should be. Allowing for the fact that Native Constables would supply their own clothing and equipment from the lump sum, a figure of £12 per annum was flagged. This was challenged by the Minister of Education, who considered such a sum

> more than is necessary and it certainly would not be desirable to place any
> such sum in the hands of a blackfellow at one time. Surely there is no
> necessity to provide them with boots unless it be with [the] idea of adding
> dignity to their appearance. A native as a rule both rides and tracks better
> barefooted.[17]

Finally a lump figure of £7/10/- was approved. To the degree that the officers and the Native Constables shared many of the living conditions which, it seemed, contented no one, it is perhaps not surprising that Willshire, at least, would project a sense of affinity with the Native Police, however elastic that could be: at different times, the Native Constables were described by him as his protégés, his brothers in arms, and the thorns in his side, not to be trusted.

The Interior Police Patrol

By the early months of 1887 cattle killing was on the upswing. Between February and April Willshire and his Native Police were especially active in the region between Owen Springs and Undoolya. In March Willshire received a report that an Aboriginal worker on Undoolya station had been murdered. On 13 March he and four Native Constables travelled to the station and secured the suspect, returning that night, as the station journal recorded, 'with a wild nigger in chains'.[18] The following day the prisoner, Jacky, was brought before Skinner JP and remanded for eight days to permit further police inquiries. The extra time was not required. On 18 March Willshire recorded that while Native Constable Peter was escorting Jacky into the bush to 'ease himself' the prisoner made his escape. Willshire, Archie and Collins saddled up and gave chase, overhauling Jacky several kilometres from the Heavitree Gap station. He was repeatedly called upon to stop, but to no effect. 'If this notorious cattle killer got away altogether,' reported Willshire, 'no one in the country would be safe.' He gave his trackers instructions to shoot, and on the third shot Jacky fell. Ross and Skinner JP, local station managers, were informed of the death, but 'knowing the prisoner so well they deemed an inquest unnecessary'.[19]

While Willshire continued to patrol in the area of Undoolya and Love's Creek, a new front was opening up to the west. At Charles Chewings' relatively new Tempe Downs station, cattle killing was becoming a recurring problem. According to the station's manager, Robert Thornton, about 12 head of cattle had been killed since the station had been established. With Wurmbrand absent on a patrol to Barrow Creek, Mounted Constable Daer was ordered up from Charlotte Waters to render Willshire assistance. He patrolled in the region for two months between May and July, gauged that there were about 80 Aboriginal people about the run, but reported that owing to 'the very rough nature of the country' he was 'unable to affect any arrests'. The cattle killers would raid a mob, kill two or three beasts and take the meat, and then retreat into the ranges where the police found it infuriatingly difficult to follow them.[20]

On his return trip to Charlotte Waters, Daer diverted to Erldunda after receiving news from the station manager Robert Warburton that a large mob of his cattle had been driven off. On 25 July Daer, his Native Constables and a party from the station followed tracks for 150 kilometres until they came upon an encampment of around 30 men, including two suspects of an attack against Warburton some weeks previously. 'Of late,' he reported, 'the natives at Erldunda have become so daring, that on several occasions they have sent word to Mr Warburton that they intended burning the station & killing all the whites.'[21] When the party attempted to arrest the two suspects, reported Daer, they were met by a volley of spears, one of which passed between his left arm and body. With more spears pointed at him and a Native Constable, wrote Daer, 'I was compelled to shoot ... in self-defence,' as was the Native Constable who was 'similarly situated'. In this one encounter, two Aboriginal men died by police rifles. In contrast to Willshire's reports of violence, there is a tone of contrition in Daer's account, as well as a consciousness of administrative form. He was 'sorry to report the death' of the two men, he wrote, and added that whenever circumstance brought him 'into collisions with the Natives I have always tried to avoid taking violent measures'. The deaths of the two men had been reported to the nearest magistrate, a formality rarely undertaken by Willshire.[22]

Throughout the winter and spring of 1887, cattle killing continued on the stations on the western fringe of pastoral settlement, Tempe Downs and Erldunda in particular. Over the course of 1887 Robert Thornton, on

Tempe Downs, wrote frequently to the station's owner, Charles Chewings, complaining that while beasts were only being killed in ones and twos, the raids were constant, and the cattle, made nervous, were becoming difficult to control. 'A good many of the missionary blacks' were about, he observed, and 'they are not to be trusted'. The police at Alice Springs were of limited assistance; their presence required a 600 kilometre round trip. What was needed, he suggested, was a constant patrol.[23]

In response to the complaints of Thornton and others, the station owners again began petitioning the South Australian government for greater police protection of their pastoral interests. This time, enhanced protection was conceived not only in terms of police numbers but, most particularly, in terms of extended freedoms to patrol at will. Hitherto, police patrols had largely been in response to specific reports of aggressions, and they did not have the authority to take anticipatory action in regions where Aboriginal cattle killers were suspected to be 'troublesome'. This was about to alter.

In November 1887, Charles Chewings, the owner of Tempe Downs station, sent a letter to the Commissioner of Police to press his view 'that it is absolutely necessary for the police to have liberty to patrol the district at any time, by this means they could pop in on [the Natives] when least expected. The present system of having to send to the Alice for them is of no use whatsoever'.[24] In another letter intended for publication, he pressed the point further, praising the police constables' work but criticising the legal form that restrained their powers. The effect, he argued, was that settlers needed to take matters into their own hands:

> For a long time the Police protection has been inadequate to the
> requirements of the Macdonnell Ranges, the Finke and Palmer Rivers &
> the country to the north . . . The chief difficulty has arisen through the
> hard & fast rules the police are bound to follow . . . It is not right that
> stockowners and those employed by them should be forced to protect
> themselves and their stock by means of rifle. Humanity cries out against

this sort of thing and rightly too. Are we, as stockowners, justified in instructing our managers and men to ruthlessly shoot these natives . . . We are not allowed to do this and rightly too. But what are we to do? We cannot develop the country when our stock are being killed & driven away off the run as fast as we put them there. One of three things must come about, & that right speedily.

1. we must leave the country & dispose of the stock that are left.
2. we must take the law into our own hands & dispose of the natives as opportunity offers.
3. or we must have proper police protection to successfully carry on the development of the interior.[25]

Asked for his response, Willshire endorsed Chewings' suggestion for greater police freedom as 'a very good one'. He argued that freedom of the Officer in Charge to patrol 'any station that he knows where the blacks are nearly always doing something wrong ... would give more satisfaction than the usual way of waiting at Alice Springs until a report came re some offence'.[26] The argument for expanded police freedom was supported by Besley, who recommended the addition to the force of four Native Constables and four camels for the purpose of continuous patrols.[27]

Within months Reverend Heidenreich, the Lutheran mission superintendent based at Bethany in the Barossa Valley near Adelaide, was reporting further protests from Hermannsburg about the failure of the law in regard to the treatment of Aboriginal people. Reverend Kempe had complained to Heidenreich that on the Finke River,

the Acts of Parliament in regard to Aboriginals are not carried out like it is with white men, and as these blacks on the station & neighbourhood are partly civilized, and Christians, I cannot see any reason why this should be, and respectfully request, that you will be pleased to instruct the police stationed there to enforce the act as it is enforced down here.

Willshire was invited to respond to Kempe's complaints. He had visited the mission 11 times, he reported, and no such complaints had been raised with him. His response was passed on to Heidenreich, and there — for the moment — the matter rested.[28]

The year 1888 saw considerable rearrangements in the Centre's police force. A new Mounted Constable, Robert Hillier, had arrived to work with Willshire. In May, Wurmbrand was posted to Port Darwin, and left the Interior.[29] Other changes were happening in the district as well. It was believed that rubies had been discovered in country to the east of Alice Springs and by the end of the year between 150 and 200 miners were working the fields.[30] To meet these new demands Mounted Constable William Garnett South was transferred from Barrow Creek to take charge of the Alice Springs station and to serve as Mining Warden. In October he wrote to Besley, partly in response to settler entreaties, requesting even greater police presence in the Centre, especially for the district west of Alice and north-east of Barrow Creek, to enable continuous patrols around the pastoral stations and mining grounds.[31]

In November the Commissioner of Police Peterswald informed Willshire that the government intended to appoint one Constable and four more trackers to the Territory, and invited him to be transferred to the Territory's police force and take charge of the re-organised Interior Police Patrol. Willshire replied that he would be pleased to do so, and from 1 January 1889 his salary was transferred to the Northern Territory. Under these new bureaucratic arrangements, Willshire now had two chains of command: as well as reporting to Sub Inspector Besley, he reported to the Minister for Education, as the Minister controlling the Northern Territory.

In keeping with his new role as head of the Interior Police Patrol, and in response to the changing nature of the Central Australian frontier, Willshire established his base at Boggy Waterhole on 1 August 1889. For Willshire, it was a strategic location, situated 120 kilometres west of Alice Springs and roughly central to a circle that encompassed the Hermannsburg mission, and Owen Springs, Henbury and Tempe Downs stations. The waterhole, as Willshire may have been aware, was a significant one, located near the western boundary of Arrernte country. According to John Mulvaney:

> Aranda people knew Boggy Hole by a more poetic title, Alitera, named for two ghost-gum serpents and an ancestral wallaby who came here. As they had travelled west from the Hale River, during the Dreaming, they linked different Aranda groups through associated ceremonies.[32]

It is, Mulvaney writes, 'a beautiful place of tumbled red rocks (one of which is the ancestral wallaby), massive cliffs, water and related life-forms'. By establishing his base at such an 'economically and ceremonially significant waterhole', Willshire was denying the Arrernte 'free access to both its resources and to the route along the Finke gorge'.

Willshire's camp at Boggy Waterhole must have been a veritable caravanserai: there was Willshire and his four Native Constables, a cluster of tents to accommodate them and their supplies, at least a dozen horses tethered nearby, and at least five camels kept a secure distance from the horses. When the caravan moved, it must have been an impressive sight – and a logistical nightmare. According to later reports each of Willshire's trackers 'had a wife, sometimes two or three', and when the police 'go away on duty the lubras of trackers very often follow on foot'. One of the reasons they followed was because they were afraid to stay behind, 'as they often belong to hostile tribes'.[33]

In Willshire's official reports of patrolling with his four – later six – Native Police, he never reports that each of the Constables, and Willshire himself, was accompanied by an Aboriginal woman, together with other relatives. However, in his account of a patrol to Lake Amadeus, in *A Thrilling Tale of Real Life in the Wilds of Australia*, he describes the party: Willshire and his female 'guide' Chillberta 'rode the leading camel', a senior Native Constable and Ungellean 'rode together on another camel, the others followed in rotation', while Chillberta's father 'and thirty-seven other aboriginals came on behind on foot'.[34] Willshire had become the headman of a strange frontier tribe, enmeshed in a web of responsibilities and obligations grounded in the expectations of his followers, and the consequences of his own behaviour. A sense of his recognition of this comes in a report requesting more clothes for his trackers. 'I don't want them to leave me,' he pleads, 'so I must do something for them, so as to make my party worth remaining in.'[35] Willshire had become a sort of antipodean Lord Jim, and with that authority came a complex set of obligations: to his police superiors who provisioned his party and sanctioned his actions; to the pastoralists for whom he patrolled; and to his Native Police, in whose network of sexual and social relations he was becoming inexorably entwined.

By this time, Willshire had been based in the Centre for seven years. His position as Officer in Charge of the Native Police force had come within two years of his arrival there, and was now consolidated. He enjoyed the support of the pastoralists in the region, and considered himself on familiar terms with the country, as well as with the character of its indigenous inhabitants. His reports of patrols conducted extensively around the region had been accepted and filed by his superior officers in Port Augusta and Adelaide, and despite some recurring complaints about police activities by the missionaries at Hermannsburg, he had suffered no reproach. He was at the height of his personal and professional power. His confident sense of the critical role he was performing in opening up the Interior, up until now, was not challenged.

ETHNOGRAPHY AS SURVEILLANCE

The 'museological era'

By the 1880s anthropology was emerging as a popular and increasingly influential social science. There had been a brief flourishing of ethnographic work in early colonial South Australia, recorded mainly by the first wave of German Lutheran missionaries, but the interest had flagged. The early work was largely motivated by utilitarian questions of how best to 'civilise and Christianise' Aboriginal people, but in light of a general unwillingness to negotiate cultural difference, it was soon realised that the mechanisms set up to control the indigenous population required no deep knowledge of their culture. After Clamor Schürmann's account of the Port Lincoln Aborigines was published in 1846, very little work of ethnographic significance was produced for a quarter of a century. The decline in interest was mirrored in other colonies, as well as in Europe. In London, for instance, the Ethnological Society, which had been founded in 1843 as a breakaway from the Aborigines Protection Society, struggled with declining membership for the next two decades.[1] However, the publication of Darwin's *Origin of the Species* in 1859 sparked a resurgence of scientific interest in Aboriginal culture.[2] As the idea of natural selection was increasingly applied to the evolution of human societies, indigenous peoples once dismissed as 'savage' were now feted as 'primitive'. Aboriginal peoples now represented 'the childhood of humanity', modern survivors of the dawn of time whose present condition held clues to the origins of man.[3]

The impact of this international revival of interest in 'primitive' cultures began to be felt in the Australian colonies during the 1870s. Gentlemen anthropologists like Alfred Howitt and Edward Curr were making public calls for people to collect information on Aboriginal culture before the tide of history washed away any trace of their living presence.[4] Not surprisingly, missionaries were among the first to respond. George Taplin, who had worked as a Congregationist missionary at Point McLeay in southern South Australia since 1859, published *The Narrinyeri* in 1873 and shortly afterwards began work on a general survey of South Australian Aboriginal people which was published in 1879 under the title *The Folklore, Manners and Customs of the South Australian Aborigines*. Ethnologist Max Muller, of the Royal Institute, London, called for 'Literary Missionaries' to combine their religious calling with ethnographic work. 'What is wanted,' he exclaims, 'is more facts and fewer theories, and those facts can only be obtained by patient study of the lowest races of mankind.'[5]

The work produced in this era of 'compilers and collectors' typically drew its information from questionnaires distributed throughout the colony.[6] It was not sophisticated: isolated postmasters and policemen, for instance, were asked questions such as 'Are these people cannibals?'

The scientific interest in Aboriginal culture was matched by a growing popular interest. In May 1885 a corroboree was held for the public's entertainment on Adelaide Oval. The participants were Aboriginal people from the mission stations at Point McLeay and Point Pearce, and to everybody's surprise the event attracted a crowd estimated at 20,000.[7] By this time Aboriginal people were a rarity in the city and, for this generation of South Australians, their culture was a novelty. South Australia's contributions to colonial and international exhibitions now routinely included artefacts and dioramas of Aboriginal life, alongside displays of local produce and industry.[8]

Aboriginality and its material signs were being commodified. For the first time, the South Australian Museum began soliciting ethnographic material from the frontiers of settlement, where Europeans came into contact with supposedly 'pristine' and 'uncontaminated' Aboriginal tribes.[9] The rise of this 'museological era'[10] coincided with the first phase of pastoral expansion, and frontier conflict, in the Centre. So it is no surprise to find William Willshire, while engaged in 'dispersing the natives', also engaging in the late colonial fascination with Aboriginal culture.

In 1888, at a time when his autonomous authority in the region around Alice Springs was at its height, Willshire responded to the call for ethnographic information with the publication of the first of his three books, *The Aborigines of Central Australia*. While ostensibly an ethnography – an account of the 'manners, customs and languages' of Central Australian tribes – it is more tellingly a literary reconstruction of his experiences and opinions as a Mounted Constable in the Interior. Part memoir and part polemic, its writing provided Willshire with an opportunity to enter respectable posterity as a self-made anthropological 'expert'. But equally its writing facilitated something more self-referential: an exploration of the role of the frontier constable as a heroic one, one that – like the role of those earlier heroes of the colonial frontier, the explorer and the pioneer – contributed to the making of white nationhood.

The Aborigines of Central Australia

When first published, *The Aborigines of Central Australia* was received as a valuable contribution to ethnographic work, conducted under frontier conditions of 'great difficulties'. A reviewer for the *Adelaide Observer* praised Willshire's 'modesty and brevity', and gave due credit to his 'considerable attention' to the subject of 'the languages, customs, and traditions of the Australian aborigines'.[11] Willshire was certainly not the first or the last frontier police officer in the Northern Territory to publish his insights about Aboriginal culture. His colleague Samuel Gason, who had led the punitive expeditions following the attack on the Barrow Creek telegraph station in 1874, had published his pamphlet *The Dieyerie Tribe of Australian Aborigines* in 1874, and Inspector Paul Foelsche had also written an ethnographic paper about Aboriginal people in the Territory.[12] Ernest Cowle, who arrived in the Centre just before Willshire left it, would become a significant ethnographic collector for the anthropologist Baldwin Spencer. Notable about Willshire's book, however, is the service to which the slim ethnographic content of *The Aborigines of Central Australia* is put.

Its opening chapters are devoted to a description of Willshire's own arrival in the Centre, the advantages and difficulties of frontier policing, and the nature and state of pastoral settlement. The country itself – its timbers, grasses and ranges, the fertility of its soil, the plenitude of its game, its mineral wealth, its 'natural richness' – is described with considerable affection. The extent of pastoral settlement is outlined in full detail: the size and capacity of all of the pastoral properties, their owners, and the nature of their business. The putative subjects of the book, the Aborigines of Central Australia, are introduced at this stage in terms of a moral scale that is measured by their effect on the pastoral industry: the Aborigines around Owen Springs are 'addicted to cattle killing, and are otherwise "bad"', those near Anna's Reservoir are 'very bad', while those about Henbury are 'quiet'.[13]

Having outlined 'the state of settlement in Central Australia' thus far, Willshire engages his professed purpose, a description of Aboriginal culture. His commentary is prefaced by a reminder to his reader of his first-hand authority on the subject, an authority that supersedes that of either the explorer or the pioneer: 'what I state herein as facts, *are* facts . . . [and] were gathered during years of close study and communion with the natives, and from a more intimate acquaintance with "wild" blacks than falls to the lot of either explorers or even pioneer settlers.'[14] What follows is an account of their 'absurdly superstitious' character, their 'taboos', their 'nomadic instinct', their common crime of infanticide, their 'skirmishes' with the police, and, finally, a vocabulary. He closes with the modest reiteration that his research on the subject was 'prosecuted under considerable difficulties, and with steady persistence during six years of my life, spent among the natives of Central Australia'.[15]

A characteristic of this first, short work is the way in which the object of Willshire's literary attention shifts mid-chapter, mid-paragraph, or mid-sentence. He begins a chapter devoted to a description of Aboriginal hunting practices, but quickly it becomes an account of Aboriginal cattle killers and, in due course, his expertise in tracking them, a matter 'in which I take a deep interest':

> The tracking goes on, day after day, from water to water . . . The ranges are carefully scanned with field glasses for the smoke of camp fires, or other indications of aboriginal life . . . The chase is getting warmer now – and as the children say in their 'hide and seek' game – the pursuers are presently 'burning'.[16]

Finally 'the pursuing party abandons the tracks and divides, one section galloping off at full speed to get round the fugitives and cut off their retreat, while the other section spreads out and closes in'. Sometimes, a 'hot pursuit' will lead to a scrimmage, which may provide an opportunity for gathering collectibles of ethnographic worth; 'it is only after one of these chases that there is a chance to collect native weapons, by going back over the ground when the scrimmage is over'.[17]

The power of Willshire himself to ascertain, judge and affect Aboriginal cultural life is never far below the surface of the narrative, and he presents this power with odd good humour. Relating an anecdote in which he compelled his 'black boy "Jack Harrison"' to eat turkey, which was 'taboo', he writes: 'to break down his superstitious fears I insisted, and stood over him while he slowly worked his jaws through the worst part of a turkey I had shot. I must confess that I acted the "old man nigger" on this occasion, having taken the breast and choice parts of the bird for my own share. My boy informed me that only "Arilta" (circumcised young men) could eat turkey, but after violating the greedy law of the old men, he laughed to find that no evil consequences followed.'[18] 'Jack Harrison', who was Willshire's sole companion in this trip from Port Darwin to Alice Springs, is no doubt the same 18-year-old boy who, Willshire earlier tells us, 'died, I regret to say, of some internal complaint' within days of their arrival.[19]

Willshire's exploitation of the power that ethnographic knowledge gives him is evident in his account of sacred places and the cultural taboos surrounding them. Describing the 'rude' drawings in the gorge around Emily Gap, he relates:

> These drawings are called by the Alice Springs natives 'En-dull-inga' and they are 'taboo' to lubras – as I have personal means of knowing. In March 1883, when coming . . . through the Emily Gap, three lubras followed close behind my horse, saying that they were going to Alice Springs. Just as I reached the entrance to the Gap, five blackfellows appeared and ordered the lubras to go over the range – as no women were allowed to go through the Gap. The range was 500 feet high, and as the lubras had walked 25 miles that day I told the blackfellows that they should follow me through the Gap. At first they assumed defiant and bellicose attitudes, but I cleared them out and passed on, followed by the lubras, who, to my great astonishment, picked up some rags, bushes and grass, and made coverings to their faces, and walked blindfolded, by the sound of the horse's footsteps.[20]

Ethnography as surveillance

These literary moments, offered as ethnography, might be described as what Deborah Rose calls 'trophy moments' in which Aboriginal cultural life is captured and put to the service of European conquest. They are moments that relegate the living Aboriginal social world to the history of colonialism, that dismiss that social world from the present and shift it to the realm of classifiable or contemptible relic. The trophy moment is, writes Rose, 'a trophy of nationhood', produced for the purpose of spectacle or science, and each moment contains, simultaneously, the display and the eradication of Aboriginal culture.[21]

The Aborigines of Central Australia concludes with some diverse notes. There are brief sections on infanticide and cannibalism, doubtless produced for sensational effect, and two appendices. The first is a vocabulary of Aboriginal words, a curious feature of which is a long list of 'Lubra's Names'.[22] Unaccompanied by a parallel list of men's names, its purpose is opaque. The second appendix is a detailed account of the 1874 attack on the Barrow Creek telegraph station, which had occurred eight years before Willshire's arrival in the Centre. Apparently prepared 'from the statements of Mr S Gason', it enables Willshire to explore his taste for adventure narratives, but its place in this apparently ethnographic study is obscure. To the extent that this is ethnography, it is the ethnography of surveillance and control.

Willshire was not alone in combining his role of surveillance with a role of ethnographic collector – a dual role which is, perhaps, best exemplified by his description in The Aborigines of Central Australia of collecting native weapons when a 'scrimmage' was over. Philip Jones has speculated that the collection of culturally significant objects, such as the sacred tjurunga, became a form of social surveillance and control that might not have been as fatal as the rifle, but was just as effective.[23] In this sense, ethnographic collection emerged as another form of policing on the Central Australian frontier. Mounted Constable Cowle apparently considered his collecting of sacred objects for Baldwin Spencer not only as a contribution to the late nineteenth-century discipline of human science but also as part of his policing role 'to maintain an authoritative presence throughout the region'.[24]

European motives for collecting such material signs of 'Aboriginality' were varied, but such 'relics' fed late colonial society's sense of its own superiority. Sacred objects were also hard currency. Even Francis Gillen, who was considered to be unusually sympathetic to the Arrernte people, became a keen collector of Aboriginal cultural objects, and sold sacred *tjurunga* through anthropologist Baldwin Spencer's European market networks in order to supplement his stationmaster's income.[25] The Hermannsburg missionaries also trafficked in *tjurunga*, though no doubt for other motives. In the early twentieth century Carl Strehlow and his successor F W Albrecht amassed collections as part of the process of monitoring and substituting Arrernte religious practices in favour of Christian ones – but the monetary value from the sale of these items was useful in supplementing the mission income.[26] Under these circumstances it is not surprising that individual Arrernte people might barter *tjurunga* in return for securities of other kinds.

In this amassing of cultural information, people who otherwise had little in common kept each other company. Some years after writing *The Aborigines of Central Australia* Willshire was invited to contribute information about Arrernte culture to an ethnographic survey on Aboriginal peoples of Central Australia, to be published in the *Royal Anthropological Journal*.[27] The survey's 'Questions on the Manners, Customs, Religions, Superstitions, &c., of Uncivilized or Semi-civilized Peoples' had been formulated by the anthropologist J G Frazer and circulated by the South Australian Museum's director Dr E C Stirling to a variety of contributors, including Willshire. The range of contributors reveals a fascinating combination of ethnographic 'experts': included with Willshire are his police colleagues Samuel Gason and Paul Foelsche; Lindsay Crawford, the station manager at Victoria River Downs pastoral station; the stationmaster at Powell Creek; and the Protector of Aborigines, Edward Hamilton. Willshire may only have known Hamilton through correspondence, but he certainly had personal contact with each of the other contributors in his capacity as a Mounted Constable in the Territory. Lindsay Crawford's qualification to write on the Victoria River region is introduced by his own curious explanation that 'during the last ten years, in fact since the first white man settled here, we have held no communication with the natives at all, except with the rifle. They have never been allowed near this station or the outstations, being too treacherous and warlike'.[28] Reverends Schulze and Kempe of the Hermannsburg mission both published extensive studies of the Arrernte during the early 1890s, outlining their habits, customs and languages from the missionaries' point of view.[29]

It is in this capacity as an expert on Aboriginal culture that Willshire introduces *The Aborigines of Central Australia*. He was motivated in offering his contribution to scientific knowledge, he writes, after seeing a notice in the *Adelaide Observer* that the Royal Geographical Society of Australasia was anxious to record information about Aboriginal culture before it was too late.[30] As Willshire explained it:

> It has been said that the Australian aborigines are fast dying out. If that be true, this little brochure will help to preserve the language of the natives of the western territory of Central Australia. Those two admirable institutions, the Australian Natives' Association and the Geographical Society, will no doubt be pleased to see that the author . . . has tried to do something for his countrymen.[31]

The making of white nativeness

Given the climate of the times, Willshire's ethnographic interests were by no means contradictory with his role of surveillance over Aboriginal people in the Centre. Notable about Willshire's enactment of those roles, however, is the extent to which they unfolded in extreme and ambivalent relation to each other. He was an officer notorious for the violence of his patrols, yet he projected a sense of himself as connected by indigenous links to the country he patrolled. In *The Aborigines of Central Australia* he writes unrelentingly of his subject with a combination of dismissive contempt and qualified admiration. Yet the perceived qualities of nativeness that he either dismisses or admires are different ones; Aboriginal bodies are to be dispersed; 'nativeness' itself is to be mythified and remade.

In this sense, the most important implicit subject of *The Aborigines of Central Australia* is not Aboriginal cultural life but rather the sentiment of burgeoning nationalism. Willshire was familiar with the symbols of nascent

Australian nationalism and used them knowingly. In 1891, he republished *The Aborigines of Central Australia* through C E Bristow, the South Australian Government Printer. This contains some interesting differences, including a new preface, in which Willshire identifies himself as 'an Australian native' who is providing a benefit to the nation through ethnographic study of the 'natives'.[32]

Earlier in the nineteenth century, the term 'Australian' was often used interchangeably with the term 'native' to refer to Aboriginal people.[33] Yet in the same period, as early as the nineteenth century's beginning, the term 'native' was applied to Australian-born descendants of British emigrants.[34] By the mid nineteenth century, the term 'native' became extended to the idea of a white 'native race': 'that is to say,' as *Sidney's Emigrant Journal* put it in the 1840s, 'Australians born in the country, of European origins.'[35] Australian-born whites were thus attributed with a specifically eugenic distinction. However, 'the natives' is still the phrase used most often to signify 'Aboriginal people' in letters, government reports and the literature of the nineteenth century. By the time Willshire was re-editing his first book, then, 'native' had become a most peculiar term, a collapsing category: it could signify the new 'Australian race', the progressive nation, or the 'dying race', the displaced people. Depending on the context, nativeness was a racial category to eliminate, or a racial category to celebrate.

The aspiration to white nativeness that Willshire identifies in his preface to *The Aborigines of Central Australia* relied on a simultaneous borrowing from and repulsion towards Aboriginality. This, by the late nineteenth century, was the logic of Australianness in the making. Nicholas Thomas puts it this way: 'On the one hand, a self-conscious national culture that has seemed permanently in the making required Aboriginality for its sense of place; on the other, Aboriginal sovereignty and autonomy diminished the authority and coherence of the settler nation, and were persistently suppressed.'[36] Within this logic, there is no contradiction in Willshire's ethnographic fascination with – even, indeed, his qualified appreciation of – the Aboriginal people he shot down during his patrols.

He asserts his credentials as 'white man born under the southern cross'. He took an interest in the Federation debate and was a member of the Australian Natives Association, membership of which was limited to Australian-born whites, testimony to the growing nationalist sentiment of late colonialism.

In his next book, published four years after the reissued *Aborigines of Central Australia*, Willshire makes liberal use of the wattle as the symbol of the white Australian nation. He relates an anecdote, for instance, in which he makes a farewell speech to the Aboriginal people of Lake Amadeus, urging them to remember, when the wattle next blooms, 'how I adorned my hat and my camels with that emblem of my native land, and how I taught you to adorn yourselves with it'.[37] The irony of this gesture is unmistakable: a policeman who was actively engaged in a war of dispossession lectures Aboriginal people on love of country. His articulation of white nativeness extends beyond such references to generic natural symbols. More intrinsically, his writings perform a steady eulogy to the 'bushman', or white frontiersman, as the authentic expression of a unique Australian identity.

In his book *The Australian Legend* Russel Ward traces the origins of the Australian national character, or mystique, to the nineteenth-century bushman. The bushman was a member of what Ward called the 'nomad tribe' of pastoral workers, describing his attributes as follows:

> . . . a practical man, rough and ready in his manners. . . . He swears hard and consistently, gambles heavily and often, and drinks deeply on occasion . . . . He believes that Jack is not only as good as his master, but . . . probably a good deal better, and so he is a great 'knocker' of eminent people.[38]

Most importantly, the bushman 'knew' the bush: he was not only comfortable in that environment, but was master of it. His very identity was shaped by his relationship to the environment: he was not the settler of the pioneer legend battling with an alien land, he was an Australian in his environment.

Ward has relatively little to say about the relationship between the bushmen and Aboriginal people, but he suggests that they felt 'some indebtedness' to the Aborigines. He writes,

> many bushmen felt themselves to be, in some sense, the heirs to important parts of Aboriginal culture. After all, no white man has ever been the equal of the Aborigines in essential bush skills, in tracking, finding water, living on bush food, and so on. And it is doubtful whether white men have ever equalled Aborigines in some purely European-derived arts, such as horse-breaking or cattle-mustering. . . . If, as has been argued, the bushman's *esprit de corps* sprang largely from his adaptation to, and mastery of, the outback environment, then the Aborigine was his master and mentor.[39]

While it is undoubtedly true that bushmen like Willshire expressed admiration for Aboriginal bush skills, be they tracking, finding water, or living off the land, they also articulated a bitter contempt for all sorts of imputed Aboriginal characteristics – savagery, treachery, immorality, ingratitude and so on. This ambivalence, this constant shifting between respect and contempt, derives from an uneasy interplay between the bushman's self-identification and his lived relationship with the Aboriginal people. The bushmen, that is to say the pastoral workers and their associates – people like Willshire – were in the front line of settlement. It is they who were responsible for the greatest violence against Aboriginal people – intimidation, murder, as well as sexual violence and exploitation. It is hardly surprising that in their writings they should portray the Aborigines in a way that served to rationalise or legitimate their behaviour. Yet the bushman's self-identification was built upon his adaptation to and mastery of the Australian environment – characteristics perceived to be typically Aboriginal. Given the importance of these characteristics to the bushman's identity, they could hardly be denigrated in Aboriginal people. Yet the bushman, despite what Ward argues, had no desire to identify with the Aborigines, nor acknowledge them as masters or mentors. Quite the reverse.

These contradictory preoccupations dominate the revised edition of *The Aborigines of Central Australia*. The 1891 edition includes a new chapter on 'The Aborigines of Lake Amadeus and the George Gill Ranges'. In it, Willshire again illustrates his affection for the country: its springs and claypans, its native fruits, its cotton-bush plains and ranges. 'The character of the country', he writes, 'may be imagined when Mr. Giles, who discovered it, thought it proper to name one part of it the "Vale of Tempe", another the "Vale of Amber", and a third "Glen Edith".'[40] Such affiliation with the country is also made, Willshire intimates, by long familiarity with its isolation and dangers: 'Travelling many years with blacks only, hardened by disappointment, travelling by night a wild, devious, and untrodden track to reach water I once knew, to find the hole dry – these are the experiences that make the bushmen of Australia.' Willshire's depiction of his knowledge of the country, which is his passport to membership within the nomadic tribe of bushmen, is equalled by his vitriol towards Aboriginal people themselves:

> The ingratitude of the aborigines is well known and understood by all the white people who may have anything to do with them. They have few and limited ideas, and are destitute of anything like sentiment. They attach themselves to the whites from motives of self-interest only, and, as a rule, they will return evil for good . . . It need hardly be averred that they are cannibals, and sometimes eat each other . . . From a very long experience of the blacks, and careful observation of their character and habits, the author cannot speak much in their favor. They are ungrateful, deceitful, wily, and treacherous. They are indolent in the extreme, squalid and filthy in their surroundings, as well as disgustingly impure amongst themselves . . . [If they] ever were superior to what they are now . . . they have lost all the good qualities which their progenitors might have possessed, and have sunk down into a dirty, mean, and thriftless condition.[41]

Within the world of flux described in *The Aborigines of Central Australia*, the central stabilising force is the police patrol party, whose duties are 'to see that the wild natives do not interfere with the white settlers'.[42] Willshire's account of Aboriginal deceit and ingratitude is followed by an account of police patrols: the difficulties of 'undergoing many privations, such as the want of water, meat, &c.', and the preparations that become necessary when 'encountering hostile natives'. 'The spears of the natives are not very effective out in the open, and of course would be of little avail against the Martini-Henry, with which the police are provided.' In this opaque description of policing duties, Willshire is careful to uphold police precautions: 'If there ever is any trouble [the police] must not be the aggressors'. But equally he laments the encroaching limits on police power: 'It is hardly safe now to chastise the blacks, or to punish them in any way'. And, most particularly, he laments the interference in police matters by missionaries: 'Their sympathies would at once go with the oppressed native, and the circumstance would be reported in some direction so that something might arise out of it.'[43]

Representations in Port Augusta

In January 1888, Willshire's colleague Wurmbrand was completing a long patrol which had culminated in the arrest of Toombana and Nitri Nitrinia, men implicated in the attempted murder of Robert Warburton on Erldunda station during the previous May.[44] Neither Willshire nor Wurmbrand had often taken prisoners, and rarely had they transported them south for trial, but they did on this occasion. Given their history, one might speculate that there was an ulterior motive for the long and tedious journey. Willshire's book *The Aborigines of Central Australia* was published at Port Augusta in 1888 and it is likely that he used this trip to deliver the manuscript to his publisher. In January 1888, not long after Toombana and Nitri Nitrinia were sentenced to two months' gaol for common assault, Willshire, Wurmbrand and the Native Police posed for a series of studio portraits.

Each of these photographs, taken in Port Augusta and replicating life on the frontier, recalls Deborah Rose's notion of the 'trophy moment'. Shortly after the photographs were taken *The Port Augusta Dispatch* published a lengthy description of the scene depicted. At the centre of a recreated bush scene is Mounted Constable Willshire, one hand resting on the Martini-Henry carbine that supports his pose. His eyes follow the sightline of the Native Constable who stands at his side, bare chest strung with ammunition, pointing out a target beyond the frame. Around them in poses of attention, rest or recline are Mounted Constable Wurmbrand and other Native Constables, who are partly dressed in the uniforms of the Native Police, carbines at ease.

The commentary on this photograph in *The Port Augusta Dispatch* offers direction on how to read its storyline. Apparently, it was intended that the 'picturesque' group should include two Aboriginal prisoners, Nitri Nitrinia and Toombana, who had been brought down to Port Augusta after their capture by Wurmbrand and the Native Police, but the prisoners had, 'through some misapprehension, been handed over to the custody of the Greenbush gaoler before the arrangements were completed'. However, 'the tout ensemble did not suffer much from their absence, and, indeed, in the scene represented they would have been dramatically *de trop*, for what is shown (with the aid of scrub accessories skilfully arranged), is the police camp near Erldunda on May 26, when MC Willshire and Wurmbrand were "out" with their sable subordinates after the blacks who had attacked the station about a week before'. The target in the sightline of Willshire and his Native Constable 'Chickylia', the article informs us, is smoke which marks out 'the camp of the hostile blacks'. Willshire 'bend[s] towards his Aboriginal henchman and keenly scrutinis[es] the smoke in the distance'. Wurmbrand half reclines 'in an attitude suggestive of fatigue' while behind him squats Undundna/Billy, 'the best shot in the native police force, who clasps his carbine as if he loved and relied upon it'.[45] It should be noted that Willshire is the central figure of photographs which purport to recreate a scene on Erldunda in May 1887 when 'Wurmbrand and the

Native Police' captured the prisoners 'Nitranitrinyana and Toombana' – he is portrayed as the central figure of an incident at which he was not present. Wurmbrand, who made the arrests depicted in the scene, is almost hidden in the background.

As anthropologist Nicolas Peterson has written of the photograph, it is a characteristic instance 'of the colonial ideology in action'.[46] While there is a superficial appearance of equivalence and camaraderie between the white and black police officers in the group – both white and black squat, or stand, and their attention is drawn to a common target – the comfortable assurance of Mounted Constable Willshire's pose, and his central place within the photograph's implied narrative, point to the fact that he is this visual story's key figure, its centre of control and authority. Moreover, of course, and as would be well known to its local contemporary audience, the role of the Native Constables in this recreated scene is, under the direction of the Officer in Charge, to pursue and capture the 'hostile blacks', on whose distant camp the attention of each subject in the photograph is directed. The photograph's sole plot, then, revolves around the enlistment of Aboriginal people by white officers in the violent suppression of other, 'hostile' Aboriginal people.

Another studio photograph depicts a variation on the same storyline. In its centre, again, Willshire stands prepared for action, his chest strung with ammunition, Martini-Henry carbine at the ready. He is flanked by two Native Constables, their mixed status marked out by the combination of the police trousers they wear and the traditional scars of initiation that line their bare chests. Willshire's line of vision follows the sightline of one of the Native Constables, who stands with his rifle raised and aimed. At their feet, two figures occupy the foreground. One is a third Native Constable, posed on one knee with his rifle held upright before him. On Willshire's right sits a more ambiguous figure: an Aboriginal woman, who gazes out of the frame in the direction of the raised gun. A camp fire smoulders on her right, at Willshire's feet. Does her presence serve some ethnographic function? As repeated missionary complaints had attested,

Aboriginal women were often present in the police camps, as partners of the Native Police, temporarily as the surviving 'spoils of war', or perhaps as the mistresses of the police. To which 'camp' does this woman in the photograph 'belong'?

The photographic portraits are evocative of the types of illustrations that graced the pages of imperial adventure novels of the period, such as Rider Haggard's popular novel *She*, a novel which Willshire knew and to which he refers in *The Aborigines of Central Australia*. In an illustration from a nineteenth-century edition of *She*, the white hero stands before a smouldering fire, his clenched fists on his hips and his chest strung with ammunition. To his right and slightly behind stands his native 'henchman', on whose loyalty the white hero can rely. The hero's gaze is held by the 'she' of the title, the erotic/destructive force whose power he has overcome in his confident possession of the country.

The lost patrol

While Willshire was writing up his experiences for the sake of science and posterity, he sometimes failed to keep journals of his policing activities. The maintenance of such records was a routine part of his job and was required for both administrative and legal purposes. In 1889, shortly after forming his new Interior Police Patrol, he undertook a three month patrol into the Musgrave Ranges in search of killers of a Chinese station hand. Willshire returned with his prisoners, but kept no journals of the expedition. Notwithstanding this breach of administrative requirement, it is surprising that Willshire, who represented himself as an explorer and writer, kept no record of what was possibly his most adventurous and remote patrol. Besley was astonished. At the end of the year, he wired Willshire with the message: 'your journals required from the time you were transferred to Northern Territory department, in future enter correspondence received & sent, state date formed camp.'[47] Willshire replied with a belligerent letter expressing a feeling that such details were beneath his real role:

I had no recognised place of abode, no books. I had been informed that I would not be allowed any travelling allowance, & from all those facts mentioned how could I keep Journals. It will be remembered also that I did the work of Daer and James who let their witnesses escape & I caught them again.[48]

Besley had, from the time of Willshire's arrival in the Centre, been his active supporter, commending him for the role of Officer in Charge of the Native Police, and taking up his requests for more resources with Police Commissioner Peterswald. On the question of Willshire's erratic reporting, however, Besley displayed a new irritation with his constable, and pursued the requirement of record-keeping into the new year.

I am wiring again today for your Journals from the date of your transfer and I must have them. It is no use saying you had no Books. I did not expect you to have & carry a set of Police records with you, but you <u>ought not & must not travel without a memo book</u> and in it enter shortly every days work. Otherwise your officers or yourself will have no record of what duty you perform.[49]

In reply, Willshire displayed his own impatience with Besley and his formal procedure. Alluding to a hypocrisy within an administration that demanded his action and yet complained about paperwork, he makes it clear that what matters to him is not regulatory details but material outcomes:

it is impossible for me to furnish Journals I have no record, you were continually writing me whenever I was available to lose no time, but get Jimmy the important witness in the Chinese murder case, I worked very hard, and about 5 months were spent by me in travelling between the Peake & the Musgrave Ranges, I got the witness & other witnesses that Daer & James failed to capture . . . I kept no record whatever, but nevertheless I got the witness that I was after, the one the Comm of Police said must be got.

Perhaps Willshire felt that he had gone too far in alienating his best supporter. Soon he was writing again to Besley on the issue of his journal keeping, in a more conciliatory tone. His letter reveals a longing for recognition of his own value, and resentment that it is not fully given.

In reference to the journals from January 1st 1889 up to July 31st I shall try my best to write them out, but I have no record, I know that I did work for months in the Musgrave Ranges to get that witness a most wonderful thing it was too, getting one single blackfellow alive in the midst of a wild tribe, I kept no record never knew the day or date was allowed no travelling allowance.

... It takes me days & days to do writing ... I have to do the cooking in fact everything devolves upon me. And after staying in a close little tent writing by a slush lamp till midnight. ... Can the Inspr let me off of all this correspondence or of some of it, I understood, that I was to be a patrolling Constable, but here I am in the midst of a lot of correspondence ... & now preparing to start again with the Trackers to Tempe Downs ... On this occasion I shall take the books with me, & write up the days work every time I get a chance.

Forwarding this letter of lament to the Commissioner of Police, Besley suggested forgiving Willshire for his neglect: 'I ordered Willshire to lose no time in trying to get witness. This he desires great credit for doing but kept no record for a long time. I now respectfully ask that his Journal may be allowed to commence from the August 1st 1889'. It seems that the Commissioner and the Minister for Education were satisfied with that suggestion, but not without a shadow having been cast over Willshire's record. As Willshire was to find, a new era of administrative surveillance was encroaching on his autonomy in the Centre.

THE MISSIONARIES UNDER SCRUTINY

The murder of Nameia

During the last months of 1889, Willshire was settling into his newly established police camp at Boggy Waterhole, not far from the Hermannsburg
mission. As he had done for much of the year, he spent a good deal of
energy writing requests to his superiors to properly outfit and supply his
Interior Police Patrol. In December he submitted a requisition for 116
items, including soap, leggings and looking glasses 'to keep the Native
Constables clean and tidy'. In reply, the secretary to the Minister complained to Besley that the order would 'nearly stock a country store' –
would he please strike out any items not reasonably required.[1]

Meanwhile, Willshire's tension with Besley about his poor record-
keeping practices continued to simmer. In December Willshire was challenged about his unauthorised subscription to a private mailbag. (A post
office receipt indicated that his last delivery had included six letters and 16
newspapers.) This was not a private mailbag, he responded, but one he
used for government business and, he confessed, a most tedious business at
that: 'if there was such a place where no mail ever came I should like to be
there as I am a very poor hand at clerical duties.' He noted that Besley had
just returned all his journals by the last mail for correction, and countered
that the 'hours I spend in a small hot tent on a sandbank writing that lot out

caused me some trouble, doing all the cooking and a host of other jobs, and dust storms blowing day after day in the hottest months of the year, writing on a clothes box, it is no easy matter to keep up correspondence'.[2]

In the same batch of correspondence is a report written on 8 January 1890 about a fresh outbreak of cattle killing on Tempe Downs. Over Christmas and the New Year, Willshire wrote, hundreds of head of cattle were driven off, and while he was 'working one part of the run, blacks were killing cattle on another part'. The following day, his report resumed with an account of an attack on the police camp during the previous night by 'a mob of Tempe Downs natives'; the deaths of two Henbury cattle within a few kilometres of his station at the hands of the same group who, he complained, could then take refuge at Hermannsburg; and – the necessary point – a request for more constables to stabilise the region:

> I commenced this yesterday afternoon and of all the remarkable
> coincidences I have ever experienced this is one. My camp was attacked by
> a mob of Tempe Downs natives in the night and during the day I am
> writing to the Inspector for more protection for myself and every white
> man in the West, two of the Native Constables have just returned &
> reported to me that this same mob of natives killed two of the Henbury
> cattle within six mile of the Police Camp, the owner of Henbury will be
> annoyed when he hears of it, killing cattle and attacking the police camp
> the same day shows how daring they are, they think nothing if one or two
> of their clique are shot dead, they come again . . . being inadequately
> manned watching night after night comes hard on the trackers, and worst
> of all, these demons seek refuge at the mission station when pursued hotly,
> it is the refuge for all outlaws in the whole district.[3]

Curiously, not reported in this letter is a key event that occurred during the night's attack on his camp: the killing of Nameia, who was also known as Peter. According to Willshire, the killers were 'a mob of wild blacks from the westward' who had intended to kill one of his Native

Constables but had killed Nameia instead. According to Ted Strehlow, Nameia's death was the final episode in the long-running history of paybacks that had been exchanged between the Southern Arrernte and the Matuntara, beginning with the breach of traditional law by Nameia's clan at Irbmangkara. Nameia's key role in the assassination of Matuntara leaders, following the massacre of his kinsmen at Irbmangkara in about 1878 – no more than a few kilometres from what Willshire would later make his Boggy Waterhole police camp – had its fulfilment when the Matuntara learnt, in early 1890, that Nameia was camped there, close to the boundary of their tribal territory. Nameia was there to visit his son, Aremala, or 'Larry', one of Willshire's Native Police.[4]

When Nameia's murder was discovered, the attackers' tracks were identified and within days a patrol party, led by Willshire, was organised. Willshire and his Native Police tracked through the country until they came across 'a mob with the two men who had actually murdered [Nameia]'.[5] They gave chase, but were compelled to give up when the pursued men fled into the surrounding gorges and ranges. While he does not name the two men, Willshire seemed to be in no doubt that he knew who they were.[6] He was aggrieved that such a brazen attack would be carried out in his police camp, and he may well have desired to re-assert an authority that had been patently undermined; possibly, too, he was conscious of having a place within a complex network of allegiances which, if sustained, would ultimately maintain his Native Constables' loyalties to himself. However, events transpiring in Adelaide on the very same day that the murder occurred took matters in a different direction.

Accusations and counter-accusations

On the very day that Nameia's murder took place at Willshire's police camp on the Finke River, a public meeting was held in the Young Men's Christian Association parlour in Adelaide 'to consider matters relating to the condition and treatment of the blacks of the colony'. Friedrich

Krichauff, a prominent member of the German Lutheran community, chaired the meeting, which was convened principally to air the grievances of his fellow Lutherans from the Finke River mission, and with the intention of urging on the government 'a complete change in the manner of dealing with and protecting the aborigines'.[7] Charles Eaton Taplin, son of the Congregationalist missionary George Taplin and member of the influential Aborigines Friends Association, was the first to speak. He claimed that 'in the interior especially the natives were subjected to very harsh treatment' and that the government should be urged to set aside reserves for their 'exclusive use and protection'. Without such protection, he argued, Aboriginal people 'would soon die out'.

Reverend Schwarz, one of the two founding missionaries who had served at the Finke River settlement since its establishment and who had only recently returned south, addressed the meeting through a translator. Schwarz was less concerned with the matter of the Aborigines 'dying out' and more with the matter of potential genocide: 'the actions which were taken against the blacks,' he began, 'were so taken with the object of exterminating them, and especially the men.' The squatter's guiding principles were simple, he argued. If he 'kept cattle, and there were blacks on his run, either the blacks or the cattle had to go'. Schwarz related the incident of an Aboriginal man who was ordered to leave a pond where he was fishing or be shot; he was shot. He also recalled the case from November 1884 of the Mounted Constable who had taken three men away from the mission in chains, whose bodies were found, shot and still chained together, on the boundary of the mission station.

The missionaries' remaining allegations concerned the prevalence of 'immorality' and the keeping of Aboriginal women on almost every station 'for shameful purposes'. Mission girls, Schwarz said, were enticed away by white men. He reported that three girls who had run away from the mission were now to be found in Willshire's nearby police camp. Schwarz levelled another serious charge when he referred to a policeman – Willshire, implicitly – who was sent out to 'arrest some blacks, but instead shot them, and brought back against their will two young black women, who lived with him, and one of whom came to the city with him'.

These were exceptionally serious charges. Not only did they allege apparently unrestrained violence and exploitation by Europeans, but they portrayed the police as being among the chief offenders. The meeting concluded with a recommendation that the government appoint a commission to investigate the claims. This was to be pursued by Charles Taplin, who closed with the cautionary comment that 'it would be very difficult to gather evidence on the spot on account of the complicity of the police'.[8]

Over the following two months, Willshire was active not only in refuting such claims, but in putting into disrepute the people who made them. Writing to Besley from his Boggy Waterhole police camp on 21 February, he reacted strongly against the 'damaging assertions' to come out of the Adelaide meeting, and denied that they had any foundation 'as far as I know'.[9]

> Taking these German missionaries altogether, (viz) Kempe, Schultz and Schwarz, they never go about, hardly ever leave their home, consequently what they say against the white men is only what they hear from the blacks, and what they invent . . . And I can say, the missionaries are no more the friends of the blacks than I am. I treat them kindly & will bring witnesses to prove, that I spend my own money liberally in buying rations to feed them, and I know just as much about the Aborigines as they do.
>
> . . . We take for instance that person, Taplin, who spoke at the same meeting as Schwartz, he has never been in this country, what can he know? . . . it simply lies in this, that the blacks kill the squatters cattle wholesale, they spear his horses, they attack his homestead & burn it down, they ruin his wells by throwing windlass and bucket to the bottom, they murder his civilised black boys & they attempt to murder him and his employees. How many murder cases & attacks have I been called upon to take the necessary action, why the answer is, several, I go out in the bush and track up the offenders day after day.[10]

On the issue of the three chained prisoners who were shot, he points out his own uninvolvement: 'I was a thousand miles away, and all I know about it is what the white men told me when I returned, and I saw by the letterbook of the Alice Springs station, that Wurmbrand had only done his duty and exonerated himself.' The issue of white men who take Aboriginal women, he admits,

> is very unbecoming . . . but I do not know an instance where they have any of the lubras belonging to the mission station, & in the cases I have met with, the lubras are properly cared for & treated with the tenderest compassion and would not leave that state of life if they had their own way.

His letter closes with a mixed appeal to his own feeling that he has always been keen to 'get on well' with the missionaries at Hermannsburg, and that the mission is an unnecessary and unwanted institution in the region:

> apparently to my face they are allright, but behind my back they write assertions that are not true . . . I would draw the attention of my Superior Officers to the fact that I will be ready any time to assist the missionaries in any way they like to suggest.
>
> I could, if I were asked, bring natives to their place, even the blind lame and otherwise infirm [but] natives will not remain there, they have a difficulty to keep the Aboriginals that belong there . . . the fact is there are so few natives in the locality of Hermannsburg that a mission station is not required.[11]

Within two weeks, on 10 March, Willshire was again writing to Besley ridiculing the Lutheran missionaries. Forwarding a copy of a letter he had received from Kempe requesting the return to the mission of the two Aboriginal girls who were staying at the police camp, he writes:

I have the honor to forward you a sample of the letters I got from the Revd H Kempe the manager of the mission station. In one letter to me he wrote and spelt like the following fac-similie,

'I was tinks that a bag of vegatibles was do your stummick more good as tew bottils of grog at the same price'.

Now the Revd. Gentleman never saw me drinking grog. I might be a teatotaller for all he knows.

I have seen these Revd. Gentlemen get up from the verandah where Mr Flint and their wives were sitting, and go a little way, say about 7 yards, and make water, and talking all the time about how decent people ought to be.[12]

With this letter to Besley he included an additional report defending himself from any suggestion of wrong, assuring the Inspector of his sound relationship with the missionaries, and simultaneously seeking recognition of their disreputableness:

Since writing the attached report I have been to the mission station & have seen both Mr Kempe and Mr Schultz. They treated me kindly & Mr Kempe told me he was much obliged to me for sending the children back that had run away. He is perfectly satisfied with my conduct towards Aborigines, & offered to take my part if ever it became necessary, & he said that Schwartz mentioned things in Adelaide that had occurred long before I came in the country. I then told Mr Kempe that I never heard in all my travels all over Central Australia, of any blacks being ill treated by white men . . .

I can assure Insp. Besley that I want to keep my billet by doing my duty & therefore I will not offend the missionaries if I know it, but would go a lot out of my way to please them. Somehow or other the blacks wont stop there, consequently they go in all directions & the missionaries are wroth about it, I wont let them remain at my camp for fear of offending the missionaries . . . These missionaries come to peoples camps with long whips & revolvers looking for a few harmless lubras.

They are strange Reverends, I asked them why the boys & girls ran
away & they could not give me a satisfactory reply, I always thought that
missionaries were supposed to be kind & gentle, but these Germans up here
are rude and Uncouth, they acted very friendly towards me when I was
there last, that is for them, because they are naturally uncourteous.[13]

A further letter by Willshire to the Commissioner of Police refuting
the missionaries' claims was published in the *Advertiser*. In it Willshire
charged the Aborigines who lived at the mission with being 'the greatest
liars and blackguards amongst the blacks'. He added that he made it his
business 'to be courteous to the missionaries', but 'at the same time, it
behoves me also to look out that they don't injure me. As I am desirous of
doing my duty and keeping my position, I write this to my superior officers
for their perusal, and to let them know that these missionaries do not treat
the blacks as they should be treated'.[14]

Clearly, a war of white relations was heating up in the Centre. After
the *South Australian Register* reported the outcomes of the 9 January delegation, letters from the Centre's pastoral community were published
refuting the missionaries' allegations and supporting the police. 'Shame on
Mr Schwartz,' wrote Ben Rogers, the cook on Tempe Downs station, 'to
accuse these men who have done their level best to keep the blacks quiet.
The police are respected and admired by every one.' As for the mistreatment of Aboriginal people in the Centre, the blacks 'on all the stations . . .
are fed well, dressed well, and have plenty of time on their hands', while
the mission blacks are 'sulky, miserable wretches, no life in them whatever,
in fact they are nothing else but slaves'. If a commission were to be
appointed, he concluded, 'things will then come to light that will not be to
the credit of the missionaries'.[15] Another correspondent – 'Old Hand', the
pseudonym of Erldunda's owner and manager Robert Warburton –
mocked the 'gentle philanthropists' who vilified their 'fellow-colonists
with vague and garbled accusations'.[16] A 'Resident of Seventeen Years'
from Glen Helen station wrote to remind Adelaide's metropolitan readers

of the 'hardships and privations' endured by mounted patrol officers like Willshire, little dreamed of by 'those unacquainted with bush life'.[17]

Ben Rogers and Robert Warburton also took up Willshire's case in letters to the Minister. Warburton was less circumspect than he had been in the press. 'These Reverend gentlemen,' he wrote, 'try to pose as little kings.' They were 'puffed up with conceit'. The Hermannsburg mission was 'nothing but a farce, and a nuisance to everyone'.[18] Ben Rogers promised revelations about the missionaries that 'will astonish the public of South Australia'.[19]

While the dispute simmered, the Centre's pastoralists were mounting a case for increased police protection. In February 1890 representatives of the Tempe Downs Pastoral Company waited upon the Minister for the Northern Territory, John Gordon, arguing that the 'blacks in that part of the country were numerous and mischievous', and that the police force available was not strong enough. The Minister, while unable to meet their request, nonetheless expressed his 'unqualified sympathy'. Much to the surprise of many, including the delegation, he then launched 'a vigorous attack' upon the missionaries, attributing to their influence 'much of the mischief done by the natives'. The missionaries, he asserted, did more harm than good, while the Aborigines on the mission – 'outlaws', 'black scoundrels' and 'demons' – were among the worst cattle killers in the district. According to the press, the source of the Minister's allegations was Mounted Constable Willshire.[20]

The relationship between the police and the Tempe Downs Pastoral Company was a close one. From the time he established his camp at Boggy Waterhole, Willshire's Interior Police Patrol had spent much of its time policing the Tempe Downs run which, south-west of Alice Springs, had become a primary site of conflict on the shifting Central Australian frontier. Willshire joked about his almost domestic familiarity with the Tempe Downs station in January when he wrote that 'I have been so many times to Tempe Downs re the cattle killings that Mr Stokes [manager of the Glen Helen run] asked me if I intended to live at Tempe Downs altogether'.[21] Back in January, when reporting the outbreak of cattle killing on Tempe Downs and the attack on his police camp, he asked the Inspector if the events could be kept from the press, 'as the station is now formed into a company and the foregoing if known may prove detrimental to their interests'.[22]

The missionaries wrote to the press to 'correct some untruthful statements made by Mounted Constable Willshire which the Minister had cited'. They rejected as a lie the claim that the worst cattle killers came from the mission. Addressing Willshire's charge that the mission was 'the refuge of all the outlaws in the district', they wrote that they never tried to shield Aboriginals whom they knew to be cattle killers but wanted to see the guilty ones punished, 'not the innocent, and punished justly according to the law, not, as some whites have done, to go at night into a black's camp and shoot down every one they can reach with firearms'. They responded to the Minister's claim that the 'mission blacks' were the 'curse of the Northern Territory' by countering that the real curse was shooting Aboriginal men down like 'wild dogs', 'using their wives and girls for immoral purposes', and boasting about it.[23]

The editor of the *Register* fielded these claims and counter-claims. The charges levelled against the mission by Willshire were, he argued, of a very general nature, and as such difficult to answer, but the missionaries had done so in a 'straightforward and manly way'.

The onus, it seemed, was now on Willshire to make good his statements. He began by discrediting the entire substance of the missionaries' charges as hearsay, nothing more than stories told by 'wild Aborigines, who had no idea of day, date, time, or number'. Then he laid his counter-charges. Aborigines ran away from the mission because they were so badly treated. He had seen a 'lubra chained to a heavy log in the hot sun at the Mission Station', and had been asked by the missionaries to tell her not to run away. The mail man George King had told Willshire that he had also seen Aboriginal people chained up on the mission.

The picture of Aboriginal mission life portrayed by Willshire, and corroborated by some in the Centre's pastoral industry, was a most disturbing one. He had, Willshire wrote, seen the missionaries 'in the blacks camp threatening them with firearms and breaking all their spears up'. If one of their charges should run away, 'they ride after them with long whips and revolvers up and down the Finke'. When 'boys' ran away from the mission and were unable to find employment, they joined the cattle killers and became 'notorious outlaws'. The missionaries, he concluded, did not 'treat the blacks as they should be treated'. On the charge of European mistreatment of Aboriginal people, it seemed, no one was exempt.

The tension building between the missionaries and the police in the Centre had become a public affair in Adelaide. In the *Lantern*, it was satirised with a cartoon depicting a police constable and a missionary squaring off for a fight, while in the foreground an emaciated Aboriginal man – one of the putative subjects in this struggle over different visions of colonial civilisation – watches laconically.

In his allegations against the missionaries, Willshire devoted little space to defending the charges levelled at the police, and this did not pass un-noticed in the press. In an editorial preamble to Willshire's letter, the *Register*'s editor noted that it was chiefly of the '*tu quoque*' order, and in other respects unsatisfactory; it touched only the 'fringe of the question in dispute', which was 'the extraordinary charges made by Mr Schwarz against the police'. The controversy springing from the January meeting, the editor noted, was now a 'painful sensation' that had 'thrilled the hearts of Australians, much as Australians have unfortunately been accustomed to hear of outrages against the blacks', a sensation exacerbated by the fact that the news was circulating in the English press. London's *Daily Chronicle* had reported Willshire's allegations against the missionaries, and insisted on 'the necessity of an enquiry into the truth'.[24] It was unfortunate, the editor commented, that the Minister had already revealed himself as partisan in any resulting inquiry, making it all the more important that the 'utmost publicity' be given to the evidence.[25] Half the world, it seemed, was watching.

While the controversy gathered steam, Willshire seems to have done little policing, but his attention to 'clerical duties' improved. In the aftermath of the attack on his camp in January, his request for two additional Native Constables was approved, but by the following month he was complaining that the clothing allowance for the Native Police was insufficient. He was having to spend his own money on their outfitting. Over the course of the previous year he had complained mightily about the government's financial resourcing of his corps and was becoming conscious that his motives might be misconstrued. In early May he felt compelled to write:

> I don't ask for money that I can make anything out of it, I ask for more clothing . . . the weather is now bitterly cold and good useful trackers are in my camp poorly clad, I don't want them to leave me, so I must do something for them so as to make my party worth remaining in, and what I do by writing to the government is solely for the blackfellows' benefit.[26]

In the same letter, he expressed surprise about the fact that the Native Police corp he had formed and taken to Port Darwin was being disbanded. Fearing perhaps that the government's commitment to a Native Police force might have run its course, he observed, 'if that is so it should not be a precedent'.

Commission of Inquiry

By June, after several months of public controversy about the state of affairs in the Centre, the government decided to appoint a Public Service Commission of Inquiry into the treatment of Aboriginals in the Interior. Its composition was the source of considerable discussion. How could police, or even people in government service, be engaged, when public servants were the subject of allegations? How could missionaries or their sympathisers be appointed when their own people were under suspicion?[27] The government decided that rather than exclude such representation, they would balance it. In June, it was announced that H C Swan, a Stipendiary

Magistrate with some experience in the Interior, and Charles Taplin, a member of the initial January delegation in Adelaide and of the Aborigines Friends Association, would be the two commissioners.[28] They were to be assisted by Sub Inspector Besley, representing the police, and Reverend Heidenreich, representing the Lutheran missionaries.[29]

Swan and Taplin were issued with their instructions on 13 June 1890. They were to investigate the allegations made by the missionaries at the January public meeting, which had been published in the press on 1 April 1890, as well as the counter-allegations made by Mounted Constable Willshire. The commissioners departed by train for the Interior on 20 June 1890. At the end of the line they were joined by Sub Inspector Besley and travelled the remaining distance by camel.[30] They commenced their inquiry at the Hermannsburg mission on 21 July 1890 and over the course of the next few weeks took evidence from 21 witnesses at Owen Springs pastoral station, the police stations at Alice Springs and Heavitree Gap, the mines and in Adelaide. The handwritten report of evidence is tellingly headed the 'Finke River Mission Inquiry'[31] – its object had shifted, apparently, from being an inquiry into the activities of police to being an expose of the operations and actions of the missionaries.

The two key allegations raised by mission representatives at the Adelaide meeting were those concerning immorality and violence. Using those complaints as their starting point, the commissioners quoted from statements made at the meeting and asked witnesses at Hermannsburg to respond. The missionaries responded very poorly; their evidence was often vague, dated, second-hand or circumstantial. Kempe, for instance, elaborated on claims of 'immorality' by saying that on three occasions he had seen Europeans driving buggies containing Aboriginal women, and that he had seen 'or had reported to him' that Aboriginal women, dressed in men's clothing, went out mustering with European stockman. Schulze, addressing this same question, referred to a case where an Aboriginal man had complained to him about a white man taking his two wives, but conceded that this had happened 10 or 11 years previously. Some of their charges of violence were likewise vague or dated. Kempe recalled a case where three Aboriginal men and a woman had taken refuge at the mission with bullet wounds, and the woman had later died, but he added that this had occurred eight or nine years previously.[32]

On other points at this stage of the inquiry, the missionaries' compelling evidence against police and settlers was obscured by revelations about their own practices at the mission. What could they say about the allegations that they had chained up Aboriginal women on the mission? Yes, Kempe replied without embarrassment, in October of the previous year, three girls had committed adultery with visiting Afghan camel drivers, and had to be punished. He himself had punished Maria with a 'little whip', giving 'her a good hiding'. Schulze likewise punished Martha. Thomas, an Aboriginal man, punished his own wife. Later that evening, Kempe's evidence continued, the women ran away from the mission, but they were tracked and brought back. To prevent them running after the Afghans again, they were chained up for several days. When finally released they fled, together with Thomas, taking refuge at or near Willshire's police camp.

Willshire was present at Hermannsburg and was allowed to cross-examine the missionaries on this evidence. They conceded that when they went to Willshire's camp to seek out the women, they were in fact to be found in the nearby hills; Willshire had assisted in finding them. Schulze stated that, on the journey back to Hermannsburg, he had at one stage whipped Martha because 'she would not go on', and he had tied Hannah with a rope around her chest and led her in that way for three quarters of a mile. Back at the mission, he had ordered the women to remain inside, but could not recall if he had locked them in. In response to another question posed by Willshire, Kempe agreed that he did beat the children in class, if they were 'naughty'.[33]

In response to further cross-examination by Willshire the missionaries, without any apparent sense of shame or apology, elaborated on other incidents that had occurred at Hermannsburg. Kempe admitted that two cases of 'immorality' of which he was aware had been committed on the mission, by lay workers. In one of those cases, he had been satisfied with 'severely rebuking' the lay worker for having had a 'connection' with an Aboriginal woman. The other case was one in which a lay worker, Mr Schleiser, had in December 1888 come to Kempe entreating him to look after his Aboriginal wife and children. Kempe, in response, had immediately dismissed him for crimes of 'immorality'. Shortly afterwards, Schleiser shot himself.[34] Willshire also elicited a case in which a mission worker, Jurgens, in the company of Thomas, had pursued and captured two 'Tempe Downs blacks' who, they believed, had been spearing mission cattle. The two men had been tied to a post in the harness room and 'beaten with the broken piece of a stockwhip'. As one missionary put it, they were given 'a good hammering'. Then, to shame the men before their community, they cut off their beards. Finally, they conceded that they had asked Willshire 'to beat the blacks who run away if they come to your camp'.

Willshire was examined for the first time on the third day of the inquiry. In reference to the allegation that, late in 1884, three Aboriginal prisoners were taken from the mission and shot while still in chains, he simply noted that he was not in the district at the time and that the Mounted Constable involved, Erwin Wurmbrand, had explained the circumstances perfectly well in his report. On the charges of immorality: yes, he had taken Aboriginal girls or women down to Adelaide with him, but only under reasonable circumstances. On one occasion he took with him a seven-year-old girl, but only so that she could be placed as a servant with his brother-in-law, the Commissioner of Forests Mr Brown. Another time he had allowed his tracker, and the tracker's wife, to accompany him, but while in Adelaide they had all been accommodated at his father's house in North Adelaide.[35] Poorly advised, or perhaps secure in their own righteousness, the missionaries took little opportunity to cross-examine their accuser.

The only witness besides the missionaries to give evidence critical of

Willshire was Mounted Constable Robert Hillier, who had served with Willshire and Wurmbrand at Heavitree Gap for 12 months. Now posted at Gawler, near Adelaide, Hillier was sympathetic to the missionaries, and freely admitted that 'Willshire and I were not the best of friends'. Most significantly, Hillier contested Willshire's portrayal of himself as a chivalric protector of Aboriginal women. On two occasions while he was at Heavitree Gap, Hillier said, Willshire travelled to Port Augusta and on both occasions took Aboriginal women with him; on neither occasion did the husband of the women accompany them. Willshire, he added, 'was in the habit of taking lubras about with him when he was on the station & went away on duty. On every occasion he had black trackers with him & Willshire sometimes took the wife of one of the trackers, but invariably took the one about the place'. In response to a question from Besley, he made particular reference to Mary Ann.[36]

The evidence of the station managers and their men was uniformly supportive of the police, and damning of the missionaries. In response to the missionaries' allegations of 'immorality', the evidence of Thomas Magarey, manager of Crown Point station, was typical of that collected by the commissioners: he tried to 'discourage [immorality] as far as lies in my power'; he had seen Aboriginal women dressed in men's clothing in the company of stockmen, but this was less common than it had been some years ago.[37] Francis Gillen, on this point, added that Aboriginal women dressed as stockmen was 'a fashion brought from Queensland', but seemed to be dying out.[38] The station managers and their men had a low opinion of the mission, which they regarded as a waste of resources. Most witnesses from the pastoral industry commented that there were few Aboriginal residents on the mission: 'I never saw more than 50,' observed one. During the inquiry, the missionaries had been asked to list all the Aboriginal people connected to the mission; there were 38 in total, 17 men and 21 women.[39] Evidence from the pastoral industry's witnesses suggested that there were typically between 50 and 100 Aboriginal people resident at any one time on most of the Centre's pastoral runs. The general impression conveyed of the missionaries was a cynical one of holy men wholly lacking in compassion. James MacDonald, station manager of Glen Helen, recalled that when in 1885 he had 'asked Mr Schwarz to relieve me of all the old and helpless blacks', the missionary had replied: '"we will take all the young women from your station and you can keep the old people".'[40]

In reference to the allegations of violence against Aboriginal people, most pastoral witnesses denied that it occurred, or indicated that it was something of the past. Indeed, the impression conveyed by most was that the district was largely 'quiet'. Charles Gall, the overseer of Owen Springs, the first station established in the district, noted that he had experienced a great deal of trouble with cattle killing back in the early 1880s, but after Wurmbrand and his trackers were brought in to patrol, the cattle killing had almost immediately ceased, and 'we have had peace since'.[41] Most of the station managers attested to the same pattern and, moreover, pointed out that much of the work on their stations was now being carried out by Aboriginal people. The only outstanding trouble, it was argued, lay with the 'outside' stations, in the west. Willshire himself made this point. In his evidence he described his methods of patrol, and how, after driving the cattle killers into the hills and securing their weapons, the killing would stop for a time. He continued:

> Besides Tempe Downs, cattle are occasionally killed at Erldunda & Glen Helen. The country I patrol is 400 miles from North to South and 150 miles to the Westward. The Native Patrol has been established at my present camp twelve months. Six months previous to this I had no fixed camp but was continually patrolling. There is not so much cattle killing in Tempe Downs and Erludunda since the patrol.[42]

Willshire and the station managers were nonetheless keen to point out that the work of policing the runs still needed to be done. Charles Gall commented that he 'was sure the cattle killing would increase if the police were withdrawn'.[43]

Swan and Taplin's report was presented to parliament at the end of September 1890. The first issue it addressed was the allegations made by Reverend Schwarz at the January public meeting. Regarding the claim that 'the whites wanted to exterminate the natives', they found nothing to support the charge. It was a matter of importance to the leaseholders, they considered, that Aboriginal people should be kept away from the water-holes, and it was for this reason that they were 'ordered off their hunting grounds', but there was no evidence that violence was practised in affecting this dispersal. The claim that three prisoners in chains were shot while trying to escape was next considered, and dispensed with on the grounds that the case was sufficiently investigated at the time. Of the claim that Aboriginal men on the stations were maltreated, the commissioners reported that the Aboriginal men they visited on the stations seemed 'happy enough', and 'those employed were both well fed and clothed'. Of the claim that women were kept on the stations for 'immoral purposes', they conceded that there was reason to suppose that 'a considerable amount of immorality does exist', but the Aboriginal women on the stations were legitimately employed 'in housework, milking, etc.'

One of the specific charges against Willshire was that he had shot Aboriginal men he had been sent out to arrest, and had taken two girls who had been with the victims back to his camp. The shooting charge, the commissioners wrote, was unsupported by the evidence collected during the inquiry. Willshire had taken Aboriginal women with him to Adelaide, but he had been accompanied by Native Constables, and there was no evidence to prove that he was guilty of immorality.

None of the charges against the police or the squatters were found to be proven. The evidence of several German Lutheran missionaries, who probably spoke Arrernte better than English, had been pitched against that of the entire pastoral and mining communities of the district, which had stepped forth in support of the police in general, and of Willshire in particular, as its front line of protection against 'troublesome' Aborigines. The charges found to be proven were those against the missionaries. It had been established, the commissioners reported, that chains had been used to detain Aboriginal people on the mission station and that 'thrashing was resorted to as a punishment'. These actions, 'while showing a lack of judgment', were excused on the grounds that they were 'prompted by the kindest motives'. In summing up, the commissioners reported that the missionaries had made their statements against settlers and police 'without careful consideration' by acting upon the unreliable testimony of the Aborigines. Willshire's conduct, according to most witnesses interviewed, was praiseworthy: he had done his work well and given 'satisfaction to the majority of the public'.

The commissioners concluded with a number of recommendations regarding Aboriginal policy in general. Their report was highly critical of the fact that, at the time of their visit, six missionaries were supervising a handful of Aborigines in a district that had a population of approximately 1000 people. It would be of greater advantage, the commissioners suggested, if missionary labour was better utilised. They recommended that reserves of between 800 and 1600 square kilometres be established, and that these be stocked and placed under the control of a manager and schoolmaster. In recommending the plan, they cited one of the inquiry's pastoral witnesses, who had argued that 'if the Australian people could once recognise the difference of cost at which they had obtained their magnificent country as compared with the cost of, say, the South African or New Zealand wars, we feel sure that much greater provision would readily be made for smoothing the path to the inevitable extinction which seems to await the Australian Aboriginal'.[44]

When Willshire published his revised edition of *The Aborigines of Central Australia* the following year, he gave some space to the previous year's war of relations in the Centre. In the reissued book's new chapter on 'The Aborigines of Lake Amadeus and the Gill Ranges', it is not only the character of Aboriginal people that is found to be wanting but also that of the missionaries. While in the 1888 edition of *The Aborigines of Central Australia* his description of Aboriginal culture and character is at worst patronising, Willshire's account in the 1891 edition reveals a new degree of invective. The Aboriginal women, he writes, 'exhibit the worst types of unchastity'. As for the Hermannsburg missionaries, they are unwittingly complicit with Aboriginal people in making the Interior a more dangerous place. Interference of the missionaries only makes the life of the police and pioneering pastoralists more difficult: 'The settlers hardly know what to do in this kind of country, where the wild natives kill their cattle whole-sale . . . Unless they have adequate protection they must act for themselves, for otherwise there is nothing before them but to abandon the country and leave it to the blacks.'[45] The settlers have a difficult enough time dealing with the aggressions of 'wild natives', but the 'views and the influence' of the missionaries make any 'serious repression of these outrages' impracticable. The mission station itself, he argues, has become a base and place of retreat for Aboriginal raiding parties.

In his assessment of the poverty of the missionaries' arguments he is at pains to outline his own superior ethnographic knowledge, particularly in relation to Aboriginal sexual roles: 'Much has been written by the Lutheran missionaries upon the outrages committed by white men taking black women from the aboriginals . . . [but] statements of this kind do not deserve much consideration when the habits of the natives are properly understood and weighed.'[46] Native tribes, he writes, commonly steal women 'one from the other'. Indeed, Aboriginal women often prefer the chivalric treatment of a white man, because it is of a kind that 'they never would receive at the hands of the males amongst whom their lot was cast. All the efforts of the missionaries can never stop the practice'.[47] Willshire closes with an implicit parting shot: he has described Aboriginal people 'as they were found, lazy, treacherous and impure, and on the Finke River, where they ought to be better' – in short, at the Hermannsburg mission – 'they are worse than the other tribes which live in the surrounding country'.[48]

The greatest benefit to Aboriginal people in the Interior, he argues, comes from the distribution of rations and work at the pastoral stations, 'and that is all that can reasonably be required'. Indeed, the happiest

Aboriginal people are those to be found at the police camps. 'Those who come about the police camps are allowed to move about as they think fit, and when they come back after such a length of absence as they have been disposed to indulge in, they are in good spirits and are quite contented. Those who wish to see a number of blacks who seem really happy should pay a visit to the interior police patrol camp.'[49]

After the Commission of Inquiry findings, Willshire could feel confident that the trials which had dogged his reputation and that of the police force throughout 1890 had passed. In fact, they were just beginning.

THE POLICE
UNDER SCRUTINY

On 26 February 1891, Willshire despatched a report describing a series of dramatic events that, four days earlier, had culminated in the deaths of two 'notorious cattle killers'. Cattle killing, he began, had been on the increase for the last few months. He had 'tracked and toiled over ranges for twelve months in pursuit of them', he wrote, and all the while they 'kept a constant watch for me, and when I had passed, they came down on the flats below, and killed cattle, they were hard to get, on account of so many ranges, therefore they got cheeky and slapped their behinds at my party'. He was at his 'wits end how to stop it' but, he added portentously, 'I knew the day would come when they would be got'.[1]

He and his Native Constables continued to track the cattle killers to Tempe Downs station, where they were camped near the homestead. The police party mounted a dawn raid on the morning of 22 February and endeavoured to make their arrests. A number of the suspects fled, but two put up a violent struggle and, as a last resort, were shot by the Native Police. Other 'bad and daring natives' remained at large in the district. Indeed, Willshire had received notice that 'the Tempe Downs natives are going to kill us all, and burn down the huts'. He concluded by stressing that firearms had only been used as a last resort and then only against 'notorious cattle killers who were impossible to arrest'.

As circumstance would have it, the two 'notorious cattle killers' who were shot in Willshire's dawn raid, Donkey and Roger, were among the party who had entered his camp the previous January and killed Nameia. Willshire knew this, and elaborated on the pair's criminal history in his report of their deaths. Roger, he stated, had thrown the spear that had killed Nameia, and Donkey had further been involved in the murder of the father of one of his Native Constables, Joe, also known as Thomas. He added:

> No man could catch these natives alive if it was his duty to track up native cattle killers, they are as wily as wild ducks and as cunning as it is possible to be, ever on the alert, watching my movements for 18 months, but there was one movement of mine they did not see, that was the last one.[2]

In a few short paragraphs Willshire's pursuit of these cattle killers had escalated from a 'few months', to 'twelve months', to '18 months'. He followed this report with another, a week later, in which he requested warrants for the arrest of two further suspects in the killing of Nameia in January 1890, Chookey Chook and Dick, as well as warrants for Dick, Arabi, Peter and Racehorse, for cattle killing on Tempe Downs.[3]

In the month that it took for Willshire's correspondence to make its way through official channels to the Minister's desk in Adelaide, Central Australia became a focus of press attention in the south. The South Australian government, worried that the development of the Northern Territory was stalling in a climate of drought and economic recession, despatched the Governor, the Earl of Kintore, to investigate the Territory's settlement prospects and to generate much needed publicity. The Governor toured the Top End in April, and was scheduled to finish his trip at Alice Springs in early May.[4] At the same time as it was boosting the Territory's public profile through the Governor's tour, the government appointed a Pastoral Lands Commission to investigate ways of consolidating pastoral development there. The appointed commissioners, parliamentarians

Robert Caldwell and Frederick Holder, arrived in the Centre to take evidence in early April 1891.[5] Also in April, the Elder Scientific Expedition was about to depart Adelaide for the Peake, where it would commence its exploration of the country west of the Overland Telegraph Line.[6] Each of these almost simultaneous events – the Governor's tour, the Pastoral Lands Commission, and the Elder Scientific Expedition – brought an unprecedented concentration of public attention on this region of the Interior.

As these events were being daily reported in the press, another item appeared, on 11 April in the *Adelaide Observer*, under the heading 'Trouble with the Natives'. The Minister responsible for the Northern Territory, it reported, had received a report from Mounted Constable Willshire of 'conflict with blacks' on Tempe Downs station. Willshire's report was 'a long complaint as to the depredations made by the blacks of this tribe'. The Mounted Constable had requested warrants for the arrest of two who had escaped during the police raid, and of three others sought for cattle killing on Tempe Downs. Papers had been sent on to Attorney-General Homburg so that the requested warrants could be prepared, but, the report finished, the Attorney had given the opinion that warrants were 'really not needed' to enable a Mounted Constable to arrest alleged murderers.[7]

Robert Homburg became Attorney-General in August 1890, just a month before Swan and Taplin's 'Finke River Mission Inquiry' report was tabled in parliament: a report that had exonerated Willshire and the police, and publicly humiliated the Hermannsburg missionaries. Homburg, educated at a Lutheran school in the Barossa Valley and former president of the German Club, may have felt some sympathy for the way his country-men had been treated. He was clearly puzzled by Willshire's request for warrants, and decided to do some detective work of his own. Judging from a few pages of handwritten notes by him, it appears that Homburg pulled out the file of evidence taken before the Finke River Mission Inquiry and combed it to see if there were any references to the individuals involved in the recent police shootings. He looked at Willshire's evidence, and made notes on its inconsistencies. On page 37 of the document, Homburg recorded, 'Willshire reports that Namia killed about March 1890', yet on the very next page, Willshire had said that Nameia was killed in November 1889, and in the report of 26 February he had stated that the murder occurred on 9 January 1890. Clearly dissatisfied with the inconsistencies in Willshire's testimony and reports, Homburg wrote: 'I think it would be improper for me to direct the issue of any warrant against these Blacks at least so far as the murders said to have been committed 15 mon & 2 years ago's concerned'. Of the recent shootings at Tempe Downs, he expressed even more doubt about the accuracy of Willshire's report:

> I am however very doubtful whether the shooting by the black trackers can be justified by Mr Willshire. In July last when Mr Willshire was [examined] at 23 July at the Finke River before the Finke Mission Commission he mentioned (at page 23 of the Exam') 7 blacks but none of those agst whom warrants are sought as notorious cattle stealers – & on 28 July he mentioned the murder of Naimi before the Com stating that the Tempe Down Blacks murdered Naimi at his Camp in November 1889 & nothing whatever is said by him of the murder of Joe's father. [8]

On the basis of these suspicions, and taking advantage of the imminent arrival of the Pastoral Lands Commissioners in Alice Springs, Homburg drafted a message to be forwarded to the Officer in Charge of the Alice Springs police, requiring an inquest into the deaths of Donkey and Roger:

> Send messenger to Willshire that Attorney-General and Minister of Education have determined that an inquest shall be held on the two blacks shot by the Native Trackers on 22nd February last. That Mr Caldwell or Mr Holder members of the Pastoral Commission will be in Alice Springs on Wednesday and one of the members of the Commission will be asked to hold an Inquiry. That Willshire must be present without fail with all witnesses having any knowledge of the circumstances under which the blacks were shot and that if possible the bodies must be exhumed and the

shot wounds shown to independent witnesses to be present at the inquiry. Let Constable start at once.[9]

At the Alice Springs police station, Mounted Constable South received Homburg's instructions and despatched a messenger to Willshire's Boggy Waterhole police camp, 150 kilometres distant, to bring him in. Realistically, South responded, an inquiry would take some time to organise: it would take Willshire at least a day to travel on horseback to Alice Springs, and it would also take some time to gather witnesses and exhume the bodies.

The commissioners, Holder and Caldwell, were willing to conduct the inquiry into the police shootings if it could be held immediately, but, explaining that their business in the Centre was almost finished and they were on the verge of departing south, they wired to Homburg that Francis Gillen would be an equally appropriate person to conduct it. Gillen, a Justice of the Peace and stationmaster at Alice Springs, was the most senior civil servant in the district and one of its longest serving. Homburg wired back accepting their suggestion, and asking if they could, nonetheless, gather what information they could on the police shootings while they were there. He was especially keen to know if there was any connection in the deaths of the two men at Tempe Downs with the 1890 Finke River Mission Inquiry into the mistreatment of Aborigines; whether, in short, 'the blacks who were shot at Tempe Downs were present at the Finke Mission Inquiry'.[10]

On 15 April, having finished taking evidence on the conditions of the Centre's pastoral industry, the Pastoral Lands Commissioners began their journey home. Willshire, who had instructions to provide them with a statement, hurried after them with Native Constables Larry, Archie and Jack, each of whom had been party to the dawn raid on the Tempe Downs Aboriginal camp on 22 February. The fourth Native Constable who had also been present, Thomas, was not with them on this day. Willshire's party intercepted the commissioners' party between Ooraminna and Mount

Burrell on Friday 17 April. Willshire then gave them his statement on the events of 22 February. In large part, it repeated the contents of his report of 26 February, but included some additional information. The Aborigines who had attacked his camp on 9 January 1890 and killed Nameia, he stated, had also tried to burn the camp down. For their part in those events, he added, he had gained warrants for the arrest of Donkey and Roger from Charles Gall JP. His statement included the new information that the bodies of the deceased had been given to their tribal enemies, who had taken them away and burnt them. Remembering Homburg's request, the commissioners inquired as to whether the dead men had been interviewed during the previous year's Finke River Mission Inquiry. Willshire replied that Roger, or Erraminta, had been a witness, and that he was a 'very bad character'.[11]

Willshire and his Native Constables returned to Alice Springs. The commissioners continued to Adelaide. When they reached the telegraph station at Charlotte Waters, they wired Homburg that 'having carefully considered the statements which will accompany ... we are of opinion that no blame attaches to MC Willshire so far as concerns the death of the two unfortunate native offenders Donkey and Roger on Fey 22nd last, according to information given firearms were not used by the native constables until violence had been done by the natives'. The matter might have rested there but, by the time Homburg received this telegram, he had already directed Francis Gillen to conduct an inquiry.

Gillen's inquiry

Aided by Mounted Constable South, Francis Gillen began his inquiry on 19 April at Heavitree Gap police station, just outside of Alice Springs.[12] Willshire was the first to give evidence. He and his four Native Constables were tracking cattle killers around the Tempe Downs run, he stated. On 21 February they came across a recently killed beast near Walker's Creek, in the vicinity of which the Native Police recognised the tracks of 'Donkey' and 'Roger'. He already held a warrant for the arrest of those two men, signed by magistrate Charles Gall, on suspicion of murdering Nameia a year previously.

That night, Willshire's patrol party camped about a mile from the head station. Just before sunrise he instructed his men to 'walk into the Blacks camp with neckchains and handcuffs and use our best endeavours to arrest Donkey and Roger':

> we parted company at 4 a.m. to surround the camp and at 5.30 a.m. I heard the trackers telling Donkey to sit down, we would not hurt him. While this was going on I came close to Donkey with a pair of handcuffs and spoke to him, he then took a spear and threw it at N. C. Larry. While he was doing that I caught him by the wrist, he got away, took up a big yamstick and made a vicious blow at my head. I put my arm up for protection and the blow hit my thumb smashing the nail, it was so painful I fell down. The pain prevented me from knowing what transpired for the next minute.

After knocking Willshire down, Donkey had hurled spears at Native Constable Larry, and started to run away. 'I called out several times to the trackers,' Willshire said, 'to try and arrest them.' The next thing Willshire recalled was a shot being fired, and he saw Donkey lying flat on his stomach. Native Constable Larry had shot Donkey in self-defence, perhaps saving Willshire's life.

Meanwhile, about 150 metres north of Donkey's camp, Native Constable Joe (Thomas) was trying to arrest Roger. Willshire saw Joe leap to avoid Roger's spear. 'I heard N. C. Joe tell Roger in his own language to sit down. Joe then produced handcuffs and attempted to arrest Roger, who then threw another spear at him. N. C. Jack then came up. Roger shipped another spear and was shot by Joe while attempting to throw it at Jack'.

When the affray was over, Willshire stated, he examined the bodies. Donkey had been shot through the heart. Roger had been shot in the thigh and the head. The shot in the thigh, Willshire explained, was 'caused by

N. C. Joe who attempted to wound him to make capture easy'. Ordering his men back to their camp, Willshire went to the head station, some 300 metres away from the scene of the affray, to obtain a shovel. On his return he noticed four Aborigines on the range south of the station. They were signalling to him, and he instructed them to come down. They told him they wanted the bodies: 'The Natives explained that deceased Roger and Donkey were tribal opponents and as such it is customary to burn the bodies. When they started to carry the bodies away I returned to the Station.'

After Willshire made his statement he was examined by Gillen. From whom had he obtained the warrant for the arrest of the two men? It was obtained from Charles Gall, a Justice of the Peace at Owen Springs station, replied Willshire; and it was for the murder of Nameia at his camp on the Finke River on 9 January 1890. Could he expand on the circumstances of the attempted arrests? The intention, Willshire said, was to arrest the suspects who were known cattle killers, and the Native Constables had been cautioned 'not to use firearms, except in the last extremity'. But in reiterating the events, Willshire introduced a new piece of evidence: 'when I spoke to Donkey I said you shot Larry's father and I am going to arrest you, if you run away you might be shot'. Were there witnesses to the events? Willshire recalled that there were four Aborigines camped nearby but they had cleared out when they saw his men coming, and he didn't think they witnessed the affray. Of the others at the station, none, 'either black or white, put in an appearance'. Regarding the burning of the bodies, Willshire said that he didn't think it was part of his duty to prevent it. In short, given the circumstances, he was of the opinion that the deaths were unavoidable.[13] Willshire left the room and waited while the Native Constables were called.

The next witness was Native Constable Larry. In his evidence, Larry recalled that they discovered a bullock killed near Peterman Creek, and identified the tracks of Donkey and Roger. They camped near the station overnight. Willshire had told the Native Police to take the men alive, and had handcuffs and neckchains ready for the purpose.

Larry recounted the struggle to capture Donkey. He grabbed Donkey by the wrist, but Donkey broke away and threw two spears at him. Willshire then entered the struggle, but was felled by the blow from a yamstick. Then 'Donkey more come up longa spear and I shot him' because 'I was afraid he would kill me'. He added, 'Donkey killed old man Naimi (my father) in the night time at Willshire's camp'.

Meanwhile, continued Larry, Native Constable Thomas had been ordered to Roger's camp to arrest him. 'I heard Thomas sing out that Roger had spears and that he was frightened, I was then at Donkey's camp and heard rifle shot'.

Gillen then questioned Larry about the wounds Donkey and Roger had received. Donkey had received one gunshot wound to the chest, as Willshire had tesitifed. But Roger, said Larry, had been shot four times, in the thigh, the hip, the chest and the head. Willshire had reported a thigh and a head wound. How many shots had Larry heard? Four shots, he testified. With the shooting over, they returned to the station for breakfast. Asked about the fate of the bodies, he said, 'I heard Blackfellows burned Donkey and Roger.'[14]

The third witness was Native Constable Archie, or Coog'nalthika. Like Willshire and Larry, he recalled the discovery of a speared bullock, although he stated that they found it near Palmer Creek, whereas Larry had reported its discovery at Peterman Creek and Willshire at Walker Creek. They identified the tracks of three men, including Donkey and Roger, and a third man, Chookey Chook. Like Larry, Archie recalled that Willshire had instructed them to take the men alive and that they had handcuffs and neckchains with them for this purpose. Donkey was asleep, he said, when they arrived at his camp, but he jumped up quickly and grabbed his spears. He claimed that he tried to catch Donkey (neither Willshire nor Larry had reported Archie's presence in their accounts). Archie then described the struggle that ensued when Larry and Willshire tried to take Donkey. Larry, he said, shot Donkey in the back as he tried to flee, while Willshire was lying on the ground, having been struck by the yamstick. In Roger's camp, Archie recalled seeing Native Constable Jack try to make an arrest, but Roger broke free. Roger threw two spears at Jack and one at Thomas, before Thomas fired two shots, bringing Roger down. Was he sure about the number of shots, asked Gillen? Yes, Archie said, only two shots were fired, one striking Roger in the leg and the other 'above the hip near the ribs'. He subsequently examined the body 'and there were no bullet holes in the chest or head'.[15]

Gillen was clearly concerned about this contradiction in what should have been straightforward evidence, and concluded his examination of Archie by asking if he had been told what to say. Archie said he had not.

Native Constable Jack was the last to be examined on this day. His statement adhered closely to Archie's account. A dead bullock was found near Palmer Creek and the tracks of three suspects, including Donkey and Roger, led them to Tempe Downs. They were instructed to capture Roger and attempted to do so, but Roger pulled away. After throwing several spears Roger was shot by Thomas, once in the leg and once in the back. Jack then described what he saw of the struggle in the other camp: Willshire was knocked down with a yamstick and Larry shot Donkey as he attempted escape. Gillen asked Jack if he had been instructed in his statement. No, replied Larry, he had not.[16]

The first day of Gillen's inquiry was concluded. The broad picture of events described by those involved was largely consistent. A speared bullock had been discovered in the vicinity of the Tempe Downs head station, together with the incriminating tracks of Donkey and Roger, suspects in the murder of Nameia. At dawn the next day the police party endeavoured to capture the suspects, both of whom were shot and killed while resisting arrest. The bodies of the dead men were removed and burnt by Aboriginal strangers who arrived to claim them. There were, however, some significant variations in the testimonies. Where was the dead bullock found: Walker, Palmer or Petermann Creek? How many tracks did they discover? Willshire and Larry reported only the tracks of Donkey and Roger; Archie and Jack reported the tracks of a third man,

Chookey Chook, who had not been involved in the affray. Most seriously, how many times had Roger been shot: four times or twice? Gillen, it seems, suspected the Native Police of repeating a version of events in which they had been coached.

The following day, 20 April, the inquiry moved to the Owen Springs station to interview its manager Charles Gall, the Justice of the Peace from whom, Willshire had testified, he obtained his warrant for the arrests of Donkey and Roger. Gall, however, told Gillen that he had not 'issued any warrants for the arrest of Natives' since the beginning of 1890, nor had the police applied to him for any. Indeed, 'Mounted Constable Willshire has never applied to me for a warrant for Donkey or Roger, or any other Natives'.[17]

The next day Gillen travelled to the police camp at Boggy Waterhole, where Willshire had returned after his testimony at Heavitree Gap. It was here that Willshire presented a new and voluntary statement regarding the question of the warrant. 'When I gave my evidence,' he told Gillen,

> I was under the impression that the warrant was signed by Mr Gall JP but since I have discovered that the warrant was not signed, though the body was filled up as usual and only required the signature of the Magistrate. I went into Owen Springs for loading and intended to get it and another signed, but being busy with the loading I forgot it and came away under the impression they were signed, hence the mistake.'[18]

It was an awkward explanation, given that Gall had pointed out that Willshire had *never* applied to him for a warrant, for these or any other Aboriginal suspects. This was the start of a bad day for Willshire. Next, Gillen heard an account of the events that did not square at all with the previous testimony.

On this day Native Constable Thomas, also known as Joe, gave his testimony for the first time. He recalled the patrol to Tempe Downs. He did not see any dead bullock on the road and, as for tracks, he saw a lot of them, but not those of Donkey or Roger, which, he said, he would have recognised. According to Thomas, 'Mr Willshire been yabber (tell) longa road he look out for Donkey and Roger, him been kill old man "Naimi".' At daylight the police party approached the station. Willshire, Larry and Archie headed for Donkey's camp, and Jack and Thomas headed for Roger's. 'Mr Willshire been yabber,' said Thomas, 'suppose Roger run away, you shoot him'. The handcuffs remained in the packbags. As they made towards Roger's camp a gunshot from the other camp alerted their suspect, who began to flee:

> I then fired at him and he fell, after which N C Jack fired two shots with the revolver. My shot hit him in the back and Jack's shot hit him in the leg ... Roger did not throw any spears, he had no weapons when he was running away. Jack and I did not try to catch Roger as Mr Willshire been yabber, want to kill him.

As for the events in Donkey's camp, Thomas recalled seeing Larry and Archie close to the camp, hearing a shot fired, and Donkey crying out. 'Donkey was shot in the camp and did not run away.' Thomas was not aware that Willshire had been struck by Donkey. 'I heard Mr Willshire tell Larry to shoot Donkey – he told him this the previous evening.' When the shooting was over, said Thomas, Willshire, Jack, Archie, and Billy Abbott, a prospector staying at Tempe Downs station, took the bodies away on a camel. Thomas had seen the smoke from two fires, and Jack and Archie had later told him that they had assisted in the burning of the bodies.[19]

If, as Thomas' account indicates, Willshire had stood on the sidelines during the melee, where had his thumb injury come from? By Willshire's own account, he had injured a thumb while loading camels during his Musgrave Ranges expedition early in 1889. Indeed, in June of that year he sought re-imbursment from the government for having to travel to Adelaide for an operation to repair the damage.[20]

Gillen now had reason to believe that the accounts given by Willshire,

Attack on Barrow Creek telegraph station, in the *Illustrated Sydney News*, 28 March 1874. Courtesy of the National Library of Australia.

Trooper W H Willshire, reproduced from Norman A Richardson, *Pioneers of the North-West of South Australia*, W K Thomas & Co., Adelaide, p. 102.

BELOW: Police Inspector Brian Besley.
Courtesy of the South Australian Police Historical Society.

Hermannsburg missionaries, W F Schwarz, L G Schulze and A H Kempe.
Courtesy of the Lutheran Archives, South Australia.

Alice Springs telegraph station, c. 1900. Spencer Collection, courtesy of the South Australian Museum.

Missionaries' residence at Hermannsburg, late nineteenth century. Courtesy of the Lutheran Archives, South Australia.

Chambers Pillar, in the *Report of the Horn Scientific Expedition to Central Australia*, Part 1, London, Dulau and Co., 1896, opp. p. 49. Courtesy of Special Collections, Barr Smith Library, University of Adelaide.

Crown Point, in the *Report of the Horn Scientific Expedition to Central Australia*, Part 1, London, Dulau and Co., 1896, opp. p. 33. Courtesy of Special Collections, Barr Smith Library, University of Adelaide.

Lake Amadeus, in the *Report of the Horn Scientific Expedition to Central Australia*, Part 1, London, Dulau and Co., 1896, opp. p. 33. Courtesy of Special Collections, Barr Smith Library, University of Adelaide.

Palm Creek, in the *Report of the Horn Scientific Expedition to Central Australia*, Part 1, London, Dulau and Co., 1896, opp. p. 114. Courtesy of Special Collections, Barr Smith Library, University of Adelaide.

Native Constables and witnesses brought down to Port Augusta for Willshire's trial before the Supreme Court in 1891. Courtesy of the South Australian Police Historical Society.

Mounted Constables Willshire and Wurmbrand with the Native Police, taken in a studio at Port Augusta in 1888. According to the *Port Augusta Dispatch*, 24 January 1888, the tableau illustrates a police camp at Erldunda after an attack on the station in May. Courtesy of the South Australian Police Historical Society.

Mounted Constables Willshire and Wurmbrand with the Native Police, taken in a studio at Port Augusta in 1888. Variation of the scene described in the *Port Augusta Dispatch*, reproduced in the *Report of the Protector of Aborigines for the year ended June 30, 1906*, Adelaide, C E Bristow, Government Printer, North Adelaide, 1907, after p. 8. Courtesy of the South Australian Museum.

Mounted Constable Willshire with four of his Native Police and an unidentified Aboriginal woman, probably taken at Port Augusta in 1888, reproduced from Reginald Mayes, *A Pictorial History of Port Augusta*, Rigby, 1974, p. 43.

The Port Augusta studio photographs of Willshire and the Native Police are reminiscent of the sorts of illustrations found in late nineteenth-century adventure fiction, such as the books of H Rider Haggard. This illustration is from Haggard's *Black Heart and White Heart*, Longman's, Green and Co., London, 1900, facing p. 18.

'Alone in the Desert', in Ernest Giles, *Australia Twice Traversed*, vol. 2, London, 1889, p. 39.

OPPOSITE PAGE: Cartoon in the Adelaide-based newspaper the *Lantern*, 10 May 1890, p. 25, commenting wryly on the accusations and counter accusations flying back and forth between Mounted Constable Willshire, his supporters, and the Hermannsburg missionaries. Courtesy of the State Library of South Australia.

'The way Lindsay should explore', in the *Quiz and Lantern*, 23 October 1891, p. 9. Courtesy of the State Library of South Australia.

RECENT DISPUTES BETWEEN MISSIONARIES AND POLICE *RE* ABORIGINAL
Edifying for the aboriginal converts on the Finke River.

A THRILLING TALE

OF REAL LIFE

IN THE

WILDS OF AUSTRALIA.

BY

Mounted-Constable Willshire.

J. BRUER.

FREARSON & BROTHER, PRINTERS, NORTH TERRACE, ADELAIDE.
1895.

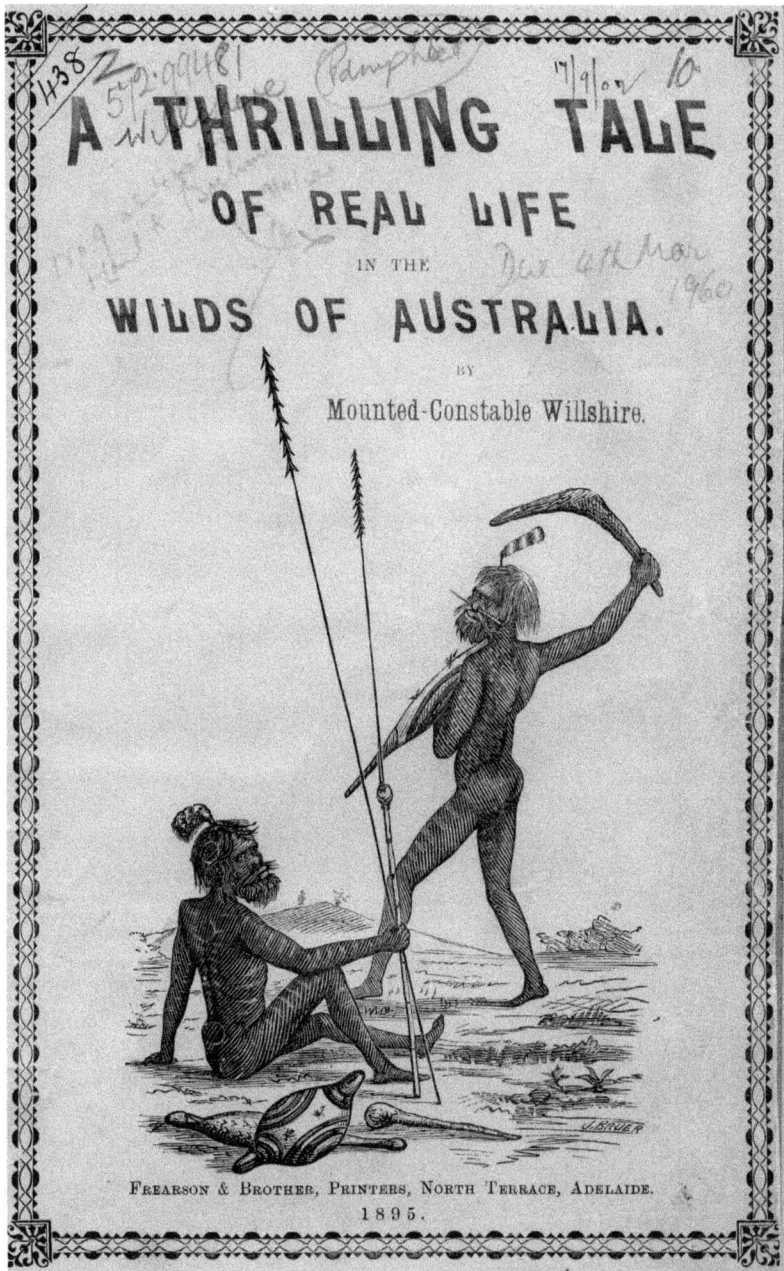

Cover of W H Willshire, *A Thrilling Tale of Real Life in the Wilds of Australia*, Adelaide, 1895. Courtesy of the State Library of South Australia.

Native Police Camp, Gordon Creek, Victoria River Downs.

Illustration printed at the head of a letter written by Willshire, 10 February 1896, SRSA GRS 1/1/1895/121. Courtesy of State Records of South Australia.

'Matters are getting tropical', extract from Willshire's Police Journal for 18 March 1895, Police Station, Timber Creek F 302, Police journals, 1894–1977. Courtesy of the Northern Territory Archives Service.

'M C Wiltshire [sic], River Katherine', copied from album associated with W S Anderson. Photographer believed to be Floreng Bleeser. Courtesy of Philip Jones.

The 1901/1902 expedition team at Alice Springs. Left to right: Purunda, F J Gillen, Harry Chance, Baldwin Spencer and Erlikilyika. Spencer Collection, courtesy of the South Australian Museum.

'The Author and a Boy Native', frontispiece to W H Willshire, *Land of the Dawning*, Adelaide, 1896. Courtesy of the State Library of South Australia.

TOP: Ruins of the Owens Springs homestead. Owen Springs was one of the Centre's first pastoral stations. Photo: R Foster.

BOTTOM: View towards Mount Sonder, Central Australia. Photo: R Foster.

TOP: Alice Springs Telegraph Station Museum. Photo: P Clarke.

BOTTOM: Missionaries House, now a cafe and museum on the Hermannsburg Mission Historic Precinct. Photo: R Foster.

Memorial to the men who were killed by Aboriginal people during the
construction of the Overland Telegraph, West Terrace Cemetery, Adelaide.
Photo: R Foster.

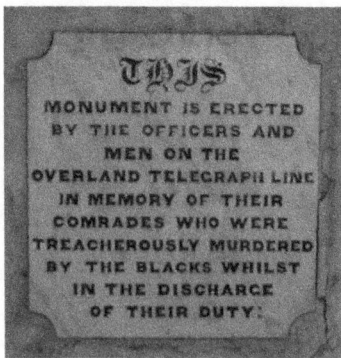

THIS
MONUMENT IS ERECTED
BY THE OFFICERS AND
MEN ON THE
OVERLAND TELEGRAPH LINE
IN MEMORY OF THEIR
COMRADES WHO WERE
TREACHEROUSLY MURDERED
BY THE BLACKS WHILST
IN THE DISCHARGE
OF THEIR DUTY.

JAMES
LORENZO STAPLETON,
STATION MASTER,
BARROW'S CREEK,
SPEARED FEBRUARY, 22, 1874,
DIED 23, FEBRUARY, 1874,
AGED 40.

JOHN FRANK,
SPEARED AT BARROW'S CREEK,
22, FEBRUARY, 1874,
DIED THE SAME DAY

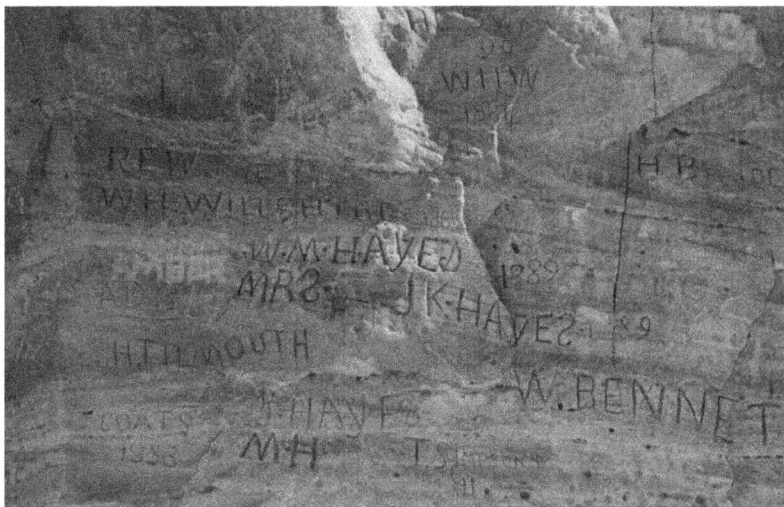

Graffiti on Chambers Pillar. In this section Willshire's autograph appears twice, once as 'WHW 1884' and again as 'W H Willshire 1885'. 'H C Swan 90' appears just above Willshire's 1884 inscription; Swan was one of the commissioners who held an inquiry into Willshire's activities in 1890. Photo: B Gammage.

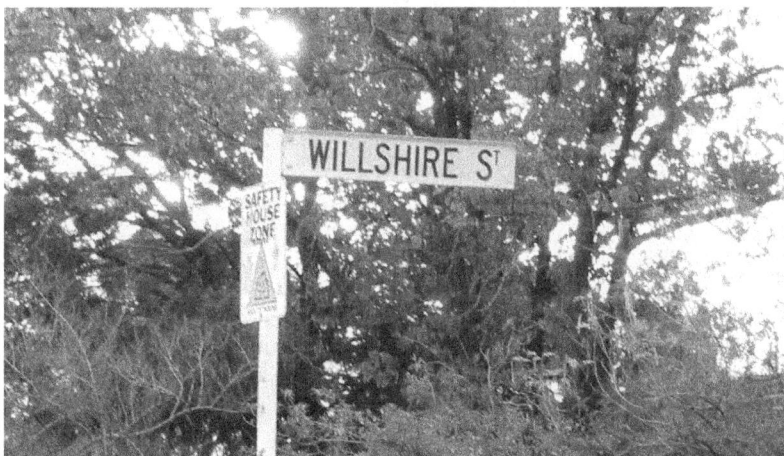

Willshire Street, Alice Springs. Photo: P Clarke.

Memorial plaque, Coniston, Northern Territory, in memory of the 1928 Coniston Massacre. Photo: G Serras. Courtesy of George Serras and the National Museum of Australia.

Larry, Archie and Jack had been contrived. At the conclusion of the inquiry that day he sent a telegram to Homburg outlining the developments. There is nothing to suggest that Gillen, a resident in the Centre since 1875, had found any reason until now to query the actions of Willshire or his Native Police. He had been one of the petitioners recommending Willshire's appointment as head of the Native Police in 1884. In his testimony to the Finke River Mission Inquiry in 1890, he had no criticism to make of the police and in fact described them as a 'smart and efficient' body. In his telegram to Homburg, however, Gillen seemed genuinely shocked: 'Case most serious and revolting, police should be instructed [to] arrest Willshire who is here at once'.[21] He summarised the evidence against Willshire: Gall's denial that he had issued any warrants to Willshire at any time, despite Willshire's evidence to the contrary; and Thomas' statements. Unlike the other Native Constables, he observed, Thomas 'had not seen Willshire' since the time he had been given instructions to attend the inquiry.

Gillen concluded his wire by asking if he should re-examine the other trackers. Homburg wired back immediately to concur: 'the government greatly appreciate your efforts to obtain information & anxiously await the result of any further inquiry you may deem necessary'. [22]

The investigation was suspended, and resumed again on 23 April. Most of the employees on Tempe Downs were gathered for interview. When asked for their testimonies, the European employees were uniformly unhelpful in their recollections. One stockman, Michael Devlin, could not recall when the events took place; he did not remember seeing the police in Donkey's or Roger's camps; he did not remember hearing shots fired. Another stockman, Charles Tucker, did recall hearing shots being fired, but he was in bed at the time and did not get up to investigate them. He had subsequently learnt that Donkey and Roger had been shot, but not by whom. Donkey, he said, was working at the station at the time, and Roger had worked there recently. In his opinion Roger was a bad character, but he knew nothing about Donkey.[23] Denis White, the cook at

Tempe Downs station, similarly had little information to offer. He recalled hearing something that morning, but could not be 'sure the noise was caused by shooting'. He was later told by Aboriginal women on the station that Donkey and Roger had been shot. He considered them bad characters, 'very bold and determined', and 'should not have liked to try to arrest either of them'. He was of the opinion that 'Mr Willshire kept the Blacks in check, they were afraid of him. He will be very much missed'.[24] Billy Abbott, the prospector who had allegedly helped remove and burn the bodies, also remembered very little. He had not heard the shooting, and although he had seen the bodies in the distance, he did not know what happened to them. He had not listened to accounts of the shooting 'as I did not want to know anything about it'.[25]

The station manager Richard Thornton was not on the station when the shootings occurred. When he returned to the station three days after the affair, he told Gillen, no one had informed him of what had happened. Donkey, he said, was employed as a temporary hand at the time of his death, and in Thornton's view neither Donkey nor Roger could be considered 'dangerous natives'. [26]

While interviews with the European station employees offered nothing to contradict the accounts of Willshire and the three Native Constables, interviews with the Aboriginal employees did. A number of Aboriginal women, who were in the 'Lubra's Camp' near the station's kitchen, recalled what they had seen that morning. Mary Ann, who described herself as 'Donkey's Lubra', said that when they heard shots fired, 'all the lubras jumped up and I saw Roger running away and heard him call out "Come on Nimi my lubra you and me run away". He had no weapons in his hands. I heard a shot and saw him fall immediately afterwards'. Chiuchewarra, who was with Mary Ann, saw Roger attempting to flee and being shot down. Both testified that Willshire, Billy Abbott and two Native Constables took the bodies away on a camel and burned them.[27]

On 25 April, the investigation shifted to the Hermannsburg mission station where, just nine months before, Willshire had detailed the mission-aries' ill-treatment of Aboriginal people on the station. Now those same people witnessed Willshire's examination.

The first witness called was Roger's wife, Nungoolya, also known as Naomi, who had been living at Hermannsburg since the events at Tempe Downs. She gave evidence in her own language, with Reverend Kempe interpreting. She had been asleep with Roger, she said, when she was woken by gunshots.

> Roger jumped up and started to run away and was shot by Native
> Constable Thomas. I saw Thomas shoot. Before Roger was shot he sang
> out to me "get up, get up, the Policemen are shooting". Roger had neither
> spears or boomerang. Thomas did not speak to Roger before firing. I ran
> away to lubra's camp near kitchen.

The bodies, she said, were taken away by camel. Willshire had subse-quently told her 'not to look out for my "noona" [husband] any more, and took me into his camp at Boggy Water'. Further Aboriginal witnesses who had been present at Tempe Downs on the morning of the shootings were interviewed at Hermannsburg. Peter and Friday were sleeping in the cart shed when they heard the commotion. Friday told Gillen that later 'I went along Donkey's camp and saw him dead with a bullet hole through chest'. Peter said that Willshire warned them not to 'walk longa creek'. 'By and by been see Willshire, Billy Abbott, and Blackfellow Policeman Jack and Archie take em Donkey longa camel longa sandhill. Then piccaninny time big fellow smoke jump up and then they came back and took Roger'. Jemmy and Dick, the two remaining Aboriginal witnesses, were away from the station when the incident occurred, but on their return a few days later they followed the camel tracks to the remains of two large fires where they found broken and charred bones in the ashes.

On 27 April, Gillen began his re-examination of the Native Constables at Alice Springs. Archie was the first to revisit his testimony, and he began, in my 'previous evidence I did not tell the truth Mr Willshire having told me to say what I did. I will tell the truth now.' There was no dead bullock on the road, he said. At daylight, 'Mr Willshire said to Larry and I go longa Donkey's camp and shoot him in the camp . . . We did not take any hand-cuffs or chains & Mr Willshire did not tell us to catch Donkey'. He did not see Roger shot, but he heard three shots come from the other camp. 'Mr Willshire said he wanted to kill Roger & Donkey because they killed a blackfellow at his camp.' When the men were dead, he and Jack assisted Willshire and Abbott to remove the bodies by camel, and burn them in separate fires. He took part in the shooting, he concluded, 'because I was afraid Willshire would shoot me if I disobeyed him'. [28]

Native Constable Jack also confessed to having lied in the previous evidence. He claimed that Willshire had instructed them to shoot Donkey and Roger. When the men were dead, Willshire and the four Native Constables went into the station and the cook fixed them breakfast. After breakfast Jack collected their camels from the police party's previous night's camp. They placed Donkey's body on one of the camels and took it to some sand-hills, where they burnt it. They returned for Roger's body, burning it in a nearby creek. The motivation for the raid was that Donkey and Roger had killed old man Nameia at the Boggy Waterhole police station. Jack admitted that he didn't like 'shooting Blackfellows but Willshire told me shootem'.[29] Native Constable Thomas was re-interviewed next, and he repeated the account he had earlier given. 'Willshire told us to shoot them,' he said, 'and I was frightened not to shoot.'[30] Larry was last to be re-examined, and on this occasion he gave his statement to Gillen's assistant Mounted Constable South. He explained that he originally lied to Gillen 'because Mr Willshire told me what to say and I was afraid. All us trackers were afraid Mr Willshire would shoot us if we did not obey him'.

At the first opportunity that day, Mounted Constable South wired the Commissioner of Police: 'Evidence against Willshire appalling, shews he went into Donkey and Roger's camp at Tempe Downs at Daybreak with trackers Archie, Jack, Larry and Joe. Donkey shot whilst asleep,

Roger whilst running away.' He advised that Willshire had been placed 'under strict guard' at the Alice Springs police station until further direction. Some of the station employees were re-examined but, having already stated that they had seen and heard nothing, they simply attested to the bad character of Donkey and Roger. With this evidence, the last day of Gillen's inquiry was concluded. At six o'clock that evening, at the Alice Springs police station, Mounted Constable South arrested Willshire on a charge of wilful murder. Willshire made no statement.[31]

Several days later Gillen wrote to the Attorney-General: 'This enquiry has been to me a painful and unpleasant duty but I have carried it out to the best of my ability and with perfect impartiality.' He respectfully recommended that Willshire's Boggy Waterhole police camp be abolished, and the work of patrolling the district be carried out from the Alice Springs police station. He further noted that a Sub Protector of Aborigines was needed for the district, 'and would be a great check on native abuses'.[32]

Shortly after arresting Willshire, South wrote an unusually candid note to Besley on the events described at the inquiry. South had joined the force a mere six months before Willshire and had known him for almost 14 years. He had 'always considered him eccentric, with an inordinate love of Notoriety', but had hardly taken these 'peculiarities' seriously. He simply could not account for Willshire's alleged actions

> unless the result of insanity, as surely no sane man, however wicked he may be, would go into Native's Camps within 200 yards of a head Station and shoot them; 4 men and other natives being there at the time, afterwards go and have breakfast at the Station, then take the bodies away on a camel and burn them within 1/4 of a mile of the Station, and not take, even, the precaution of reporting the matter to a Magistrate.[33]

Several days after Willshire's arrest Reverend Heidenreich wrote a letter, in German, to Attorney-General Homburg offering him 'the latest facts concerning the occurrences at Tempe Downs Station', which he had received from Reverend Schwarz at Hermannsburg.[34] The testimony provided by Schwarz, who was about to depart to a new missionary field in New Zealand, suggests deeper layers of social and sexual politics than those revealed by Gillen's inquiry. Willshire, according to Schwarz, 'alienated' Erraminta's (Roger's) wife from him, 'keeping her in his own hut for a considerable time'. Heidenreich himself, he wrote, had 'seen Ereminta's former wife in Willshire's hut, and that she appeared from her deportment to be "master" of the house'. Schwarz was of the view that Erraminta was so 'provoked by Willshire that he retaliated by killing cattle and indulging in the usual acts of violence', but he had subsequently settled down, marrying Naomi at Hermannsburg. Erraminta then moved to Tempe Downs where he became the station manager's 'best and most trusty blackboy', and it was here that he was shot down – Willshire having 'for years sought his life'.

According to Heidenreich, Mounted Constable Thomas, who shot Roger at Tempe Downs, was a promising convert gone astray. He had been instructed by the missionaries in God's word, baptised and married, but he ran away to Glen Helen, and 'took part in the murders and acts of reprisal against the Tempe Downs tribe'. He returned for a time to Hermannsburg before falling 'under Willshire's influence' and being enlisted as a tracker:

> Willshire knew well that the two tribes were at enmity and took delight in acts of violence against each other. It is an undoubted fact that in this way, and the responsibility resting with Wurmbrand and Willshire, the poor savages are shot down like wild dogs.[35]

Heidenreich's letter concludes by suggesting that the Native Police be disbanded, and that the government funds which had resourced them be devoted, in future, to developing the mission. The complex web of relations that pertained in the Centre between the mission, the police and the Aborigines emerges opaquely from Heidenreich's letter. To the missionaries, it must have seemed, especially after the Public Service Commission inquiry of the previous year, that the time of Willshire's 'payback' had arrived. Probably Willshire himself, in his self-aggrandisement, over-estimated the degree to which he commanded the loyalty of his Native Constables. And what of the Aboriginal people themselves, who moved between the world of the mission, the stations and the police camps that now occupied their country? The history of Native Constable Thomas suggests that Aboriginal people would still pursue their own cultural and social interests, despite either the mission's or the police's assumptions of their role in the new colonial order.

Just days before Homburg ordered Gillen to conduct his inquiry into the deaths of Donkey and Roger, the Pastoral Lands Commission had begun their inquiry into the state of the pastoral industry in the Centre. Where Willshire's reports of February and March conveyed the image of a still-dangerous frontier in need of subjugation, the evidence presented to the commissioners suggested a very different picture.

On 6 April, David Breaden, manager of Mount Burrell station, was asked if the Aborigines were helpful on the station, to which he replied, 'Yes; very.' 'Formerly the Natives were troublesome' to the station's development, he said, but those times were largely past. Asked if the station could be worked without their aid, he replied, 'No; probably not.' Asked if Aboriginal reserves were a good idea he dissented, but suggested that the provision of government rations would help them a lot. Francis Gillen, questioned as to the value of Aboriginal labour to the squatters, observed, 'I don't know what they would have done without them.' Mounted Constable South was of like mind: 'I do not know how their services could be dispensed with'. The Chairman went on to ask, 'The blacks are not troublesome in this district, I presume?' South replied, 'Not at all. They may kill a beast occasionally, of course, but nothing more'.[36]

As they answered these questions, all the witnesses would have known of the recent police shootings at Tempe Downs, and Gillen and South, at least, knew that an inquiry was about to be held into the matter; yet no one mentioned that event. All the witnesses suggested that the violence between Aboriginal people and settlers, which had so worried the Centre's pastoral industry a few years earlier, was now subsiding. Importantly, the Pastoral Lands Commission evidence was uniform in its agreement that the industry had become dependent on Aboriginal labour. This, too, had been the overriding impression to emerge six months earlier from the Finke River Mission Inquiry.

The nature of the district had changed; the era of 'dispersal' was ending. The tools of control that the pastoral industry perceived as necessary were different, by the turn of the 1890s, from those demanded during the previous decade. Whereas a few years before settlers had petitioned the government for officers with Martini-Henry carbines and Colts revolvers, now they wanted flour, tea and sugar to attract Aboriginal labour. The fact that Aboriginal people 'may kill a beast occasionally' was of little significance when weighed against the growing importance of their labour to the pastoral industry. Cattle killing was still prevalent on the stations to the west, such as Tempe Downs and Glen Helen; but one cannot help but wonder how self-referential Willshire's frontier had become; how much of the violence was dependent upon the presence of Willshire, his Native Police, and the entanglement of social relations they brought in their train.

THE TRIAL OF
WILLIAM
WILLSHIRE

The arrest of the Officer in Charge of the Native Police on a charge of murder could hardly have come at a worse time for the South Australian government. The Governor was, at that very time, travelling through Central Australia on his publicity tour, and was due any day for a formal visit to Alice Springs. A plethora of telegrams flew over the following week between Adelaide and Alice Springs as Police Commissioner Peterswald and Willshire's former supporter Besley made arrangements to smooth the Governor's visit.[1] 'Make what arrangements you like,' wired the Commissioner of Police to the Sub Inspector, 'so that there is no hitch in the other matter. Willshire is to be sent down to Adelaide as soon as possible.' It was planned that Mounted Constable Ernest Cowle would meet and escort the Governor, while Mounted Constable Chance would escort Willshire south to Oodnadatta, from where he would be transported by train to Port Augusta.[2] On Friday 8 May, as Willshire was being discreetly taken south, the Governor arrived in Alice Springs where he was met by Gillen and a corps of the Native Police, now under the command of Mounted Constable South.[3]

While at Oodnadatta Willshire may have witnessed the Elder Scientific Expedition, under the command of David Lindsay, assembling and preparing for its explorations of South Australia's north-west and adjacent regions of Western Australia. It was Lindsay's discovery of what were believed to be rubies in the country east of Alice Springs (they were in fact garnets) that had led to the modest mining boom in 1887.[4] Lindsay's new expedition would track through country Willshire had travelled only two years before, undertaking the epic patrol of which he had failed to maintain a record. The Elder expedition would herald in a new style of Central Australian exploration: the scientific expedition, which counted geologists, botanists and, eventually, anthropologists among their number.

In a nostalgic memoir of his 1889 patrol to Lake Amadeus – country Lindsay was only now about to traverse – Willshire makes an anachronistic reference to the Elder expedition. He recalls sitting in camp 'overhauling my plans for scaling distances', when he chances upon an issue of the *Quiz*, an Adelaide monthly, featuring a cartoon of the 'quondam explorer [Lindsay] sitting in a palanquin carried by a couple of Australia's dusky savages, with a host of others behind carrying water'. On explaining the joke to his Aboriginal companions, he reports that they 'laid down' and 'laughed extravagantly'.[5] Had he had his chance again, he wrote, he would have been an explorer.

Willshire was received at Her Majesty's Gaol, Port Augusta, on 14 May 1891, his name entered into the prison register next to the charge that he did 'feloniously, wilfully and of his malice aforethought kill and murder two aboriginal natives Donkey & Roger'.[6] Willshire's father, who had already been advised of the content of Gillen's inquiry, wrote to the Attorney-General and requested that 'in the interest of justice and fairness, no published statement' of its content 'be issued the Press prior to the trial'.[7] In the meantime, Willshire was applying to the Commissioner of Police to employ counsel on his behalf. He would, he told Besley, like Sir John Downer to take his case. Besley's telegrammed response was curt: 'Government cannot employ counsel. Willshire's solicitor must make all necessary applications for bail . . . Police must not interfere.'[8]

Sir John Downer did take his case. More influential counsel would have been difficult to find. Downer, who had only recently returned from

a Federation Convention in Sydney, had already been Attorney-General
and Premier, and his brother, Edward, was Attorney-General when the
Finke River Mission Inquiry was ordered in 1891. Such high-powered
representation came at a cost, and was largely paid for by subscription
raised by Central Australian pastoralists.[9]

Willshire's trial

On 23 July 1891, Willshire's trial was held at a Circuit Court sitting of the
Supreme Court in Port Augusta before Justice W H Bundey. Representing
the defence was Sir John Downer, and representing the Crown was Mr J M
Stuart. The case opened with a statement to the jury by the Crown
Prosecutor, an address which might just as readily have been presented by
the defence. There was no doubt, Stuart began, that Donkey and Roger
had been shot by the Native Police under the control of the prisoner at the
bar; but unless the prisoner could be proved by evidence to be guilty of
murder, then he must be discharged. The prisoner at the bar might have
been compelled to use drastic measures, situated as he was in the centre of
the wilds of Central Australia, for the protection of the whites and for the
prevention of cattle stealing, but still deliberate killing was not allowable.
Virtually alone 'amidst a savage nomadic race', the accused presumably 'had
to exercise a certain amount of arbitrary power to protect the whites and
prevent the commission of outrage; but it must be borne in mind that no man
had the right to take life except under the most extreme circumstances'.
Stuart then turned his attention to the evidence of the Aboriginal witnesses,
upon which his case as Crown Prosecutor depended. The case was rendered difficult, he said, 'because the evidence of Aboriginal natives must be
weighed very carefully ... Simplicity of character, a not too retentive
memory, and a tendency to adopt a course which they considered would be
most agreeable to the person questioning were features in the aboriginal
disposition, and made their evidence subject to suspicion'. The victims in
the case, he continued, were known as 'notorious offenders' who had been
involved in cattle spearing; they were also allegedly involved in the murder

of one of the Native Constable's relatives, and it was possible that their deaths might have occurred 'in obedience to some tribal law of retaliation'.[10]

The most serious charge presented against Willshire, it seemed, concerned the disposal of the two bodies. It was 'a singular fact', said Stuart, that Willshire's report on the case to his superior officer 'did not mention the burning of the bodies of Donkey and Roger'. He added, however, that he believed 'it was a custom of the blacks to demand that the bodies of those killed in obedience to their law of retaliation should be burnt'. The source of this piece of 'customary' evidence was Willshire himself, from the depositions taken by Gillen in April. Stuart concluded his opening address for the prosecution with the odd statement that there 'was no doubt that cattle-killing and cattle-stealing had been prevalent in the district, but that Donkey and Roger were the delinquents was not proved'. The victims, it seems, were the ones whose criminality was most at issue.

The first witness to take the stand was Native Constable Jack, who was described in the press as a 'rather well-built native trooper, with a typical aboriginal head and a rather intelligent face'. Jack described how the police party had travelled to Tempe Downs and raided the Aboriginal camps at dawn. Jack and Thomas had shot Roger. Willshire had told them to 'shoot him Donkey and Roger'. The police party then went to the station and had breakfast. After breakfast they collected the camels from their camp and returned with them to the station. Willshire, Billy Abbott, Native Constable Archie and Jack made two trips, firstly taking Donkey's body to the sandhills and then taking Roger's body to the creek. 'Billy Abbott makem fire of dead tree. We all cut wood for fire – one axe – brought axe on camel – this was just after breakfast.'

Sir John Downer then began his cross-examination. His defence strategy was clear: to portray the Native Constables as liars, whose testimony had already – before the trial began – been contradictory, and whose credibility was necessarily in doubt. Downer's interest was in tracing over the earlier accounts that had been taken in the April depositions, and his invitations to repeat those accounts revolved around an uncovering, not of *what* occurred, but of what the witnesses had initially *said* occurred. Willshire's defence, then, relied upon the principle that the responsibility for the entangled relationship between 'truth' and 'lies' lay not with the accused but, rather, with the Native Constables.

Jack said that the evidence he had first presented at the April inquiry 'was a lie'. He elaborated: 'I tell em lies cause Mr Willshire been tellem me to tell em.' Encouraged by Downer, he recounted the list of lies he had, as he had subsequently told Gillen, been required to tell:

> Tellem Gillen spear sticking in a bullock, a lie. Told Gillen I saw Donkey's and Roger's and Chuck a Chuck's tracks along a bullock, a lie. Tell Mr Gillen I follow tracks to Tempe Downs Station, a lie. Told Mr Gillen that I and Thomas have a yabber, to put handcuffs on a Roger, a lie. Told Gillen I saw Donkey knock down Willshire with a yamstick, and saw Donkey running away carrying a spear, and saw Larry shoot him with a rifle, and that Mr Willshire was down when Larry fired, and that if Larry had not fired Donkey get away. All a lie.[11]

According to the press report on the case, this witness's 'free admissions of mendacity' were so liberal they 'became monotonous'.

Downer's second strategy concerned motive for the shootings, and in this respect there was no attempt to portray the witness as a liar. Under Downer's questioning, Jack agreed that Donkey and Roger were cattle killers and, more importantly, the killers of Native Constable Larry's father Nameia, as well as Native Constable Thomas' brother. The case was put that Donkey and Roger were killed by the Native Constables in the prosecution of a blood feud.

Thomas was the second witness called. He confessed to shooting Roger. Asked why he shot the man, he replied, 'because Mr. Willshire tellum.' In his cross-examination, Downer was brief. He confirmed with Thomas that Donkey and Roger had killed his brother, and that he himself had shot Roger while he was running away.

The third witness was Archie. Under Downer's examination, he repeated his two earlier testimonies of what had occurred on the day of the shootings and of what he had told Mr Gillen during the taking of the depositions in April. His two testimonies were in contradiction with one another; yet he was not asked to explain how, in the April inquiry, he had come to fabricate and then retract his initial testimony.

The proceedings adjourned for lunch and resumed at 2 pm, when Larry was the last of the Native Constables to be called. Questioned by Stuart, he bluntly related a sequence of events: he had gone armed to Donkey's camp, had shot Donkey through the chest, and had done so because 'Mr Willshire bin tellum day before after dinner'.

At this point Willshire was granted the right to ask a question of the witness in Larry's own language and to interpret his responses to the court. Willshire asked Larry to relate what he, Willshire, had said to the Native Constables when they were approaching the camp on Tempe Downs. Larry, whom Willshire personably referred to as 'Milla', gave his reply, which was translated for the court by Willshire. Unfortunately, neither the judge's case notes nor the press report describe the contents of that exchange. What is most telling is that the accused was allowed to question the witness, and to act as that witness's interpreter, in his own murder case.

Downer began his cross-examination of Larry with some humour. He was afraid, he said, 'to attempt the mixed English and Aboriginal dialect, because being a native himself he might not be able to break himself of it'. Larry's testimony in Aboriginal English was translated by Sub Inspector Besley, who 'knew the vernacular'. While the previous witnesses had been provided little opportunity to distinguish between their first deposed testimonies (what they had 'told Gillen') and their second (what 'had happened'), Larry attempted to do so, perhaps because he was the only witness aided by a translator. When Downer asked for confirmation of what he had told Mr Gillen, Larry replied, 'No; that a lie in that one yabber,' and in the subsequent questioning he persisted in trying to distinguish for the court between his original 'false' and his subsequent 'true' evidence. On the occasion of the first testimony given to Gillen at Alice Springs, when Willshire was outside the police station, Larry recalled: 'When I first yabber Mr Gillen Mr Willshire tell me.' On the second occasion, when Willshire was absent he recalled, 'I tell Mr Gillen that what I said first was wrong'. Justice Bundey commented that 'he was most anxious to find out if anyone had been tampering with the witness'. But despite this statement, the issue was not raised again during the hearing.[12]

The next witness called was Naomi, who had been asleep with Roger when their camp was raided and he was shot. Downer objected to her examination through an interpreter on the grounds that the interpreter was 'a native discharged from the employ of the accused'. She was dismissed as a witness. Billy Abbott, the next witness called, testified that he had nothing to do with the burning of the bodies, and was discharged from the stand.

The final witness was Willshire's arresting officer, William Garnett South. In contrast to the baffled and curiously personal letter about Willshire he had written to Besley two months previously, South confirmed that Willshire 'is an able officer & I believe he has given very general satisfaction'. South also put Willshire's diary into evidence, and read his account of events to the court:

> The depredations of the blacks upon the stations, their cattle-killing and otherwise troublesome behaviour, the measures taken to arrest Roger and Donkey, the instructions to the trackers to catch the delinquents alive, their resistance, the spear-throwing, and fatal termination.[13]

As South finished his reading, the spectators in court responded with spontaneous applause. In court, the Native Constables had struggled to differentiate the truth from Willshire's fabrication. They did so in a language that was difficult for them, yet they were mocked for the manner of their speech and characterised as liars. Willshire's rehearsed account offered a familiar storyline, one the audience was always ready to adopt, and even in a court of law it carried weight.

The case for the prosecution was closed. For the defence, Downer began his closing address with the statement that the case was 'one of the most disgraceful that had ever been brought into the Court'. Willshire, he said, was a man of high character who performed 'arduous and dangerous duties', and who had been 'hurled into gaol, and put in the dock to answer on peril of his life a charge of murder because he had thoroughly done the difficult work entrusted to him'. Willshire was put at risk of being hanged by the 'testimony of two self-confessed murderers, whose statements were of the most extraordinarily contradictory character'. Such contradictory statements were to be contrasted with the 'plain, straightforward report' given by the accused, a report that was even supported by the testimony of those – the contradictory Native Constables – who had committed the fatal deed. 'There was no reason,' Downer said, 'why Willshire should want to kill the men,' but there was every reason to believe that the Native Constables had sacrificed them 'in pursuance of a tribal vendetta and a native law'. The prosecution of Willshire, Downer concluded, was 'monstrous and entirely unjustifiable'.

In summing up, Justice Bundey told the jury that it would be a terrible thing if 'poor blacks' were shot down with impunity, but at the same time, it would be a discouragement to officers of the law in the execution of their duty if they were not supported. He then reiterated the depositions and gave the case over to the jury to decide 'according to how their minds were influenced by the evidence'. Late in the afternoon the jury retired, and returned 15 minutes later. Their verdict was 'not guilty', with the addendum 'that there is not a tattle of evidence to incriminate Mounted Constable Willshire'. According to the press report, the verdict 'was received with a round of applause, which the officers of the Court checked. The accused was released, and on his appearance outside the crowd cheered him lustily, and followed him across to his lodgings in a sort of procession'.

Reporting the case in its pages two days later, the *Adelaide Observer* commented that rarely had a case 'excited so much general interest'. Public sympathy, it noted, appeared to rest 'entirely' with the accused, 'and it is said that the funds for his defence were provided by voluntary subscription. A good number of people came up from Adelaide to hear the trial, and judging from the number who went to the telegraph-office to send down the result as much interest was felt in the city as in the country over the matter'.[14]

Although letters in support of Willshire poured in to the papers both before and after the trial, the case brought forth some dissenting voices. One correspondent questioned a trial in which the case for the prosecution was virtually indistinguishable from the case for the defence. Signing himself 'Justitia', the correspondent commented that after the trial, many people from the north, including himself, had 'expressed their dissatisfaction at the way in which it was conducted. I was present, and never heard a more entirely one-sided affair'.

> Is it credible that Mr. Gillen, who was living near the scene of the murders and was acquainted with previous circumstances connected with Willshire's treatment of the blacks, should have committed him for trial without any grounds whatever? I was in the North soon after the murders took place, and the universally accepted story was that the black trackers . . . shot the unfortunate men Roger and Donkey by Willshire's orders . . . [and] finding the matter had attracted attention, Willshire instructed these men to make a statement to Mr. Gillen, which statement under cross-examination they retracted . . . Every one was determined that Willshire should be acquitted, and the speech of the counsel for the prosecution might certainly have been that for the defence.

No person, he wrote, 'ought to be entrusted with the autocratic power Willshire possessed over the lives and properties of these comparatively defenceless people'. Those unacquainted with life in the north, he finished, would be incredulous at 'the cheap rate at which human life when contained in a black skin is valued'.[15]

Days after the trial, an editorial appeared in *The Port Augusta Dispatch* cautiously examining the terms on which frontier policing in the Interior, up until this point, had been enabled to proceed:

> The trial of MC Willshire last week points unmistakeably to a necessity
> for some more efficient manner of dealing with crime in the interior than
> that at present in vogue. If no attempt is to be made to alter the conditions
> which now obtain, it would seem as though the protection of our
> aborigines might be regarded as a mere cant term. As the case stands at
> present we have a police officer appointed to take charge of a corps of
> native trackers away in the interior. The former has absolute control –
> in fact his rule is despotic. The men whom he governs are . . . armed with
> the most deadly and destructive firearms, and have every means to hand
> for committing crime secretively in regions far removed from centres of
> civilisation . . . Let us put a case plainly. Suppose the officer in charge . . .
> should be tempted in an indiscreet moment to tumble a few native
> evildoers 'heels over head', who need be any the wiser?[16]

Some of the worst violence on the Central Australian frontier coincided with Willshire's tenure as Officer in Charge of the Native Police, but to explain that violence with reference to Willshire alone, as a consequence of his personality, would be a mistake. Willshire was an aberrant personality, egotistical and narcissistic, but these traits better explain the extraordinary nature of the record he left to posterity, than the actions he undertook as a Mounted Constable. All the evidence suggests that his compatriot Wurmbrand was no less violent in his policing and operated under the same 'rules of engagement'. Their activities as Mounted Constables and Officers in Charge of the Native Police had the tacit approval of their superiors and were in accord with a well-established frontier tradition. Willshire certainly saw it in this light:

I am proud to be able to submit to paper that the Government at the time told me as the officer of police parties to go out and do as the law provides . . . and now I say, 'All's well that ends well.'[17]

That Willshire was eventually called to account might well be explained by his personality. Words gave him away, caught out in a lie while engaged in a vendetta to re-assert his personal authority over the people he commanded and those he policed.

The new rule of law

Although many people in the Centre's pastoral community had pledged their support for Willshire, the South Australian police administration was evidently chastened by what had been revealed in the inquiry and murder trial that followed. Following Gillen's advice, Willshire's Boggy Waterhole police camp was abandoned, and the Centre's Native Police force was redistributed between the Alice Springs police station, under the direction of Mounted Constable South, and the Barrow Creek station, under the direction of Mounted Constable Daer. In August 1891, three weeks after Willshire's trial, Besley drafted detailed and precautionary instructions to the new Officers in Charge in which he clarified police procedures, especially in regard to offences by Europeans against Aborigines. The trial of Willshire had clearly affected how the government conceived its task of policing the frontier. The Officer in Charge would henceforth

send a report to his Inspector immediately after each journey; briefly by wire and fully by letter giving details of events, and stages travelled. It will be the duty of the Officer on this Patrol to make enquiries into all offences committed by the natives especially cattle killing, obtain warrants where practicable for offenders, and if possible apprehend and bring them to justice. Firearms must not be used except in self defence, should any Aboriginals be killed under no circumstances shall the bodies be burned.

He is also directed to specially enquire as to the treatment of the natives by Europeans, and promptly report all offences against them and when necessary take prompt action against offender. He must report all cases where a European takes away the wife (of an Aboriginal) from her husband, or a girl from her parents or guardian without their consent, as this often leads to offences by Natives committed in retaliation, it must therefore be checked.[18]

The government made a number of other changes in an effort to bring something like the rule of law to the region. A local court was established at Alice Springs to allow charges to be heard in the district, rather than require officers to transport prisoners many hundreds of kilometres to Port Augusta or Palmerston. A Sub Protector of Aborigines was appointed for the region, in the figure of Francis Gillen. Lastly, Illamurta police camp was established to the south-west under the command of Mounted Constable Earnest Cowle, to replace Willshire's Boggy Waterhole camp.

Although the Pastoral Lands Commission of 1891 had heard that the level of cattle killing was subsiding, it still continued in the west, on Tempe Downs and Glen Helen in particular. In August 1893 Mounted Constable Cowle and his Native Constables successfully arrested 'Racehorse's Mob' on Glen Helen station, and soon they arrested another six men for whom warrants were held, including those Willshire had failed to capture in the early months of 1891. Six of the men were found guilty of the 'larceny of beef' and sentenced to six months hard labour, which they served at Port Augusta Gaol. On their release there was some discussion about whether or not their incarceration had been a sufficient lesson, and it was mooted that they be sent to Point McLeay mission for a spell. However, the Attorney-General objected that such action might be illegal and 'might lead to all sorts of abuses'. In the end, when their six months' goal term had been served, the prisoners were put aboard the train to Oodnadatta, from where they were obliged to walk home.[19]

In his Annual Report for that year Francis Gillen, in his capacity as

Sub Protector of Aborigines, congratulated Cowle and Daer on their 'clever arrest'. He observed that it would have a 'salutary effect and I do not anticipate any further trouble in this quarter for some time'. He also commented on the advantageous effect of the newly established rations depots in the district. Many Aboriginal people were coming in to the depots from hundreds of kilometres around, he noted, and 'generally remained until heavy rains enable them to procure food' more easily. Prior to the establishment of the depots, he sympathised, accessible means of subsistence for Aboriginal people were deplorable and 'one cannot wonder that cattle killing was rampant'.[20]

THRILLING TALES

After the trial

Although Willshire had been suspended from the force while awaiting trial, he was reinstated on his acquittal, and his superior officers were faced with the problem of what to do with someone of his particular skills. Willshire himself was keen to return to the Centre, but neither Peterswald nor Besley was willing to send him back, or to send him to a metropolitan station in Adelaide. He spent the following two years moving between South Australian rural postings. His first transfer after his reinstatement was to Innamincka in the far north-east of South Australia, where the absence of reports indicates a quiet time.

After arresting him at the close of Gillen's committal hearing, Mounted Constable South noted Willshire's 'inordinate love of notoriety'.[1] It is likely that his desire for notoriety had been dampened by the trial, but the attraction of it remained. While at Innamincka, Willshire collected a boomerang from an Aboriginal man, Logic, who had briefly achieved celebrity status in the mid 1880s after escaping from Yatala Labour Prison.[2] Local settlers, sympathetic to his cause, helped Logic as he tried to make his way home to Innamincka and when he was eventually captured they successfully petitioned the Governor for his release. Willshire, an avid reader of the local press, undoubtedly followed the story and now he had a memento of the 'once notorious' Logic.[3]

In March 1892 Willshire was transferred to Port Augusta, where he had a difficult time: in May he was cautioned for being under the influence of liquor (he had been fined for a similar offence in 1888); in June he was cautioned for being insolent to an officer; in October he was ordered to pay damages for a 'falsehood' about the defacement of police property. Late that year he was posted to Port Pirie, where he would again get into trouble for insubordination.[4] While Willshire wondered what his future held, a ghost from his past re-appeared.

In October 1892 Willshire's father, James, wrote to Sub Protector Besley at Port Augusta regarding a 12-year-old Aboriginal girl who had been living with his family, but whom they did 'not require' any longer. A covering memo indicates that the girl had been 'brought down by M. C. Willshire', and 'taken care of by his parents' at their North Adelaide home. Besley wrote back informing him that Mr and Mrs Parkhouse of Adelaide had been looking for a 'nurse girl' and could provide her with a good home. The Willshires, he added in a letter to the Parkhouse family, 'had taken a great deal of trouble with her', she spoke good English and was very 'handy'. It was suggested that they take her on 'a month's trial', and if she suited, an agreement to 'obtain full control' could be drawn up by Protector Edward Hamilton.[5]

Who was the girl and when did Willshire bring her down? In Swan and Taplin's 1890 inquiry, allegations had been raised that Willshire had travelled to Adelaide with a young girl. Willshire defended himself by saying that he had taken a seven-year-old Aboriginal girl down with him, but only so that she could be placed as a servant with his brother-in-law, the Commissioner of Forests Mr Brown.[6] Initially, at least, it seems that the girl was placed with his sister. Forty-four years later the anthropologist Norman B Tindale collected a genealogy from an elderly woman living at the Point McLeay Aboriginal settlement in the state's south-east. She was an Arrernte woman by birth whose father had died when she was a baby.

She told Tindale that she had been 'brought south by Mr Willshire, policeman and brought up by his sisters and mother'.[7] What motivated Willshire to remove the child is unknown – it is quite possible that he construed it as a compassionate act – but it is difficult not to see it as yet another 'trophy moment'.

That he was unhappy with the turn in his career and his relationship with the police administration since leaving the Centre was clear. In time, he would complain to John Field, Besley's replacement as Inspector of Police: 'A great many men in charge of stations in the Central Division are junior to myself – and even if I could not get a station there, I might have been permitted to do duty in Head Quarters in Adelaide, until the Commr. had time to see whether I behaved myself circumspectly'.[8]

In February 1893, Willshire saw a notice in the *Register* that a temporary police station would be established in his old patrolling territory, at Tempe Downs. He applied for the post, emphasising in his application that 'the ways and customs of wild natives are well known to me, and stopping their depredations is my special forte'.[9] Peterswald forwarded Willshire's application to Besley, asking, 'What do you say to this? It is proposed to establish a station on the Elsie River under Foelsche. Willshire will never do any good in the settled districts.'[10] Besley wrote back: 'I am decidedly opposed to MC Willshire going back to Tempe Downs – as he does not appear to get on well in the settled districts I would recommend he have a trial at the Elsie River.'[11] Situated in the far north-west of the Territory, the Elsie River, apparently, was far enough removed from the 'settled districts' to accommodate an officer of Willshire's temperament.

At the end of March 1893, the Commissioner of Police wrote to Inspector Saunders, Willshire's superior officer at Port Pirie:

There is likely to be a vacancy in the Northern Territory Police, is MC Willshire willing to go there?

From what I have seen of his disinclination to submit to authority, and his evil example to his comrades, which, the discipline of any station, where he is, is impossible, I feel I cannot do otherwise than bring his conduct under the notice of the Chief Secretary with a view to his leaving the Force.

Should he decide however on [transferring] to the Territory I will request Insp Foelsche to give him a station in the Bush on the first opportunity that offers, as though a source of trouble in a station down country I believe he would be a useful man in the interior.[12]

The Commissioner had effectively issued an ultimatum: accept the post at Elsie River, or resign from the force. Within weeks, on 25 May 1893, Willshire was entered for service into the Northern Territory police force. An 'evil example' in the down country and the settled districts, he was evidently still a 'useful man' in the far-flung country and the unsettled districts. By the following year, he was established in the Territory's far north, on the Victoria River.

In the same year, 1894, Francis Gillen met the anthropologist Baldwin Spencer, who was travelling the region with the Horn Scientific Expedition. With its genesis in this meeting, theirs would quickly become a major partnership in Australian anthropology. Between May and November of that year, the Horn expedition tracked its way through many of Willshire's former patrol sites. For part of the expedition, Spencer was accompanied by Willshire's former colleague, Mounted Constable Ernest Cowle, who subsequently corresponded with Spencer and collected ethnographic information on his behalf. The expedition was planned as an anthropological and botanical one, and was widely reported in the press. Taking place within a few short years of Federation, it ensured, as Tom Griffiths has put it, that science played a role in shaping the emerging Australian national consciousness.[13]

In his introduction to the report of the expedition, Baldwin Spencer traced the reasons why, in his view, ethnographic work in Australia, particularly of the Interior, had not hitherto fared well: 'the trained observer has lacked the opportunities for observations. To no country is the remark of a distinguished traveller more appropriate than to Australia – that "as a rule the men who know don't write, and the men who write don't know".'[14] In his own notes on 'The Natives of Central Australia', which appeared as an appendix to the Horn expedition report and were read to the Royal Anthropological Institute in 1898, Gillen outlined the complexity of Aboriginal social organisation and cautioned his audience against bringing European social understandings to it: 'tribal organisation', he wrote, 'is often of so complicated a character that, though the natives understand it clearly enough, it is most difficult for the white man to grasp. One has to throw on one side all ideas of organization and relationship, as existing amongst ourselves'.[15] The aggressive patrolling of the Centre in the service of pastoral expansion and Aboriginal pacification had turned with the Horn expedition to an interest in sifting the Centre for its ethnoscientific secrets.

A Thrilling Tale

From his new location on the pastoral frontier further north, Willshire was pursuing further 'ethnographic' work of his own. Perhaps encouraged by the reasonable success of *The Aborigines of Central Australia*, which was republished shortly after his trial, he published his second work *A Thrilling Tale of Real Life in the Wilds of Australia* in 1895. In its preface, Willshire modestly offers his 'little book', as he had *The Aborigines of Central Australia*, as a work of ethnographic interest: 'I would like the critic to be a countryman of my own – a South Australian – and then judge it on its merits, not as an aspiring literary effort, but as a work giving some information regarding the aborigines of an almost unknown and unexplored portion of Central Australia.'[16] Whereas *The Aborigines of Central Australia* had been printed with an undecorated cover, *A Thrilling Tale* appeared with a cover etching, by the South Australian artist William Cawthorne, of Aboriginal warriors, surrounded by various items of native weaponry, posed in positions of either mid-hunt, or leisurely recline.

With its location around Lake Amadeus and its reference to six Native Constables,[17] it is likely that *A Thrilling Tale* is a literary representation of a patrol undertaken in the early months of 1889 – another patrol of which Willshire left no record. Willshire's aspirations to be an explorer were strong. In the months after establishing his Interior Police Patrol, and before undertaking this journey, he requisitioned supplies that included maps of the country to the west of his Boggy Waterhole police camp.[18] On this patrol, Willshire followed in the footsteps of Giles's 1874 expedition that terminated at Lake Amadeus.[19] He had clearly read Giles's account, and records many of the landmarks Giles had visited: Mount Peculiar, the Tarn of Auber, the Vale of Tempe, Laurie's Creek and Lake Amadeus.[20]

A Thrilling Tale is Willshire's most idiosyncratic and 'literary' work, in the sense that the events are consciously plotted to conform to the conventions of colonial adventure romance novels that were becoming popular in the late nineteenth century. In *Writing the Colonial Adventure*, Robert Dixon outlines the features of this genre, and its influential place in Australian popular culture in the decades approaching Federation. Although its plots might vary, its structural features are repetitive. An explicitly masculinist genre, it relates adventures in which a group of explorer-heroes journey into unexplored regions; they encounter a lost race, often a hybrid or degenerate society, and natives 'warring among themselves'; the erotic attractions of the barbaric race are manifest when one of the white heroes is enraptured by a native woman; they establish the order that their natural superiority requires; and, with any luck uncovering a treasure in the wilds of the now-explored Interior, they return to civilisation. As Dixon argues, such colonial adventure narratives reveal 'anxieties about race, nation and empire', or more specifically, the anxieties about 'racial and cultural decline' that mark the late colonial period. They reflect an imperative to civilise – an intrinsically imperialist imperative – and at the same time an anti-empire, pro-nationalist sentiment. In this sense, the formation of a distinctly Australian nationalism was conceived in this literary genre in terms of rejecting both 'external' Britishness and local 'barbarity'.[21]

A Thrilling Tale follows many of the conventions identified by Dixon. The hero – Willshire – journeys into the western reaches of Central Australia, he lives among the Aboriginal inhabitants, is enraptured by a native woman, reveals secrets and 'treasures' in hidden caves, and travels into unexplored country. The work's literary intentions are nonetheless confused as Willshire slips almost seamlessly between different narrative voices and genres. On the one hand the work offers itself as a factual record of 'the natives and their habits', a document 'of true aboriginal life recorded as a result of actual observation by the author'.[22] On the other it is the story of heroic exploration, at the heart of which is the real subject: Mounted Constable Willshire. In the preface, the author tells us that during the book's 'compilation no house offered shelter; but in the wild bush, and principally on a camel pack-saddle for a table did the author dot down the facts and experiences which are now given to the public'.

Willshire injects his story with archetypal significance by beginning in a style more reminiscent of fairy tale than adventure romance:

> In the Western territory of Central Australia, and on the northern shores of Lake Amadeus, lived a maiden whom nature endowed with a most sweet disposition. Her name was Chillberta, which, in the aboriginal tongue, means 'Falling rain'.

In his journey his guide and muse is the 'dusky maiden' Chillberta, to whom the book is dedicated. It was Chillberta who told him of the beautiful country to the south, 'a perfect fairyland of palmy foliage' that 'inspired' Willshire to accompany her 'to this Austral paradise'.

The dual positions of narrator and hero that Willshire inhabits in *A Thrilling Tale* are played out in a slippage between narrative voices: the first chapter unfolds in the first-person narrative voice adopted in *The Aborigines of Central Australia*, that of the educated observer of Aboriginal life; but in the second chapter the narrative moves without explanation into a third-person point of view. Henceforth, Willshire tells his reader, 'the white man will be known as Oleara', a 'native' name granted to him, he says, from the local language.[23] With the passing of the frontier era that he had lived through in Central Australia, it seems as though Willshire, with this new work, aspired to regenerate himself as a character in his own mythological narrative of white nativeness.

The conceit of relating the story as 'Oleara', in a third-person narrative voice, has the unusual effect of subverting the usual panoptical vision of the explorer. We see the land and the people through Willshire's eyes, but just as often we see Willshire, as he imagines himself, being watched by Aboriginal observers. Yet, in keeping with the mode of adventure romance, the latter perspective is enlisted only in so far as it can imaginatively refract back, for the reader's benefit, the image of the narrative's real subject: the white hero, the master and natural inheritor of the environment. In this sense, in a play of double vision, Willshire presents himself both as the neutral author of facts 'recorded as a result of actual observation', and as the heroic central character of adventure romance.

> I liked the life, enraptured by scenes of desolate wildness; of picturesque beauty, gorge and glen where the wild holly and oranges wafted their perfume over the camp of the weary white-fellow.
>
> From many a craggy eminence I have seen the wild aborigine keenly observing my movements, and while meditating on these wild scenes I have fallen asleep, whilst my blackboys have prepared the usual repast of tea, kangaroo, iguano, &c.
>
> Savage life, stripped of all its fictitious ornaments has its natural and entrancing beauties, but the darker shadows of its vices dim the lustre of its virtues.[24]

Chillberta, Willshire tells us, is 'undoubtedly, the heroine of the story'. A comely virgin of 16, just 'budding into womanhood', she is a tantalising reminder of the natural treasures of the country over which the white hero is master. Like Chillberta, the land itself is ripe for plucking: it is 'a beautiful land, where very few white men have been, and where, in all its luxuriant lusciousness, flourish the ever-welcome quandong and wild orange'.[25] Chillberta becomes Oleara's girl-Friday, his 'cicerone' on his journey, warning him when danger is near and, as his protégé, moving inexorably herself towards a yearning for 'civilised' femininity.

Indeed, Willshire's Chillberta is perilously similar to the idealised white Australian Girl who captured the popular imagination in late nineteenth-century verse. Ethel Castilla's popular 1888 poem 'The Australian Girl' offered an image of the coming generation of Australians, in feminised terms, as independent-spirited, sun-kissed, and fit for the future:

> Southern sun and Southern air
> Have kissed her cheeks, until they wear
> The dainty tints that oft appear
> On rosy shells.

> Her frank, clear eyes bespeak a mind
> Old-world traditions fail to bind
> She is not shy
> Or bold, but simply self-possessed.

> . . . In sports she bears away the bell,
> Nor under music's siren spell,
> To dance divinely, flirt as well,
> Does she distain.[26]

Born of the country and 'chaste as the morning dew', Chillberta is the 'light-hearted girl who loved the free air of the ranges' and whose stoic heart always 'dispelled adversity'.[27] Yet unlike the heroine of Castilla's popular verse, Chillberta cannot represent Australianness to come unless she becomes, impossibly, white. Her role in *A Thrilling Tale* is ultimately not to bear the mantle of Australianness herself – despite her adoption of 'the habits of a refined white woman'[28] – but to provide the narrative point of entry through which Oleara, the exemplary bushman hero, is granted possession of the landscape. When her role as guide and muse is completed, Chillberta disappears from the narrative. Her only lasting presence is signalled by the book's dedication to her. She has, it seems, fulfilled her perceived destiny as a member of the 'dying race' in having 'gone to that place from whence no traveller ever returns'.

As the Finke River Mission Inquiry had uncovered in 1890, the taking of Aboriginal 'mistresses' by white men, including the police, was a controversial issue both for the Hermannsburg missionaries and for the police administration. Although missionary complaints had implicated Willshire in the practice, the inquiry found that 'there was no evidence to prove that he was guilty of immorality'. Though he clearly distanced himself from such charges in letters to his superior officers, in his literary writings Willshire alludes to his patrolling practice of sometimes taking Aboriginal women back to the police camp after a 'scrimmage' in which their men had been killed. The purpose of doing this, though vaguely framed in terms of general chivalry, is never explained, and the ubiquitous sexual undercurrent of *A Thrilling Tale* is ambivalently rendered. With her bouquet of orange blossom and necklace of quandong stones, Chillberta is the rich potential of the land itself. Yet throughout the narrative her virtue is maintained, protecting for the reader her own value as the ideal of pristine Aboriginality, as well as Oleara's necessary status as the chivalric hero. At the same time, with her 'magnetic eyes, licentious smiles and flowing hair',[29] Chillberta's 'innate' sexuality presents the civilised white hero with a sore challenge:

> Intercourse with the white man induced the desire for information as to
> the habits and peculiar characteristics of the white lubra, and it was no easy
> task to satisfy the inquisitive Chillberta. All Australians are aware that the
> aboriginals are not restrained by law or morality, therefore their natural
> born ignorance produces licentiousness and wantonness. Chillberta's

conversation with Oleara drifted, naturally, to unhallowed and impure words, hence she would be checked, much to her wonder.[30]

In a neat turn, the risks of sexual licentiousness are deflected away from Oleara and his dusky muse, to be lived out elsewhere:

There were several other girls besides Chillberta, but none so prepossessing; yet all were amorously inclined. Some of them were of irregular shape and poor looking; nevertheless, Oleara's civilized blackboys took to them very kindly and helped them to that with which nature had endowed them. The aborigines of these parts are taught from their infancy bad and wicked things. They are a wild and savage race, practice unlawful commerce with the sexes and enjoy matters as they stand . . . Oleara never intended to instruct the blacks like a missionary in what was right or wrong.[31]

Aboriginal sexuality is described in decidedly contradictory terms in *A Thrilling Tale*. While 'delectable' dusky virgins like Chillberta raise the vision of an erotically imagined Aboriginal innocence, Aboriginal women in general – savage versions of the shrew – generate more of Willshire's vitriol than he reserves for Aboriginal men: 'most of them are stubborn, obstinate and lazy, and their husbands are compelled to resort to extreme measures to get them to do anything. In a paroxysm of temper they will tear their apparel into ribbons, and throw their tucker away in the sand. The savage instinct is more largely developed in the woman than the man'.[32] '"Frailty,"' he quotes at one point, '"thy name is woman"'.[33]

In his exploration of sexual licentiousness as a feature of racial regressiveness, Willshire borrows loosely from other adventure romance novels of the day, and also from other pan-colonial stereotypes that circulated in nineteenth-century popular culture. Under the guidance of the friendly native 'Pin-pan' Oleara arrives at an isolated mountain which houses a 'harem' of women. Guided through a maze of 'cavernous hollows' and 'subterranean passages' and finally stooping through an archway of 'fresh mistletoes and beautiful creepers', he gains access to the harem and its denizens, one of whom is 'Marma-truer, or the Passion Flower of Love'.[34] With echoes of Ernst Favenc's 1880 adventure romance novel *The Lost Explorer*, Pin-pan describes Passion Flower's link to a mysterious preceding hero, now perished:

> A white man, who was lost in the bush, brought that thin silver band,
> I think he called it a dog's collar. Before he died he fastened that on the
> Passion Flower's neck, because she was the dark-winged messenger of
> peace who saved him from being killed by a horde of wild savages, who
> sighted him coming towards a stream of beautiful water. At the urgent
> request of Marma-truer, the Passion Flower, the white man was saved, . . .
> [but] he died of grief at not being able to get away from such a wild and
> inhospitable region, as he called it. Two days before he died he riveted that
> silver band of the neck of the Passion Flower of Love, and if you were to
> examine it carefully you would see some white man's writing on it, and it
> might lead to his identity.[35]

Examining the silver collar, Oleara is 'surprised to find the name of a man I knew left Charlotte Waters searching for country with water on it, and, as he never returned, he was mourned for as lost in the bush'. In this local variation on the generic adventure romance plot, Willshire's inspiration for the lost man might have sprung from the case of Mounted Constable Shirley, whom Willshire replaced at Alice Springs police station after Shirley's transfer to Barrow Creek, and who was believed to have 'died of thirst' on a lost patrol in the Interior in 1881.[36] The Passion Flower is praised for her 'courageous virtue, followed by devoted love': '"Well done, good and faithful servant"'. As for his own presence in this secreted harem, Oleara assures the reader that despite invitation, he does not 'deviate in the slightest degree from the straight path of virtue'.[37]

A Thrilling Tale proceeds according to another conventional narrative feature of colonial adventure romance: a journey through unexplored territory and encounters with hostile 'savages'. Along with Chillberta, always at hand is Oleara's Colt revolver which, when required, he is quick to draw from his belt 'with a smile ironical'.[38] However, in contrast to Willshire's first book with its focus on the violence and dangers of frontier policing, *A Thrilling Tale* contains no explicit accounts of violence, perhaps not surprisingly given the reputation he had acquired by this time. The violence however is implied, albeit in tortured euphemisms. Not long into their journey Willshire describes a run-in with a 'garrulous and loquacious old nigger'. Tired of arguing with him 'Oleara led the old gentleman away about two hundred yards, advised him to sequester himself, review his life and purify his heart'.[39] Playing on this theme of 'purification' he relates that Native Constable Ananias appears with a 'fumigating machine' and proceeds to purify the old man with the smoke it apparently generated. That night the old man died, 'the cause of death being too much fumigation'.[40] The 'machine' returns on a number of other occasions in the text, in one of which Oleara tells us that Ananias was 'itching to fumigate somebody'.[41] In a commentary on these passages the archaeologist Michael Smith speculates that the 'fumigating machine' is a euphemism for a gun, perhaps the proverbial 'smoking gun' drawn from the language of 'penny dreadful' novels of the era.[42]

Occasionally there are expressions of regret for the 'extermination' of Aboriginal cultural life by 'our boasted civilization'.[43] The cultural life whose passing is regretted, however, is a pristine one of a romantically imagined past age, one in which 'the natives' were 'happy and contented', living a life 'wild and rambling' in the fruitful land.[44] Significantly, the cause for the decline of Aboriginal life is not the explorer, the settler, the bushman or the policeman; it is the missionary. It is this 'impious villain – called missionary – who contaminates the innocent, and hitherto, unwary blacks, and I know that the natives from their innate hatred would, if they could, expel them ruthlessly from their land'.[45] Moving from adventure to polemical mode, Willshire continues: 'Mission stations are a failure . . . No sooner does the missionary loom up than the trouble commences . . . Warmly as I feel on this subject I will not indulge in expletives, I leave the reader to conjure all I mean in my wholesome contempt for some of these canting hypocrites.'[46] In *A Thrilling Tale*, Willshire's historical grievance against the Hermannsburg missionaries is equalled by his grievance against the city dwellers who, unlike himself, have no right to hard-won white nativeness. 'A white man, travelling about with aborigines, acquiring information for his country's sake, exploring unknown regions, and causing his discoveries to be published without fee or reward for the pure benefit of his countrymen' is, he laments, 'passed over for the drawing-room dandy, who lives his little life of eyeglass, ignorance, arrogance, superciliousness and failure'.[47]

Some way through chapter nine Willshire's narrative focus on Oleara slips away and he returns to the narrative position of himself, memorialising his 1889 patrol to Lake Amadeus, as the explorer and servant of science. He is back to business, the panoptical vision of the white explorer restored: on 'a hill this morning with my fieldglasses I could see, stretching away to the west as far as my eye could reach, sandhills and desert oaks'.[48] The journey ahead would be difficult: 'at 3p.m. we came to a tortuous belt of mulga scrub', and later, 'we travelled until 4 p.m. across bad and inhospitable country'.[49] As a servant of science, however, he is undeterred, and is able to collect a 'pretty good assortment of weapons and emu eggs, &c.' in the service of Australian ethnography.[50]

As Robert Dixon has noted, adventure romance fiction of the era reflects anxieties about 'racial and cultural decline'. In Ernst Favenc's 1895 novel *The Secret of the Australian Desert*, these anxieties are expressed in the character of Murphy, one of a party of explorers lost in the desert. Discovered years later by the heroes of the novel, Murphy has 'gone native'. Physically, he can barely be distinguished as a white man. He has lost his language and perhaps even taken part in cannibalistic rituals. Given these anxieties, it is interesting that one of the conceits Willshire employs in *A Thrilling Tale* is to convey to the reader that he 'went native'. This is signalled early in the book when he accepts the Aboriginal name and persona of 'Oleara'. He is given Chillberta as 'a wife'. He travels with a 'tribe' of 37 Aborigines 'who came behind on foot'. Using his rifle, he hunts on behalf of the 'tribe'. On other occasions, he takes it upon himself to settle tribal disputes and even to arrange a marriage.[51]

The most striking example Willshire gives of his entry into Aboriginal cultural life is his description of participating in a 'corroboree': 'At the special request of some of the male natives', Willshire writes, 'I stripped, and they painted me all over with red ochre and charcoal and stuck feathers and down on my chest, and then marched me to the corroborree'. As elsewhere in the book, he describes not what he sees, but himself being seen. He describes how the women admired him: 'I blushed beautifully, I must have appeared supremely attractive'. The ladies, he added, 'could scarcely restrain their genuine admiration'.[52] While he danced before them 'naked, adorned and painted … they remarked that I was their beau-ideal of manly beauty'.

While the idea of 'going native' might suggest some degree of empathy, some attraction to imaginatively entering into the Aboriginal experience, this is not what Willshire attempts. In his description of the cor-roboree, he never pauses to speculate on its meaning or significance. By his own account, his entry into the Aboriginal world is typically an intrusion, if not a violation. When he attempts to enter sacred caves near 'the native village of Okeeleebeetanna', elders reproach him: 'How dare you come here?' He responds by telling them 'how many natives had been shot dead in Australia by white men', and offers a display of his firepower by shooting a crow out of a nearby tree. With this they agreed to allow him to enter.[53] On another occasion Willshire takes it upon himself to add to the rock art beside a waterhole by painting 'a bull camel on the flat rock'. When an elder chastises him for the desecration, Willshire smears him with paint like a petulant adolescent.[54] To the extent that Willshire 'goes native', it is only to best his Aboriginal companions with his own 'white nativeness', and to reinforce his position of superiority and control.

Not long after the incident at the rockhole, Willshire begins his preparations to return to Alice Springs. His Aboriginal followers, he reported, could hardly accept his departure. His persona as Oleara now shed, he makes a speech in which he leaves them in no doubt about the 'tribe' to which he belongs:

> 'My dear countrymen and sisters, I have been roaming about with you for some years now . . . I love you all, and it is [to] your presence in this little-known part of that great Empire upon which the sun never sets, that I am indebted . . . for the position I hold under the Crown. I have sometimes written of you as lazy, ungrateful, and treacherous, but I did not mean all of you; some of you are faithful, kind, obedient' . . . At this juncture the tears rolled down [their] cheeks . . . 'If God spares me I will come back to see you all, and when the wattle blooms again you must remember me; how I adorned my hat and my camels with that emblem of my native land, and how I taught you to adorn yourselves with it, because we Australians cherish it, as do our fathers the oak.'[55]

In this extraordinary passage, Willshire brings into reconciliation his otherwise unremittingly contradictory representations of 'nativeness'. In this moment, he and the Aboriginal people he professes to address – be they treacherous or obedient to his will – are joined in communion under the emblems of the wattle blossom and the Southern Cross. If he could, he speculates, perhaps mindful of the recently completed Horn expedition, 'I would collect specimens of the fauna and flora of this Central and Western Territory, and assisted by experts in the mineralogical and geological sciences would give to the country, which I glory in calling my native home, the results of our individual and collective efforts.'[56] If he could, as a superior 'native' Australian, he would 'raise [the blacks] to a better condition . . . But no, the government would rather give a thousand miles of country to imprudent missionaries'.[57]

In the concluding pages of the narrative Willshire's authorial voice changes again. He is now Willshire the martyr, raging against the injustices he has endured. Few '*bushmen* could produce a record of such stirring incidents', or 'such personal sacrifice' in the service of the government, but his reward, was to be 'robbed of his freedom'. Again enlisting the explorer figure, he compares himself to Stanley of Africa, and finds the latter wanting. 'Stanley saw Africa; *he* and his fellow white men', while Willshire, by implication, undertook his patrols with *only* Aboriginal companions. 'Stanley was welcomed back to civilisation with the acclamations of the world, praised by princes, made the familiar of kings, idolized in the drawing-room of savants, and for the time exalted as the greatest hero of the nineteenth century'. Writing generally at first, Willshire mourns the lack of comparable recognition for the 'pioneer, the explorer and the officer of Government' in his own 'fair land of Australia'. Such men, he suggests, anticipate

> no princely reception on the completion of [their] arduous work, and though the laurel of well-earned victory be denied [them], [they are] content in the calm consciousness of having done the right, and successfully accomplishing that which was demanded by [their] country . . .

Willshire then shifts the focus to his personal experience. 'It will come as a staggerer to the reader', he writes, 'to know that Oleara met with no such gratifying reception, at the hands of his country. The flattering address took the form of a warrant on the charge of murder':

> Oleara was arrested, underwent all the indignities of an ordinary prisoner of the Crown; was manacled, ironed, and without warning, hurled remorselessly into a prison cell . . . Unjustly – a mild term in this case – robbed of his freedom; escorted by one of his own cloth evidently gratified and exultant at his downfall . . .
>
> Accustomed to adversity; travelling for years, with blacks only for companions, across sandhills and spinifex deserts of Central Australia;

143

living mostly in scenes of desolation; hardened to disappointment; he yet was free.[58]

To enlighten his readers further regarding the indignities he suffered and the public's response, he includes a transcribed collection of letters and extracts from the press as an appendix, under the heading 'Apprehension, Trial and Honourable Acquittal of MC Willshire'.

The narrative of *A Thrilling Tale* closes with Willshire's final affirmation that this has been the 'unpretending sketch of a man whose only fault was, that he served his country too well'.[59] With this final sentence, the work's rather confused literary intentions are clarified. It begins with and occasionally returns to an intention to record the kind of ethnographic knowledge that might bring reputable posterity. More consistently, within a blended structure of memoir and adventure romance fiction, it expresses a popular nationalist sentiment. But perhaps most personally, *A Thrilling Tale* enables Willshire to perpetuate in imagination an era that had by now significantly faded. It had been the age he could most successfully inhabit, and on which much of his projected identity had been established – the age of the unmonitored Central Australian frontier.

LAND OF THE DAWNING, END OF AN ERA

Gordon Creek police camp

At the time that he was preparing *A Thrilling Tale* for publication, Willshire was occupying the last frontier posting of his policing career in the far north-west of the Northern Territory. He had left Palmerston with Native Constables Jim, Larry and George on 1 May 1894, travelling by boat and barge to the Victoria Depot on the Victoria River. From there he collected police horses and travelled overland to Gordon Creek, 32 kilometres from Victoria River Downs head station, where his police camp was to be established. He arrived there after a fortnight's journey on 14 May. This would be his base for the next 16 months. His duty, again, was to patrol the region with the object of controlling cattle killing. His police journal indicates that his patrolling practices continued to involve the tracking and general intimidation of potential cattle stealers. A month after his arrival, for instance, he reported:

> 26th [June 1894]: we came upon a mob of black tracks, and on following them up into the Sandstone ranges we discovered fresh bones, fat and Hide ... we still went on their tracks and discovered them camped on the Upper Wickham ... they soon cleared out when they espied us, so we destroyed a heap of spears, and went on day after day on the tracks of other

cattle killers on the sandstone ridges . . . for the present we have made them all disappear from their old haunts we returned to station on the 26th.[1]

However, as Willshire was to experience in the coming months, the country it was now his duty to patrol was very different from that around the MacDonnell Ranges. From his well-situated police camps around Alice Springs and the Finke River, Willshire had appreciated the open plains of cotton, salt-bush and native grasses, which spread out in sight of the ranges. It was clear country, out of the gorges and ranges, that provided good potential for surveillance and suited the police horses. As he reported to Besley in 1887, he had enjoyed having 'it all to myself'.[2] At Gordon Creek, however, Willshire was soon frustrated by a country that became boggy and impassable in the wet, and was dense with sandstone ranges inaccessible to the police horses. In his report of 15 August 1894, he wrote:

> tracked up some native cattle Killers & found them with the remains of two bullocks in their camp . . . there were about 60 natives mostly men, we destroyed all their weapons, & burnt 7 cwt of beef to cinders, shot their dogs & threw the wire spear heads into a deep water hole . . . This was the first time I came in contact with the natives of Stevens Ck the rough travelling in the sandstone is exceptionally hard on the shoeing.[3]

At the end of that month he wrote:

> received a letter from Mr Crawford that the blacks were killing cattle around the locality of Mount Warburton, we went there and discovered some tracks of natives . . . so we went on their tracks up to Depot Creek and discovered they had taken to the sandstone they saw us approaching so they went on further to a most inaccessible place for horses . . . Another Tracker & another Carbine would be conducive both to my interest & the Station owners'.[4]

On 3 December: '[got] the tracks of natives . . . on the 1st of December at noon, we overhauled them all carrying fresh beef they saw us some distance away & . . . made for a big range inaccessible to horsemen'.[5] In October, one of the police horses was drowned slipping over the edge of the river bank, and the patrol's supplies lost.

In July Willshire had made a request, which was rejected, for two additional trackers. When he approached the government in December again seeking two extra trackers, Government Resident Dashwood commented that no extra assistance was necessary, 'unless it is intended to proceed to a wholesale extermination of the aboriginals'.[6] Willshire's reputation had preceded him. He was not only in country unfamiliar to him, but the Territory administration had clearly taken him on under sufferance.

By the start of the new year, the wet conditions of the country made patrolling almost impossible. On 6 February he reported: 'the whole country is so boggy that it is impossible for horses to travel in a straight line for more than a mile at a time'. Days later, on 11 February, conditions were worse: one of the police horses nearly drowned attempting to cross an overflowing Gordon Creek; the rations were rafted across, but 'everything got saturated with water, including the firearms. From VHS [Victoria Head Station] to Gordon Creek is 20 Mles of bog and one treacherous creek. The Victoria and Wickham have not been crossable for a month'.

Willshire was in country frustratingly unfamiliar to him, and responsible to an unsympathetic administration. After just seven months at Gordon Creek he had had enough. On 26 January 1895 he wrote to Inspector Foelsche requesting a transfer south: 'I have always been stationed in the remotest parts of South Australia entirely living with blacks which I am getting very tired of'. It had been a life of solitude, he continued, and, now 'getting up in years', he was 'badly wanted at home'.[7] The Inspector supported his application, but it was months before the transfer was authorised. Up to now, Willshire's policing in the district had been a mundane routine of short patrols, no arrests and few encounters, but before long matters started 'getting tropical'.

'Matters are getting tropical'

On 18 March 1895, Willshire received a report that three Aboriginal employees on Victoria River Downs, Dick, Pompey and Jimmy, ran away, taking with them two of the station's rifles and extra cartridges. Because they belonged to this country, Willshire worried, they would 'no doubt join the cattle killers'. A large fire seen in the sandstone ranges south of the police station that night, he supposed, indicated

> the runaways calling the wild tribes together. They will inhabit the gorges and caves, where it would be almost impossible to arrest or even shoot at them if it became necessary. 12 miles up Gordon Creek affords a refuge to blacks of caves & ravines on either side.[8]

One of the causes of the trouble, he felt, was Jack Watson, who had replaced Lindsay Crawford as manager of Victoria River Downs. 'Since Watson came on the run,' he wrote in his police report of 18 March,

> the whole place has been in a state of fermentation, what blackboys and lubras Mr Crawford left behind have all run away since. Watson has such a bad name amongst blacks that they are frightened to remain, nearly every white man has left, and the three that are here now will leave as soon as Watson returns.

During the Gordon Creek period, Willshire's police reports to the Inspector were strikingly confessional and anxious. It appears that the sense of order and authority that Willshire had established in the Centre had become replaced, in the Top End, with a sense of frustration and the absence of control.

The following day, on 19 March, Willshire's troubles worsened. In the evening, he found that Native Constable Jim 'had cleared out with his rifle and cartridges ... I sent [Native Constables] George and Larry to tell him to come back, at midnight they returned and told me he was frightened, and would return in the morning'. Jim, Willshire speculated, 'knew that I was all ready to go & do my duty [and] he was so afraid of meeting these Station boys out in the ranges with rifles that he cleared off, taking his rifle with him'. The Native Constables, he reported, feared that 'the wild natives in conjunction with the boys with rifles, are supposed to be coming to attack the Police Station. This will show the Inspect. what an inate coward Jim is to desert the Station at such a time & place'.[9] By the following day, Native Constable Jim had still not returned, and from the police stores he had taken 'a colts revolver, a M.H. [Martini-Henri] Carbine, a blanket'. He had also taken Willshire's valuable kangaroo dog.[10] With Mounted Constable Larry, Willshire sought out Jim's tracks, but lost them at the sandstone ranges. The next day, 21 March, they set out again to see if they could 'cut' Jim's tracks. Jim, Larry told Willshire, had planned a month ago to steal the rifles and clear out to Newcastle.

Native Constable Jim had already deserted him, and Willshire worried that Larry and George might follow. His journal entries at this time betray an almost palpable fear, and are tinged with paranoia. That day he reported in his police journal for the Inspector:

> so you see how matters are as all sorts of conspiracies are going on . . . my anxiety at present is very great, four civilised boys adrift, all good shots with three rifles & one revolver, the boys Larry and George are in a bewildered state & . . . seem confused, & I do not know what moment they may decamp in the dark . . . There is something hanging in the atmosphere that so far I have failed to discover, perhaps it is an attack on this Station, or one of the other Stations.
>
> It is not safe for one to go far away although I should like to track Jim up & get the rifle & revolver . . . as for our Jim, he is a most deceitful liar with an oily tongue . . . Whatever may be the ultimate outcome of all this I can not say, but I look to you for protection from any lying slander that this oily tongued absconder may cause. I was always kind but very firm with him, but long ago discovered that there is no gratitude in them &

friendship they are unable to appreciate . . . the only redeeming features he possessed were that he was a fairly good shot, and a fairly good tracker . . . to say the least of it, this is a rough place with treachery all around you & when blackboys belonging to the country turn out with firearms, matters are getting tropical.[11]

Willshire concludes this extraordinary report with the stated intention to

go out tomorrow & look them up & promise you I will do my duty to the very last out in the open. I am not afraid of any blackfellow with firearms but their treachery lurks beneath so many guises such as long grass, behind rocks, in creeks, and up high in gorges.

For the next several days Willshire, the remaining Native Constables and some station hands travelled up to 55 kilometres a day tracking the runaways. Willshire's crisis resolved itself on 27 March when Native Constable Jim and the station hand Dick returned of their own volition, having witnessed the murder of Jimmy and Pompey by 'wild natives'. Willshire, Walter Rees and Native Constable Larry travelled up Gordon Creek to find and bury the bodies. Willshire was relieved: '[Jim and Dick] each tell different stories & have the whole disgraceful affair so entirely complicated that I told them to go & have their food & sleep, & that I would not growl with them.'

Willshire's troubles were exacerbated by his acrimoniously competitive relationship with the manager of the Victoria River Downs run, Jack Watson. In the Centre, though his relationship with the missionaries was strained at best, Willshire had enjoyed unquestioned support from the stations' managers. Yet it does not seem surprising that Willshire and Watson should have disliked each another. Watson apparently actively encouraged the production of a bushman legend of his own. Remembered for his feats of bravado and heroics, he is described in one local history as 'the typical adventurer – a kind of northern "d'Artagnan"'.[12] He never went unarmed, and in his dealings with Aboriginal people, he was known as 'one of the most violent men on the northern frontier'.[13] Perhaps apocryphally, he is said to have shot at tins balanced on the heads of his Aboriginal employees,[14] and is reputed to have nailed 40 pairs of ears around the homestead walls, collected during raiding parties on Aboriginal cattle killers.[15] Watson, Willshire worried, undermined his own authority as the area's representative of the rule of law. When Watson took it upon himself to 'secure' two Aboriginal prisoners, who subsequently escaped, Willshire responded with contempt and anxiety, seeking to 'show the Inspr. what a fool Watson has made of himself by trying to frustrate me in the execution of my duty'.[16] His primary support in the region evidently came from James Ledgerwood, an employee on the Victoria River Downs run, whom Willshire admired as the consummate bushman and whose role at the station did not usurp Willshire's own. 'All the men know I go about all over the run continually,' he wrote to his superior officer, '& Ledgerwood says he is disgusted with Watsons conduct towards me.'[17]

This had not been the first time that Willshire felt his authority undermined by Watson. On 14 May 1895, two of Watson's station men, John Mulligan and G H Ligar, were camped midway between the Victoria Depot and Victoria River Downs, with two wagon loads of supplies, when they were attacked. Ligar was the first to be struck by a spear. Mulligan made a dash to the wagons to get his firearms, and was struck by a spear in the leg. By the time Mulligan got his rifle to work and drove off their attackers, Ligar had received another spear to the face. Meanwhile the men's Aboriginal workers, who were from this country, had cleared off with one of their revolvers. Over the course of the next day and morning the men were besieged by some 300 Aborigines, whom they kept at bay until an opportunity presented itself to escape on the wagon horses.[18]

The alarm was raised and Willshire arrived on the scene on 23 May, Jack Watson arriving the following day with ten white and six Aboriginal station hands. It was Watson who took charge, his party setting off in pursuit of the offenders and the stolen property, while Willshire was delegated the task of searching for the wounded men. When they met again, Willshire learnt that the wounded men had been found and put on a boat to Palmerston. Watson also gave into Willshire's custody 'three old lubras' whom he had discovered with stolen property. The next day Watson's party set off to return to the station, leaving Willshire in charge of the three women prisoners, and the task of escorting the re-loaded wagons back to the station. In his report on these events, Willshire no longer seems the man in charge but rather one besieged: 'the range was swarming with natives, I fired two shots to challenge them out but the cowards would not come'.[19] His three elderly prisoners escaped during the night and Willshire was suspicious that someone had released them deliberately: 'I am of opinion that someone has let them go, either blacks or whites, as they were secured by neck chain to a small tree, and the ankles handcuffed.'[20]

While Willshire was absorbed with an unsuccessful search for the killers of Jimmy and Pompey, his application for a transfer south was being considered by the Territory's administration. The Acting Minister's exasperated response was clearly informed by a knowledge of Willshire's record:

> I urgently request that MC Willshire may be immediately removed from the Northern Territory. His reputation is such that in my opinion he is the last man in the world who should be entrusted with duties which bring him in contact with the Aborigines.[21]

Moreover, having learnt from the press that very day that Willshire and his trackers were 'out in pursuit of the alleged murderers', the Resident suggested that, were Willshire to be recalled, 'no time should be lost'.[22] Willshire's transfer was approved, but it would still be a number of months before a suitable replacement could be found and despatched north.

While Willshire waited for his replacement to arrive, a routine settled in at Gordon Creek. He was occupied with the tracking of cattle stealers and the uneventful search for Pompey and Jimmy's killers. But gone was his confidence and sense of authority from the 1880s, replaced by a manifest insecurity. He continued to complain of Watson's incursions on his policing authority, and called the Inspector's notice to the ways in which he was 'frustrated in every move' by his own Native Constables.[23] Watson, he complained, 'blocks me in my work every possible chance, he curses the police all day to every and anyone. Ledgerwood absolutely refused to leave Gordon Creek without me, as he said he would stand no more of Watsons humbugging'.[24] On 21 September, Mounted Constable O'Keefe arrived from Katherine to relieve Willshire of his posting.

The land of the dawning

In 1896, the year after he left Victoria River Downs, Willshire published his third and last book. It was called *The Land of the Dawning: Facts Gleaned from Cannibals in the Australian Stone Age*, and was published in Adelaide by W K Thomas & Co. On its front cover is a photograph of Aboriginal people from Gordon Creek, the 'Pilie-nurra Tribe', posed for a conventional group portrait, indicating, as in Willshire's earlier work, an ethnographic intention, this time focusing on the people of the region around the Victoria River. The date of its dedication – September 1895, the month he left Victoria River Downs – also suggests that the work was produced during Willshire's time in the district. Part memoir, part professed ethnography, part bushman adventure romance, it elaborates and consolidates Willshire's earlier personal contributions to the literary genres of the late colonial period. In his preface, he again makes a claim to anthropological expertise based on first-hand experience: this last 'little book,' he states, 'is only intended to deal with the aborigines of the Far Northern parts of South Australia' and 'to simply inform the reader what the author knows and has personally seen of the aborigines in their normal character.' It will be admitted,' he adds, 'that the author has had an excellent opportunity to make a book, after so many years' travelling in the bush, and almost in unknown regions, the material having been obtained from the aborigines

themselves and from what he saw himself.' Willshire then offers the book
to his intended audience: its purpose is one 'of supplying information' to
the Australian Natives Association – the colonial nationalist organisation
whose members were limited to white 'Australian natives' – and to
Mr J G Frazer, the anthropologist who the previous year, through the
Commissioner of Police's recommendation, had included Willshire's contribution in an ethnographic survey published in the *Royal Anthropological
Journal*.

Having established his anthropological intentions, Willshire moves
almost immediately to the work's primary theme, the same one that had
marked his earlier writings:

> Many sleepless nights and wary anxious days have been gone through in
> doing duty amongst wild tribes, who during the writing of this book
> committed murders and killed the settlers' horses and cattle; and the
> author, being a police officer in charge of native constables, located on the
> Victoria River, received intimation of all depredations committed by the
> lawless aborigines; and those acts, being exigencies of the service, he had
> to go out with his trackers and deal with each case respectively as the law
> provided . . . he did his duty – all that was expected from him.[25]

The reader is back in the legend of the bushman, adapted to the
officer of the frontier. As part of the expression of this legend in *The Land
of the Dawning*, Aboriginal people are again the abstracted subjects of
Willshire's extravagant idealisation of the land, and the living subjects of his
vitriolic contempt. The sentiments of biological determinism that would
direct Aboriginal policy in the twentieth century, with the categorisation of
Aboriginal people into groups of blood 'degree', are given full breath in this
work from the last years of the nineteenth century. 'Half-castes' are the
target of Willshire's most virulent dislike. For the many people who
coveted a white Australia, of course, the 'half-caste problem' was deeply
unsettling. The threat of miscegenation – despite being widely accepted as

an unspoken reality of the 'unsettled districts' in nineteenth-century Australia – was a perceived threat to Australia's future nationhood. For an ardent white 'native' like Willshire, then, the 'half-caste' is 'the bastard gift of shameless Nature, conjecturally condemned'. The 'mongrel half-caste,' he writes with more virulence later, 'is born for the gallows or to be shot . . . to make the beast your own equal is a hope wild in its improbability and degrading in its possibility.'[26] In contrast, the 'natives [who are] uncontaminated, and still in their pristine vigour' are worthy of the bushman's qualified respect; as a depersonalised idea, they represent an indispensable part of the landscape of his affiliation. Also importantly, they are unobjectionable because, according to the principles of social Darwinism, 'they are gradually going to extinction'.[27] At the same time, as a potential threat to be encountered by the white bushman, they are 'a blood-thirsty lot of fierce savages, who throw the spear with unerring aim, and watch their opportunities to kill unfortunate men who are off their guard'.[28]

As becomes apparent, the only worthy companion in this landscape is the fellow white bushman. *The Land of the Dawning* carries a dedication to 'my dear friend James Logan Ledgerwood', and it is here that the book signals its strongest link to the 1890s literature of the bushmen, as well as its role as a justification and commemoration of Mounted Constable Willshire himself. As well as eulogising Ledgerwood as an exemplary fellow bushman, the dedication memorialises the hardships the author has endured in the execution of his duty as a frontier policeman. It is noteworthy, too, that in his reference to the episode of the Aboriginal runaways at Victoria River, their number has increased from four to seven:

> You no doubt remember the weary, anxious time spent on the Victoria, when there were seven civilized blacks at large in the ranges with firearms, and not one of them had any love for me . . . You remember the dark figures stealing stealthily around us, and when they were unpleasantly close the worthless vagabonds had cause to howl and shriek in the silent majesty of the night. I was prompted to select you for this Dedication as you

thoroughly understand the scheming designs of aborigines who plot and contrive to take the heart's blood of white men.

It is not the first time our names have gone forth on the wings of notoriety . . . I achieved an infamous eminence which I never deserved in doing duty assigned to me amongst murderous aborigines.

As in Willshire's previous books, *The Land of the Dawning* moves between a professed contribution to anthropological knowledge on 'the customs, religions, and superstitions of an uncivilised people' and a memoir that contributes to the literary expansion of the popular bushman myth. The bushman/frontier officer is also the explorer, taking in with his pan-optical vision the spread of his country. In this vision Aboriginal presence, when not threatening, appears as a picturesque component of the whole. 'What a sense of freedom one experiences,' he writes,

standing on high ground, with nothing above but the pure, glorious sky, and a far-spreading view of the country below, with here and there a gleam of water where the river winds, till the whole melts away in the distance against the far western sky; but nearer still, among the pandanus palms, the light blue smoke from the aborigines' camp curls up through the deep foliage.[29]

In the tradition of the 'lost explorer' literature of the nineteenth century, the soul of the country is depicted as springing not so much from the indigenous people who live in it but from the white pioneers and explorers whose bones 'lay bleaching in scenes of wildest desolation, and in scenes of picturesque beauty, at various waterholes on the overland tele-graph line, at dozens of places in the northern Territory'.[30] The potential of the lost explorer to make the country 'white' by laying down his body in the land was realised in the popular culture of the mid to late colonial period.

In both verse and paintings, lost explorers – most notably Ludwig Leichhardt, whose party disappeared during an attempted cross-continental expedition in 1848, and Burke and Wills, who died near Cooper's Creek in 1861 – became elevated to heroes of mythic proportions. In the hands of poets, painters and writers, the explorer lost in the desert became, as Roslynn Haynes puts it, 'the necessary component of a uniquely Australian form of heroism'.[31] In Henry Kendall's eulogy to Leichhardt in verse, for instance, the lost explorer's death is the very means by which the land itself becomes unified, made meaningful in a symbiotic relationship with (European) man: Leichhardt, in death, 'came to be a brother of the river and the wood – / Thus the leaf, the bird, the blossom, grew a gracious sisterhood'.[32] Artworks of the pre- and post-Federation period tell a similar story. The explorer who has sacrificed himself in the greater task of unveiling the landscape is, in such works, memorialised by a national culture fascinated with its own imminent arrival.

As in *A Thrilling Tale*, white belonging in *The Land of the Dawning* is expressed not only through the grandeur of the land's potential for white exploration, but also through its erotic offerings to the white man. Throngs of 'dusky maidens' fill almost every chapter. That they are sexually available to the white pioneers and explorers who have the stamina to penetrate the land is affirmed not only by their own guileless promiscuity but also by the rights of providence. 'Men would not remain so many years in a country like this,' Willshire asserts, 'if there were no women, and perhaps the Almighty meant them for us as He has placed them wherever the pioneers go . . . what I am speaking about is only natural, especially for men who are isolated away in the bush at outstations where women of all ages and sizes are running at large'.[33]

Yet in the tradition of adventure romance, the white hero is necessarily chivalric. With his manly authority and a heart that speaks to the landscape, he is the inevitable object of desire for the 'dusky princesses' of the forest. Several such 'dusky beauties', Willshire recalls, chose him for their attentions during one of their dances of 'wily manoeuvres' and 'barbaric sensuality', but despite the 'tremors of awe' that 'began to pervade my frame', Willshire declined their overtures, and 'bowed most courteously'.[34]

Sometimes the chaste innocents of nature and sometimes the promiscuous whores who lure the white man, the 'black Venus' and her temptations seem to be rarely absent from the narrative. Willshire could, he boasts, 'guarantee to track and round up now and again for the edification of my party a bevy of smockless black girls, as sweet in heart as the morning dew ... Just fancy my travelling companions environed by a phalanx of dusky maidens waiting for attentive consideration'.[35] 'After all my experience,' he confesses conspiratorially a few pages later, 'I came to the one conclusion – that the women will prostitute themselves during the absence of their husbands if they get the opportunity.'[36] Women are the temptresses; who can blame a bushman for the warmth of his blood? 'I believe it to be a fact,' he admits more directly, 'that there are some white men who remain sensually infatuated with what they intellectually despise.'[37]

Sometimes treated euphemistically and sometimes explicitly, Willshire takes the existence of a sexually exploitable frontier for granted. A similar shift between euphemistic and explicit reference characterises Willshire's acknowledgement of violence on the frontier. Typically, the reality of violence is enlisted not for the purposes of social verity but for its dramatic potential in elaborating the narrative of white conquest. Chapter three is dedicated to the memorialisation of Willshire's career in the Interior throughout the 1880s, and his patrols around the Finke River. His reader is back in the territory of the 'real' frontier, the frontier of Central Australia. 'I suddenly came upon one big buck, who evidently thought that I was alone,' he recalls; 'self-preservation is the first law of nature, so I levelled my shooting-iron – I don't know what became of that greasy native.'

Such encounters, as he indicated in *A Thrilling Tale*, provided ample opportunity for ethnographic collecting: 'I went back to my camp, and some of my lads came home the following day with a fine collection of spears and boomerangs – they had evidently been amongst them.'[38] Life among the 'savages', it seems, requires perpetual preparation for action: 'I always have a rifle with me and a revolver on my belt, [and] on this occasion I also had a double-barrel gun close at hand'.[39] Though never precisely explicit about what work such weapons do, Willshire is not shy in waxing lyrically about the women who remain after a 'scrimmage' with the men: 'As there was no getting away the females and children crawled into rocky embrasures, and there they remained. When we had finished with the male portion we brought the black gins and their offspring out from their rocky alcoves . . . One girl had a face and figure worthy of Aphrodite as she dwelt in a Grecian sculptor's brain.'[40] He is capable of bringing the same kind of lyricism to the remembrance of his violent patrols, as well. 'It's no use mincing matters,' he writes, 'the Martini-Henry carbines at this critical moment were talking English in the silent majesty of those great eternal rocks.' This is the country of the true bushman, for the bushman knows from tried experience that 'nothing but lead from a rifle can steady the cannibals'.[41] The bushmen 'are the brave pioneers who push out to the frontier, and are exposed to the full force of the naked barbarians. Yes, they are the brave men who discover and open out beautiful pastoral land'.[42]

In contrast to the bushmen, of course, are the town-dwelling philan-thropists, the bureaucrats, the missionaries and Justices of the Peace. They are the misled and the traitorous, who will 'protect these wild savage cannibals in the very midst of their wonton depredations'; they will make police officers 'afraid to shoot them for fear of being hanged by the Government'.[43] They are 'the oily and the soapy hypocrites' who 'know nothing about' the work of the bushmen in opening up the country for national good. If only some of these 'canting snufflers', Willshire wishes, 'were placed in some of the predicaments I have been in with the wild cannibals. Religion won't aid you then; nothing but a good Winchester or Martini carbine, in conjunction with a Colt's revolver. They are your best friends, and you must use them too'.[44] And yet it seems that in this treach-erous world of the frontier there is still room for comic enjoyments: a female prisoner can be outrun by an amorous Native Constable,[45] and Willshire himself can make an elderly 'buck' dance to the tune of his shotgun.[46] The trials of frontier life can be balanced by its entertainments.

What evils, however, do the government and the missionaries visit

upon the world of 'wild savages in the stone age'? What role in amelio-
rating the lot of the dying race is played by 'those men who call themselves
Christians, who give statues and images to adorn parks and enclosures, and
otherwise lavish their wealth around cities to gain a paltry knighthood'?[47]
Indeed, what motives can 'a poor man' like Willshire have in writing of
such things? 'None whatever, but it is my compassionate and merciful
disposition that makes me feel it so keenly.' 'Be liberal for once,' he urges
the town-dwelling cants who have had him arrested for murder, 'by
improving these poor, degraded creatures.'[48] Teach those poor creatures,
above all, that kindness only comes after subjugation. For his own part, he
cautions, 'I never relax the authority I exercise over the aboriginals in my
district, comprising as it does many thousands of square miles . . . You
must proceed instantly to work, and they will remember your firmness
in the future.'[49] Such lessons the bushman well knows, and so does
the frontier policeman: 'I am proud to be able to submit to paper that the
Government at the time told me off as the officer of police parties to go
out and do as the law provides in such cases . . . and now I say, "All's well
that ends well." '[50]

The frontispiece to *The Land of the Dawning* features another studio
portrait of Willshire. Impeccably dressed in a suit and with a fashionable
summer hat resting on his crossed knees, he sits in a rustic garden chair
while a young 'civilised blackboy', dressed to perfection in a sailor suit,
serves him fruit on a platter. Willshire is reinvented from the figure who
occupied the central position of the studio portraits taken with the Native
Police at Port Augusta in 1887. Besides the frontier hero, the man of action
in the wilds of Australia, he is a figure of respectable civilisation, and a
civiliser of men.

Willshire departed the Northern Territory in October 1895, having
secured a first-class passage aboard SS *Pathan*. When recommending his
transfer back in May, Commissioner Peterswald had commented that
Willshire was a 'capital bushman and well fitted to an up country station,
but I decidedly object to him in the settled districts for which he has proved

himself entirely unsuitable'.[51] These were the same sentiments that had prompted Peterswald to recommend Willshire's transfer to the Territory after his trial. He was now wanted neither on the frontier nor in the settled districts.

Shortly after he returned to Adelaide, Willshire wrote to his superiors requesting reimbursement for his passage aboard SS *Pathan*. The first-class passage, he complained, had been very expensive, but was the only one he could secure. In February 1896, when the reimbursement was authorised, he sent a letter asking that the money be paid directly into his bank account. The page upon which it is written features Willshire's own private letterhead: a skilfully drawn sketch of sunset at Gordon River. Whether the image was drawn by Willshire himself or under his direction is unknown, but it hints at how he chose to remember that time: it is an idyllic depiction of Aboriginal people, their shadows cast long by the late afternoon sun, sauntering untroubled about his 'Native Police Camp'.[52]

RACE AND NATIONALISM IN THE SHADOW OF THE FRONTIER

By November 1895 Willshire was back in Adelaide, serving briefly at police headquarters, before being posted to Port Augusta. He was unhappy. The day after he arrived, he offered his resignation to Inspector John Field:

> I most respectfully beg to state that after many years service in the far outlying districts, and exposed to the full force of hostile tribes, and having had to resort to measures to save my life, that no white man will ever know about, I expected a station in the central division on my return to Adelaide. My intention was to get married and settle down quietly to my duties. The Commissioner of Police directed me to go to Head Quarters Port Augusta, I obeyed his instructions and now have the honour to request that I may again be called to Adelaide where I will resign.[1]

His superiors appear to have been sympathetic to his desire to 'settle down' and in December 1895, he received a posting further south, but to Port Lincoln rather than to Adelaide. It was in Port Lincoln in September 1896 that Willshire, at the age of 44, married Ellen Sarah Howell, with whom he had two daughters and a son.[2] His first daughter he named Victoria River, in memory of his last frontier posting at Gordon Creek. 1896 was also the year that Willshire published his third book, *The Land of the Dawning*, documenting his experiences in the Top End. This would be his final publication.

In December of the same year, Willshire's expertise was sought in answering an inquiry from the South Australian Museum in relation to his knowledge of Aboriginal deaths in the Territory. The Museum Director, Dr Edward Stirling, wanted the police department's help in identifying an Aboriginal skull in the museum's collection. It was the skull, he wrote, 'of a native named "Pompey" who I believe was shot by the Police some years ago'. The department judged Willshire the most appropriate person to answer the inquiry. He responded with recollections of the various men known as 'Pompey' who each 'came to their death in my time in the far north'. One had been shot dead on a patrol with Wurmbrand to Anna's Reservoir in 1884; another had been shot dead on his patrol to Undoolya in the same year, his first official patrol as Officer in Charge of the Native Police force. A third man known by that name was one of the station employees who had run away from Victoria River Downs in 1895, and had been killed by 'wild niggers'. 'Some months after', wrote Willshire, 'when the bodies of Pompey & Jimmy had sufficiently dried I went out and brought both their sculls in and buried them in my garden at Gordon Creek, as the late John Watson . . . stated that he wanted Pompeys scull for a spittoon.'[3] Willshire's interest in 'collecting' evidently extended from vocabularies, anecdotes and Aboriginal weapons to collecting human remains on behalf of others as macabre household curios.

For the next eight years he served in a series of coastal towns on Eyre Peninsula. His surviving police journals from his time at Cowell chronicle the mundane life of a country policeman; he does his duty at the races, attends talks in the local Institute building, and deals with the occasional rabid dog.[4] A photograph from this period shows the Willshire family on the verandah of their house, posed against a lush background of potted plants. Ellen is seated in the centre of the group; Willshire, in uniform, stands to her right, his arm resting uncomfortably on her shoulder; their son sits atop a tricycle smiling at the camera.[5] Willshire is settling down to a life of respectable anonymity. What of his compatriots from his days in the Centre – the missionaries, his police colleagues, and his bete noir, Francis Gillen?

Twilight of the missionaries

At the time of the Finke River Mission Inquiry in 1890, most of the Centre's settlers regarded the Hermannsburg mission as a failure; the Lutheran missionaries soon came to the same conclusion.[6] In the same year that Willshire was sent south for trial, Schulze, Schwarz and Kempe, bowed and beaten, retreated from the Centre. Kempe, whose wife Dorothea had recently died in childbirth, was so physically and mentally broken he had to be lifted into the wagon that would carry him south. The Lutherans had struggled to make the mission self-supporting, but most importantly, they had struggled to make the Arrernte interested. The missionaries laboured vainly to attract Aboriginal people to the station, and to hold them there. The mission was established in 1877 but it was not until 1887 that the first baptisms were performed.[7] In their escalating frustration, the severity of the missionaries' discipline increased. Their station, which might well have become a refuge from the violence of the surrounding districts, itself became known as a site of violence. One of the mission's star converts fled the station in 1889 after his wife and a number of other women were chained and whipped for immorality. Known as Tekua to his kin, Thomas to the missionaries who baptised him, and Joe to the police, it was his evidence that had led to Willshire's arrest in 1891.

The Hermannsburg mission would revive a few years later but in 1894, when the Horn expedition paid a visit, it was a missionary ghost-town under the supervision of a caretaker. The expeditioners wandered through the deserted schoolroom and chapel – as tourists do today – and observed the 'effects of disuse and neglect' in the 'copy and exercise books of former pupils which were still to be found stowed away in the various corners' of the buildings. Stirling, the Director of the South Australian Museum, observed that nowhere 'on our journey did we see natives so dirty in their habits, so squalid in their mode of life, and so devoid of the usual cheery demeanour as at Hermannsburg'.[8] Baldwin Spencer, the biologist, made an unforgiving judgement of what he witnessed:

> The mission at the time of our visit was abandoned, and the whole place was more or less in ruins. A few blacks, the remnants of a larger number who were camped about the place when it was opened as a mission station, still remained, living in a squalid state in dirty whurlies. If, which is open to question, the mission had ever done any permanent good, there was no evidence of it to be seen either amongst these blacks or others whom we met with and who had been in contact with them.[9]

It was during this expedition that Baldwin Spencer first met Francis Gillen, who as the young telegraph operator in 1874 had conducted the electric conversation between the dying Stapleton at Barrow Creek and his wife in Adelaide, and who in 1891 as a Justice of the Peace had committed Willshire for trial. In his narrative of the Horn expedition, Spencer makes a simple observation that foretells the birth of modern anthropology in Australia and, in a sentence, announces a profound and abiding insight into the nature of Aboriginal culture. 'The morality of the blacks,' writes Spencer, 'is governed by rules of conduct which have been recognised amongst his tribe from what they speak of as the "alcheringa", which Mr. Gillen has aptly called the "Dream times".'[10] Impressed by his insight, Spencer invited Gillen to contribute a paper to the lavish *Report of the Horn Scientific Expedition*.

The rise of anthropology

As the 1890s drew to a close, anthropology entered a heroic age. Its practitioners experienced the sort of prestige that had once been the province of explorers, and an authority on Aboriginal matters that had once been the preserve of missionaries. In 1898 a virtually unannounced lecture by Francis Gillen to the Geographical Society was so well attended the meeting had to move to a larger auditorium, and the substance of his talk was reproduced in the press.[11] Interviews with Gillen were published in newspapers and his opinions cited on anthropological as well as social matters.[12] When Gillen criticised a proposal to establish mission stations, the *Adelaide Observer* argued that 'great weight must be attached to his criticism' on the basis of his 'intimate knowledge of the black tribes of central Australia'.[13]

After their meeting during the Horn expedition, Spencer and Gillen began corresponding on the subject of the Aborigines. It was a complicated, three-tiered partnership in which Gillen forwarded his information to Spencer in Melbourne, while Spencer, under the guidance of J G Frazer in England, organised this information and in turn passed questions back to Gillen in the field.[14] The result of this collaboration was the 1899 publication *The Native Tribes of Central Australia*, which received international acclaim and put Australia at the vanguard of anthropology.[15] The significance of the work was underlined when the governments of South Australia and Victoria received a memorial from the 'leading scientists in England' asking that Spencer and Gillen be released from their duties for a period to continue their work among the Aborigines of central and northern Australia.[16] Their work was praised as 'a model of scientific research and a storehouse of accurate observation' that ranked 'among the documents of primary importance for anthropology'.[17] The appeal was sufficiently impressive for both men to be granted leave of absence for 12 months, and for significant government and private support to be forthcoming.[18] David Syme, editor of the Melbourne *Age*, contributed a thousand pounds towards their expedition.[19] Preparations were reported in great detail and the entire editorial page of the *Adelaide Observer* was given over to a discussion of the expedition on the eve of its departure.[20] During the expedition Spencer sent regular reports, like despatches from the front, which were published in the *Age* and the *Adelaide Observer*.[21]

With the 'heroic age' of anthropology, the noble savage was reinvented. The enlightenment conception of the noble savage – one of a people living free of artificial institutional and social barriers – had been a liberating ideal, for the inventors if not for the subjects. Science's new noble savage bore an abstract nobility, born of a presumed purity of race and of pristine, evolutionary inferiority. Not only was there an urgency to study the Aborigines before they died out, but also to study those still living in a state 'uncontaminated' by civilisation. It became a badge of honour for explorers and anthropologists to contact previously un-contacted tribes.

Evolutionary anthropology's romance with the 'uncontaminated' Aboriginal tribes of central and northern Australia had the consequence of reshaping the perception of Aboriginal people who had grown up indoctrinated by European attitudes and aspiring to European values and lifestyles. In introducing 'Our Coloured Kindred: Chat with F J Gillen', the journalist played on the contrast between the 'sober savage' and the 'semi-civilised' Aborigine:

> You may break, you may scatter, the black if you will; but the charm of
> the wilderness clings to him still. The sober savage Warioota in the wild
> wastes, in his summer suit of pipeclay and red ochre, is infinitely more
> picturesque – to leeward – than semi-civilised Tommy Walker in a second
> hand tail coat and top hat . . .[22]

The 'sober savage' is charming and picturesque in his 'wild wastes', while Tommy Walker and his semi-civilised brethren are 'degenerate descendants'. A conceptual reversal was taking place. Earlier in the century, the 'semi-civilised blacks' represented the hope of transformation from savagery to civilisation, while the 'wild blacks' were the epitome of danger and moral degeneracy. By one set of rules 'contacted' Aborigines were inferior to civilised Europeans, and now, by another, they were inferior to their 'pure' brethren. These new ideas of race, informed by evolutionary theory, would play a crucial role in shaping Aboriginal policy into the twentieth century.

The era of protection and control

In 1904, Willshire was promoted to senior constable, and shortly afterwards was posted to Hergott Springs, a railway town in the far north of South Australia. There are few records of his time there, indicating an uneventful posting, but there is one letter that hints at another side of Willshire's nature that echoes the complex relationship to his Native Constables of earlier frontier days. Worrying both for their welfare and for the injury to his authority if they should leave him, he wrote to his superiors requesting that they construct a room to house the Native Police attached to the station. He complained that under the existing arrangements they we were forced to sleep in the stables, and as a consequence, were in 'a consumptive state'.[23] The situation was so bad, he added, some had already left him. Sub Inspector Clode, who had replaced Besley at Port Augusta, agreed to act on Willshire's suggestion.

In 1907, Edward Hamilton, who had served as South Australia's Protector of Aborigines for more than a quarter of a century, indicated that he was about to retire. He had been appointed in the 1870s, a time when an orthodox understanding prevailed that Aboriginal people were well advanced on the road to extinction and that the best that could be done was smooth the dying pillow. As a minor bureaucrat, he held little influence or power. He knew of Willshire. In 1884 he had questioned the constable's actions at Powell's Creek, only to be told by Besley that as these killings had occurred a long way from the centres of settlement there was little alternative but to trust the constable's word. He had fielded the Hermannsburg missionaries' complaints about 'immorality' in the district with the rather passive response that there was no legislation to deal with such matters. Throughout the 1890s missionaries and their supporters lobbied Protector Hamilton to pass an Aborigines Act that would, among other things, protect Aboriginal people from the sort of sexual abuse and exploitation that the Hermannsburg missionaries and others had been complaining of, and, equally, to allow them greater control over the lives of their Aboriginal charges.[24] In 1899 a Bill finally went before parliament but was opposed, most vociferously by pastoralists, who objected to provisions that outlined the protection of conditions for Aboriginal labour. Eventually the Bill lapsed under complaints that it had been designed for the frontier conditions of the Northern Territory, not those of the more settled south.[25]

In anticipation of Hamilton's imminent retirement, the position of Protector of Aborigines was advertised in the *Police Gazette* in June 1907. At this time, Willshire was stationed at Warooka in the midst of farming country at the southern end of Yorke Peninsula. Seeing the position of Protector of Aborigines advertised, Willshire applied for the job. In his application he wrote that he had been in the force for 29 years, and had 'great experience among the Aborigines', serving at such places as 'Innamincka, Alice Springs, Katherine and many other stations where the natives required some tact to manage agreeably'.[26] Nineteen other policemen also applied, including William Garnett South, the officer who had arrested Willshire in 1891. South left the Centre in 1895, served at Mount Gambier for three years, and had spent the last nine working at police headquarters in Adelaide.[27] The position of Protector of Aborigines went to Senior Constable William Garnett South. Willshire resigned from the force six months later.

South took up his new position on 1 March 1908 and would oversee the introduction of a new interventionist regime of Aboriginal administration. In 1911, the same year that the Northern Territory was passed from South Australian to commonwealth control, an Aborigines Act was finally passed by the South Australian government. Under this legislation, the Chief Protector became the legal guardian of every Aboriginal and 'half-caste' child under the age of 18, regardless of whether they had living parents or relatives. Aboriginal freedom of movement now became strictly controlled by the state. The Chief Protector was able to restrict any Aboriginal person to, or remove them from, a reserve or institution. It was illegal for an Aboriginal person to leave or be removed from his or her district without permission, and for a non-Aboriginal person to be on a reserve without permission. The Chief Protector could direct any

Aboriginal people who were camped, 'or about to camp', near towns or municipalities to remove to another location as directed. Any individual found loitering in any town or municipality 'and not decently clothed' could be directed to move on. And any township or municipality could be declared a prohibited area. Only those people in lawful employment were exempted from these regulations.[28] The origin of one of the more curious provisions in the Act harked back to the complaints of the Finke River missionaries: it was now an offence for an Aboriginal woman, in male attire, to be in the company of a non-Aboriginal man.[29] The Act passed easily, but not without some misgivings being expressed. In debate on the Bill, one member of parliament questioned the wide powers given to the Protector, describing them 'as arbitrary as those given to any Russian in the most blood curdling novel of the century'.[30]

Throughout his writings Willshire freely offered his opinions on issues of Aboriginal administration, reserving his bitterest vitriol for missionaries and Aboriginal people of mixed descent. While South didn't express his views with the same polemical venom as Willshire, he shared most of them. Willshire's methods of 'administering' the Centre had become obsolete, but his attitudes were becoming orthodoxies. During the term of his appointment South's principle obsessions were the missions and the 'half-caste problem' – he sought the elimination of both. South had two main concerns about the existing mission system: specifically, he objected to the divided authority between the Aborigines Department and the privately run missions; and on a general level, he regarded the existing system, particularly on the southern missions of Point McLeay and Point Pearce, as incapable of producing anything but 'idle, useless people'.[31] For these reasons he wanted the government to take over Point McLeay and Point Pearce and run them as 'industrial institutions':

> In advocating the taking over of these two stations I am not moved so much by the desire of saving tax-payers' money as by a wish to raise the constantly increasing number of half-castes, quadroons, and octoroons

from the idle, thriftless habits of the black to the level of the white race. This I regard as most important, as in the settled districts the blacks are rapidly dying out and being replaced by a race of half-castes, quadroons, and octoroons, who in turn must inevitably be merged into the general population. It is therefore desirable that nothing should be left undone that will help to convert these people into useful members of the community instead of allowing them to grow up dependants.[32]

It was under South's watch that the policy of systematically removing children of mixed descent was implemented. South's response to protests about the removal of a girl from Stuart's Creek in 1911, whom he described as 'almost white', distils the attitude of the time. The child's heart-broken mother, who was absent when the girl was taken, approached a local pastoralist who wrote to the Chief Protector on her behalf. He explained the woman's distress, pointed out that her children were 'well dressed and cared for' and asked for the child to be returned to her mother. The Chief Protector's response was that this 'quadroon girl' would in the long term be best cared for by the State Children's Council:

> I sympathise with her in the loss of her child, but no right thinking person can say that a girl of about 10 years of age who is practically white is under proper care & control while running about in a blacks' camp.
>
> It is bad enough for half-caste boys to be thus brought up, but every bushman knows the inevitable fate of the girls.
>
> It appears from your letter that the mother has had to submit to that fate as she has three children already.[33]

Typical of many cases of removal in the first part of the twentieth century, the child wasn't taken because she was neglected, she was taken because she was 'almost white'.[34]

Late colonial nationalism

In the last years of the nineteenth century, while Aboriginal Australians were being directed towards an unprecedented age of administrative surveillance, the bushman – the figure who for Willshire served to explain and justify the age of the frontier – was being bodied forth in the pages of popular literature to express the consolidation of white Australian national sentiment. The bushman, and his love affair with the bush as the site of raw Australian value, was 'among other things a useful construct for a largely urbanised population which was unable by the 1890s to entirely ignore the signs of weakness and woe within its immediate surroundings'; in the social imagination, the bush provided 'a larger vista' in which to nurture a vision of the ideal nation.[35] The bushman, as various literary historians have suggested, was hardly a ubiquitously or unambivalently celebrated character in Australia's emerging literary culture.[36] He did, nonetheless, provide pre-Federation audiences with a short-hand articulation of national belonging. In Banjo Paterson's celebratory 1892 verse, published in the 'bushman's bible' of *The Bulletin*, 'the bush hath moods and changes, as the seasons rise and fall / And the men who know the bushland – they are loyal through it all'.[37]

Willshire was a keen consumer of *The Bulletin*. It held, he wrote, 'proud sway over all Australian print productions'; even in the most remote regions of the bush it 'is handed from one man to another until all around discuss its contents'.[38] In his own writings, he consistently adopted *The Bulletin*'s literary image of the bushman as his favourite form of self-characterisation, and this was also the figure he cut among his northern-based contemporaries. When *Land of the Dawning* appeared in print in 1896, it included an appendix of admiring letters from local readers of the manuscript. The former manager of Victoria River Downs station Lindsay Crawford wrote that Willshire's style would 'please bushmen immensely', adding that 'there are one or two ordeals they perform that he has wisely left unexplained'. Thomas Cahill, manager of Wave Hill station, also admired *Land of the Dawning* as 'a rough book, by a rough author, written in the garb of a real bushman'.[39] In fiction, in verse and in the pages of the popular press, the image of the bushman gave flesh to the vision of a new Australian nation that, by the 1890s, was widely considered imminent.

However, the striking irony of Willshire's history is that, having 'gone out and done as the law provides' he became obsolete to the story he worked to shape at the very moment of its fulfillment.[40] On the same day that the *Adelaide Observer* reported the shooting at Tempe Downs that would lead to Willshire's arrest, other events of national import were jostling for space in its pages: the Governor's tour of the Northern Territory; the Pastoral Lands Commission, which reported back how 'well' the country of that region was 'beginning to look'; the Elder Scientific Expedition, which if successful, reported the *Adelaide Observer*, should bring to an end the age of Australian exploration; and most significantly, the Federation Convention, then underway in Sydney.[41] Sir John Downer, who within months would serve as counsel at Willshire's murder trial, was a participant of the Federation Convention and his comments on it were reported extensively in the press. The convention had proved, he said, that 'the feeling in favour of federation was generally strong, and the practicability of it was also recognized amongst the delegates.' Throughout April, May and June, the successes of these events – the Governor's tour, the Pastoral Lands Commission, the progress of the Elder Scientific Expedition and the Federation debate – were reported alongside the more minor story of Willshire's committal for trial on the charge of murder.

By the last year of the nineteenth century, while Willshire was serving out the remainder of his policing career in quiet obscurity at the small coastal town of Cowell, the country was anticipating the nation he had envisioned as emerging from the frontier, one free of spirit and innocent of stain. In Sir Henry Parkes' 1899 verse in celebration of the Australian flag,

Where'er it waves, on land or sea,
It bears no stain of blood and tears –
Its glory is its purity.[42]

Coda

As Australia moved into an era in which the entwined concepts of protection and control would define Aboriginal policy, one might imagine that the days of cattle killing, reprisals and punitive expeditions were over. However, events in 1928 at Coniston station, some 190 kilometres northwest of Alice Springs, present a disturbing coda to the age of Central Australia's violent frontier, and demonstrate how much of the deeply encoded culture of the frontier still remained.

Through the middle of 1928, in the midst of a terrible drought, the Warlpiri were spearing cattle on Coniston station. On 7 August they speared and killed Fred Brooks, an old 'dogger', allegedly for taking an Aboriginal woman. Mounted Constable William George Murray, with his two Aboriginal trackers, the station owner and some of his men, set off to hunt down the killers. On 16 August they came upon an Aboriginal camp where they shot down three male and two female 'suspects' before continuing on in pursuit of others. By the end of the month Murray, a Gallipoli veteran, judged the job done and returned to Alice Springs with two prisoners. Murray officially reported the deaths of 17 Aboriginal people. In the interim a station owner, Nugget Morton, was attacked and almost killed. Murray was sent out again; on this expedition he reported killing 12 people. Reliable reports suggest that as many as 70 Aboriginal people were killed in the course of the two punitive expeditions.[43]

News of the killings created a public outcry in both Australia and Britain, and the federal government was compelled to establish a board of inquiry, the membership of which included a Police Inspector, and the police magistrate who had despatched Murray on the second expedition. The Association for the Protection of Native Races sought representation on the commission to present the case on behalf of the Aboriginal people but were politely advised, after the inquiry was completed, that this was entirely unnecessary in view of the 'qualifications of the members of the Board'.[44] The inquiry completely exonerated Mounted Constable Murray. There was not, the board reported, 'a scintilla of evidence . . . of a reprisal or a punitive expedition'. The tribe coming in from the west, they found, 'had threatened to wipe out the settlers'. The situation had been worsened, they argued, by 'unattached Missionaries wandering from place to place, having no previous knowledge of the blacks and their customs and preaching a doctrine of equality'. Indeed, one of those missionaries was a woman whose presence 'amongst naked blacks' must assuredly have lowered 'respect for the whites'. They had no doubt that 'insufficient police patrols' had made matters worse.[45]

In the 1930s and 1940s the journalist Ernestine Hill travelled through the Interior and wrote admiringly of the Centre's pioneers and the hardships they had endured. In 1933 she wrote an article about the Coniston massacre under the heading 'Murray – The Scourge Of The Myalls: Man Whose Gun Keeps White Men Safe In The Wilds'. It was, as Andrew Marcus has observed, a celebration of killing; she wrote admiringly of the 'punitive police raids' which alone guaranteed the 'safety of the white man in a black man's country', assuring her readers that the Aborigines 'understood nothing else'.[46]

Willshire would have been proud: proud of his heir, Constable Murray, 'for doing what the law provided'; of the commissioners, for realising that the missionaries were the real source of trouble; and of Hill for understanding the tribulations that the pioneers faced, and the means required to protect them. Willshire had died in 1925, three years before the Coniston massacre. Up until his death, he had worked since his retirement from the police force as a nightwatchman at the metropolitan abattoirs, overseeing the killing of cattle.

EPILOGUE

How has this history been remembered? The 1874 Barrow Creek telegraph station attack was the first clash of significant scale in the Centre between Aboriginal people and white settlers, and it resulted in the deaths of three white men and an unknown number of Aboriginal people in subsequent punitive expeditions. Near the entrance to Adelaide's West Terrace Cemetery is an imposing monument to the men of the Overland Telegraph Line who died by Aboriginal spears. A broken Doric column encircled by a laurel wreath stands atop a rectangular plinth inscribed with the names of the fallen. It pays tribute to Stapleton, Franks and Flint, who were killed or wounded in the February attack. It pays tribute, too, to two others, Johnston and Augustus Daer, who were killed at Roper River in the following year. Erected by the men of the Overland Telegraph Line, it commemorates the 'comrades who were treacherously murdered by blacks in the discharge of their duty'. The memorial bears no reference to 'Jemmy', the Aboriginal worker wounded, nor does it mention the many Aboriginal lives taken in reprisal.

In 1894 Hermannsburg was sold to the Immanuel Synod of the Lutheran Church, and revived under the missionary superintendence of Carl Strehlow. Strehlow wrote about Arrernte language and culture with considerable insight, and his son Theodore would eventually become an anthropologist at the University of Adelaide. With the passage of time the Lutherans of Hermannsburg have generated an almost mythic literature of missionary courage and endurance: the epic trek to found the mission, their struggles against the violence of settlers and police, and the last tragic journey of Carl Strehlow. The story of the forlorn attempt to take the gravely ill missionary south for medical help is told by his son in *Journey to Horseshoe Bend*. It is in this book that Ted Strehlow records Willshire's part in Nameia's story, and Gillen's part in the Arrernte's story:

> Gillen's courage was never forgotten by the Aranda; and some years later their gratitude found its expression in the ceremonial festival held at Alice Springs in 1896, where the secret totemic cycle of Imanda was revealed for the first time before the eyes of white men – to Gillen and his friend Baldwin Spencer.[1]

The former mission at Hermannsburg is now a popular stop-off point on Larapintja Drive, a ring road to the west of Alice Springs that takes locals and tourists through the country that Willshire once patrolled. Visitors can wander through the former mission's many well-maintained whitewashed buildings, and enjoy lunch or afternoon tea on the shady verandah of what was once Strehlow's house. A pamphlet welcoming visitors to the Hermannsburg Historic Precinct explains that the site was restored during 1987 and 1988 as part of the Bicentennial Commemorative Program, and describes the former function of each of its buildings. A display cabinet in the museum houses photographs which commemorate the mission's founding members and an earlier age of mission life. The Historic Precinct stands self-contained on the edge of the Ntaria Aboriginal community.

Many of the sites of Willshire's former police patrols are now part of the regular tourist routes of the Centre. Glen Helen provides a camping ground, comfortable hotel accommodation and a popular bar and restaurant to visitors who use the site as a departure point for excursions into the stunning outlying gorges accessible only by four-wheel-drive. In a recent issue of *4X4 Australia*, a touring magazine that today invites four-wheel-drive explorers to discover the highlights of Australia's outback, Owen Springs and Undoolya stations are recommended for off-road and quad-bike adventure tours. The old police station ruins at Boggy Waterhole are recorded as 'a stark reminder of a violent past', but the site of this former police camp on the Finke River is beautiful, and it is recommended to visitors as 'one of the most popular remote camps in the area'.[2] Alice Springs telegraph station – the departure point for early pastoral explorations, the site of the Centre's first permanent police presence, and Willshire's base for the first several years of his posting in the Centre – is a well-maintained historic precinct, structured to capture the approving tourist gaze rather than to challenge the visitor to revisit the darker aspects of Australian history.

William Willshire died on 30 August 1925, at the age of 73. An obituary to him in the *Adelaide Observer* recalled the hardships he endured as a frontier policeman. 'The death of William Henry Willshire,' it read, 'has removed a former police officer noted for his daring and efficiency.'

> His best service was rendered in the Northern Territory, where he achieved universal popularity and esteem for his daring and efficient devotion to duty. The conditions of life in the northern settlements were then most primitive, and stern policing was necessary to preserve order and dispense justice. M. C. Willshire was eminently fitted for this exacting work. Combined with his amazing fearlessness, he possessed uncanny knowledge of bush lore, and it is claimed that there was no better bushman and horseman in the north than he. His career as a police officer was marked by good deeds, both officially and privately, and in many country centres his name is held in the highest esteem. Many of his duties were most hazardous, especially when he had to deal with cattle thieves; but he never faltered in the execution of the most dangerous tasks.[3]

No mention was made of his murder trial, or of the Commission of Inquiry his role as the Officer in Charge of the Native Police had generated. He was buried in the cemetery of St Mary's Anglican Church, then a quiet rural parish, but now a suburban church on a bustling, noisy arterial road. His gravesite is unmarked, his headstone long ago pushed aside by the spreading roots of an overgrown olive tree that separates his resting place from that of his father. Yet his name still has a physical presence in the Centre, carved by him in 1881 into the chalky limestone column of Chambers Pillar. Willshire's signature there – a personal act of graffiti on this important sacred site in southern Arrernte lands – is still visible. His signature on the land has more official memory as well, as a street name in the expanding suburbs of Alice Springs. But most significantly, Willshire's name is encoded in the Centre's social memory, a mnemonic to the culture of violence in late colonial Central Australia.[4]

This is not the only form of contemporary remembrance, however. In the 1980s, the decade which commemorated Australia's bicentenary, Willshire's story was periodically revived as a feature subject for popular newspaper articles, which brought back the colonial frontier as a theme of historical reminiscence. Though mindful of the unacceptability of violence for contemporary audiences,[5] these feature articles are noticeable for the service to which this violent history is put in nostalgically recalling a colonial romance with the country. In a feature article titled 'Rebel mountie tried to tame frontier', published in the Sydney *Sun* in 1980, a uniformed Willshire gazes from the page over the span of a hundred years, and frontier violence is enlisted in the re-creation of a frontier adventure narrative which Willshire himself might have written:

> In charge of a frontier police post, the adventurous 27 year old rebel had found his niche. Despite a love of notoriety and exaggeration, [he] won respect for his personal courage and attention to duty.
>
> . . . He was kept busy investigating settler complaints against aggressive tribesmen determined to drive out the white men and their cattle. Some

holdings were abandoned. A typical patrol with native horseboys and packhorses took about three months to cover 3,000 kilometres of rugged wilderness . . . Eternal vigilance was necessary to counter ambush and dawn attacks.

Settlers took the law into their own hands, though deploring the need. Not a man among them went unarmed. Willshire was appointed to train a native police force. The first batch of six recruits learnt the care of equipment and horses, and to shoot accurately, and the one-time rebel turned them into useful, well-disciplined men.[6]

In 1992, Austin Stapleton published *Willshire of Alice Springs*, the only biography of the Mounted Constable. It defends Willshire against 'unsustained assertions' that would have us believe he was 'a criminal of the worst kind', and omissions that overlook his 'great work on behalf of the Aborigines and science'.[7] Stapleton defends Willshire in the terms that Willshire defended himself: a frontier officer proudly protecting the advance of civilisation in the wild Interior. However, as the police historian Bill Wilson has recently argued, the Centre's policing history in the last two decades of the nineteenth century was not just one of individual but of 'institutionalised violence'.[8] The role performed by the Native Police force under men like Willshire and Wurmbrand was performed 'aggressively' and 'with minimal controls'.[9] It was a role that these officers recorded in their official reports in terms of waging a strategic and localised war with the intent of regional 'pacification'.

In 2002, writer/director Rolf de Heer explored the violence of the frontier in his film *The Tracker*. The film represents the complexities of the frontier in a series of representative types: the Mounted Constable is 'The Fanatic'; his off-sider, 'The Novice'; the local squatter, 'The Follower'; and the Aboriginal man, caught between two worlds, is 'The Tracker'. The film's dialogue tells us that the character of the Mounted Constable is based, at least in part, upon William Willshire. In the aftermath of a massacre that begins the film, the Mounted Constable congratulates his pistol for 'speaking good English'; he then consoles his distressed junior officer with the advice that the government has given them guns and ammunition with the expectation that they will use them. He is the Everyman of the frontier's darkest aspect: he is by turns admiring and contemptuous of his Aboriginal tracker; he is dependent upon his tracker's knowledge, and at the same time fearful of and disturbed by what that knowledge represents. De Heer, in reducing the story of dispossession to a set of elemental types and episodes, allows no European Australian to escape complicity in the history that he tells.

This is a story that, for some, invites a desire to forget. Copies of Willshire's and Wurmbrand's reports of their patrols with the Native Police, and Besley's receipts of them, are contained in a journal of correspondence for the Far Northern Police Division between 1884 and 1890, now held in the South Australian Police Historical Society archive. In an envelope pasted to the inside cover of the journal is a note, dated 1972, from a reader who thanks the journal's donor for its use, and offers comment on its contents. The reader expresses concern for the journal's future, partly because many such original documents no longer exist, and partly because of the social pain that exposure of the contents could cause: 'There is one extract which refers to the police shooting of prisoners – how would that be in print?' Some of the information in such old journals, this letter writer comments, 'is not fit to be put on public display'.[10]

For others, this is a story that demands an imperative to remember. On 23 September 2003, the senior members of the Warlpiri community, with the assistance of the Central Land Council, erected a simple memorial to the Coniston massacre near Brooks Soak on Mount Denison station. As an historical counterpart to the Barrow Creek memorial in Adelaide's West Terrace Cemetery, it is a reminder that the violent history of Central Australia has even a living memory, which all witnesses of the memorial are charged to acknowledge:

In 1928 near this place the murder of Frederick Brooks led to the killing of many innocent Aboriginal people across the region

We will remember them always.

Nganimparlu kapurnalu-jana manngu-nyanyirni
Tarrnngangku-juku
Nwern inenhenh kweteth iterl-arerlanetyenh
Aynanthe atewanthepe etelarerrantye

Men and women who had witnessed the events in 1928 were present. According to James Warden,

representatives of the family of George Murray spoke sorrowfully of profound regret and they apologised wholeheartedly. The apology was accepted. The Northern Territory Police were represented and spoke of regret for the harm to all involved. Community members, young and old, spoke in language and in English about the past but mostly about the future.[11]

NOTES

Preface

1 William Henry Willshire, *Land of the Dawning*, W K Thomas & Co., Printers, Adelaide, 1896, pp. 52–53.

2 Nicholas Thomas, 'Home Décor and Dance: The Abstraction of Aboriginality' in Rebecca Coates and Howard Morphy (eds), *In Place (Out of Time): Contemporary Art in Australia*, Museum of Modern Art, Oxford, 1997, pp. 24–28.

3 Deborah Bird Rose, 'Hard Times: An Australian Story' in Klaus Newmann et al (eds), *Quicksands: Foundational Histories in Australia and Aotearoa New Zealand*, University of New South Wales Press, Sydney, 1999, p. 6.

4 Ibid., p. 12.

1 Opening the Centre

1 Daniel Headrick, *The Tools of Empire: Technology and European Imperialism in the Nineteenth Century*, Oxford University Press, New York and Oxford, 1981; Shirley Shepherd, 'The Significance of the Overland Telegraph Line', in *Journal of Northern Territory History*, vol. 7, 1996, p. 44.

2 Richard Kimber, 'Genocide or Not? The Situation in Central Australia 1860–1895' in Colin Tatz (ed.), *Genocide Perspectives I: Essays in Comparative Genocide*, Centre for Comparative Genocide Studies, Sydney, 1997, p. 35.

3   D J Mulvaney, *Encounters in Place: Outsiders and Aboriginal Australians 1606–1985*, University of Queensland Press, St Lucia, 1989, p. 119.

4   Commissioner of Police to Gason, 23 February 1874 PCO, 261/1874, cited in M C Hartwig, 'The Progress of White Settlement in the Alice Springs District and its Effects upon the Aboriginal Inhabitants 1860–1894 (PhD dissertation), University of Adelaide, 1965, p. 267.

5   R S Gillen (ed.), *F. J. Gillen's First Diary 1875*, Wakefield Press, Kent Town, 1995, p. 11.

6   The events at Barrow Creek are detailed in Hartwig, 1965, pp. 265–272.

7   Hartwig, p. 265.

8   R Clyne, *Colonial Blue: A History of the South Australian Police Force 1836–1916*, Wakefield Press, Netley, South Australia, 1987, p. 173.

9   Commissioner of Police to Gason, 23 February 1874, PCO 261/1874, cited in Hartwig, p. 270.

10 *Advertiser*, 26 February 184, cited in Hartwig, p. 271.

11 A figure of around 50 deaths is cited by Alan Powell in *Far Country: A Short History of the Northern Territory*, Melbourne University Press, Melbourne, 1982, p. 116. A figure of around 90 deaths is cited by Gordon Reid, *A Picnic with the Natives: Aboriginal–European Relations in the Northern Territory to 1910*, Melbourne University Press, Melbourne, 1990, p. 65. Reid's source for this figure is Hartwig, but Hartwig suggests that as many as 90 people met their deaths at Skull Creek alone, the site of Gason's fourth punitive expedition (pp. 275–276). Other sources for this account of the Barrow Creek station attack are Richard Kimber, op. cit., and William Henry Willshire, *The Aborigines of Central Australia*, Drysdale Printer, Port Augusta, 1888.

12 T G H Strehlow, *Journey to Horseshoe Bend*, Angus & Robertson, Sydney, 1969, p, 37.

13 Ibid., p. 39.

14 Ibid., pp. 42–43.

15 Ibid., p. 43.

16 John McDouall Stuart, *Explorations in Australia: The Journals of John McDouall Stuart*, Saunders, Otley & Co., London, 1865, p. 165.

17 Headrick, p. 163.

18 Mulvaney, 1989, p. 109.

19 Hartwig, p. 282.

20 Ibid., p. 465.

21 Ibid., p. 467.

22 Ibid., p. 468.

23 F H Brauer, 'The Coming of European Man', in Gillian Cook (ed.), *Man in the Centre*, Commonwealth Scientific and Industrial Research Organisation (CSIRO), Western Australia, Perth, 1983, p. 31.

24 Kimber, p. 37.

25 Ibid., pp. 42–45.

26 Willshire to Rollison, 1 September 1880, SRSA GRG 5/2/1880/909.

27 Willshire to Besley, 22 November 1881, SRSA GRG 5/2/1881/1204 1/2 22.

2 'The Rule of Law'

1 Gordon Reid, *A Picnic with the Natives: Aboriginal–European Relations in the Northern Territory to 1910*, Melbourne University Press, Melbourne, 1990, p. 116.

2 Petition to the Chief Secretary, 14 July 1884, SRSA GRG 24/6/1884/140.

3 J H Gordon to the Commissioner of Police, 13 October 1884, SRSA GRG 5/2/1884/828.

4 Petition to the Chief Secretary, 14 July 1884, SRSA GRG 24/6/1884/140.

5 Ibid.

6 For general discussions of these issues, see John Connor, *The Australian Frontier Wars*, University of New South Wales Press, Sydney, 2002, pp. 1–21; Jeffrey Grey, *A Military History of Australia*, Cambridge University Press, Melbourne, 1999, pp. 25–37.

7 M C Hartwig, 'The Progress of White Settlement in the Alice Springs District and its Effects upon the Aboriginal Inhabitants 1860–1894 (PhD dissertation), University of Adelaide, 1965, p. 278.

8 Reid, p. 116.

9 Willshire to Besley, Far Northern Division Police Journal, 17 September 1884, SAPHS 000319.

10 Willshire to Besley, 17 September 1884, SAPHS Papers 00319 Loc 2-2/43 (Cool 87).

11 Ibid.

12 Reid, pp. 99–100.

13 Baker to Parsons, 9 September 1884, cited in Tony Austin, *Simply the Survival of the Fittest: Aboriginal Administration in South Australia's Northern Territory 1863–1910*, Historical Society of the Northern Territory, Darwin, 1992, p. 17.

14 Austin, p. 19.

15 Cited in Reid, p. 104.

16 *NT Times & Gazette*, 4 October 1884, cited in Austin, p. 18.

17 Austin, p. 18.

18 Ibid.

19 Parsons, Report for the Quarter ending December 1884, *SAPP* no. 53 of 1885.

20 Willshire to Besley, 29 September 1884, Far Northern Division Police Journal, SAPHS 000319.

21 Ibid.

22 Ibid.

23 Ibid.

24 Willshire to Besley, 29 September 1884, SAPHS Papers 00319 Loc 2-2/43 (Cool 87).

25 Paul Foelsche, Inspector of Police in the Top End, was particularly resistant to the notion of a free-standing Native Police force. See Bill Wilson, 'The Establishment and Operations of the NT Native Police', in *Journal of Northern Territory History* 7, 1996, p. 65; Austin, p. 21.

26 Alison Palmer, *Colonial Genocide*, Crawford House Publishing, Adelaide, 2000, p. 49.

27 Ibid., p. 61 passim.

28 Maurice O'Connell to the Select Committee Inquiry into the Native Police Force, *Report and Minutes of Evidence 1861*, cited in Palmer, p. 53.

29 Palmer, p. 52.

30 Cited in Reid, p. 115.

31 Petition by 18 lessees and managers to the Chief Secretary, 2 October 1884, SRSA GRG 24/61884/2479.

32 D Murray to Chief Secretary, 23 October 1884, SRSA GRG 24/6/1884/2423.

33 Peterswald to Chief Secretary, 29 October 1884, SRSA GRG 24/6/1884/2423.

34 Ibid.

35 Peterswald to Besley, 14 November 1884, PCO 920/84, SAPHS Papers 004651 (Loc: Cool 87)

36 Schwarz to Hamilton, Far Northern Division Police Journal, 24 November 1884, SAPHS 000319.

37 Hamilton to the Commissioner of Crown Lands, Far Northern Division Police Journal, 30 December 1884, SAPHS 000319.

38 Ibid.

39 Besley to Peterwald, 19 January 1885, SRSA GRG 5/2/1885/61.

40 Wurmbrand to Besley, Far Northern Division Police Journal, 26 December 1884, SAPHS 004651.

41 Ibid.

42 Besley to Peterswald, 21 January 1885; Peterswald to Besley, 26 January 1885, SRSA GRG 5/2/1885/72; Far Northern Division Police Journal, SAPHS 004651.

43 Willshire to Besley, 10 December 1884, SRSA GRG 5/2/1884/1006.

44 Besley to Hamilton, 22 December 1884, SAPHS Papers 000319, Loc 2-2/43 (Cool 87)

45 Besley to Peterswald, 19 January 1885, SRSA GRG 5/2/1885/61.

46 William Henry Willshire, *The Aborigines of Central Australia*, C E Bristow, Government Printer, Adelaide, 1891, p. 33.

47 Willshire to Besley, Far Northern Division Police Journal, 29 September 1884, SAPHS 000319.

48 Wurmbrand to Besley, 27 December 1885, SRSA GRG 5/2/1886/198.

49 See, for instance, Willshire's report of the Anna's Reservoir Patrol, Willshire
    to Besley, Far Northern Division Police Journal, 17 September 1884, SAPHS
    000319 and Wurmbrand's report of his Glen Helen Patrol, Wurmbrand to
    Besley, Far Northern Division Police Journal, 26 December 1884, SAPHS
    004651.

50 Wurmbrand's Glen Helen Patrol in December 1884; Wurmbrand to Besley
    Far Northern Division Police Journal, 26 December 1884, SAPHS 004651;
    Willshire's report of 'Jacky' shot while escaping from Native Constable Peter
    near the Heavitree Gap Police Station in March 1887; Alice Springs Police
    Journal, Officer in Charge, 1886–1889, 18 March 1887, NTAS F255.

51 Willshire's first book, *The Aborigines of Central Australia*, was printed at Port
    Augusta in 1888 and studio photographs of Willshire, Wurmbrand and the
    Native Constables were taken at Port Augusta on the same trip, see *Port
    Augusta Dispatch*, 10 and 24 January 1888.

52 Warburton to the Minister of Education, 1 June 1890, SRSA GRS
    1/1/1890/395.

53 Barry Morris, 'Frontier Colonialism as a Culture of Terror', in B Attwood and
    J Arnold (eds), *Power, Knowledge and Aborigines*, La Trobe University Press
    and National Centre for Australian Studies, Bundoora, Victoria, 1992, p. 86.

54 Ibid.

55 Willshire to Besley, 8 January 1890, SRSA GRS 1/1/1890/40.

56 William Henry Willshire, *Land of the Dawning*, W K Thomas & Co.,
    Printers, Adelaide, 1896, p. 21.

57 Willshire to Besley, 9 January 1890, SRSA GRS 1/1/1890/40.

58 Richard Kimber, 'Genocide or Not? The Situation in Central Australia
    1860–1895' in Colin Tatz (ed.), *Genocide Perspectives I: Essays in Comparative
    Genocide*, Centre for Comparative Genocide Studies, Sydney, 1997, p. 55.
    The episodes described by Kimber are in Wurmbrand's report to Besley,
    5 June 1885, SRSA GRG 52/1/1885/150.

59 William Benstead, Short Stories of my Life and Travels (typescript), private
    collection, n.d., p. 11.

60 Ibid., pp. 11–12.

3 The Native Police

1 Schwarz to Hamilton, Far Northern Division Police Journal, 24 December 1884, SAPHS 000319.

2 Kempe to Hamilton, Far Northern Division Police Journal, 13 April 1885, SAPHS 000319.

3 Ibid.

4 Daer to Besley, Far Northern Division Police Journal, 4 June 1885, SAPHS 000319.

5 Wurmbrand to Besley, Far Northern Division Police Journal, 5 June 1885, SAPHS 000319.

6 Finke River Mission Inquiry, opened 21 July 1890, SRSA GRG 1/2/1890/253, p. 2.

7 Peterswald to Besley, 2 February 1886, SRSA GRG 5/2/1886/198.

8 Besley to Peterswald, 6 March 1886, SRSA GRG 5/2/1886/198.

9 Ibid.

10 Peterswald to the Chief Secretary, 16 March 1886, SRSA GRG 5/2/1886/198.

11 Willshire's report on Undoolya patrol, March 1887: death of the prisoner Jacky; Wurmbrand's report on the Erldunda/Tempe Downs patrol, August–November 1887: death of the prisoner Wiaculla, alias Pompey, SRSA GRG 5/2/1887/65.

12 Hamilton to Kempe, 15 October 1886, SRSA GRG 52/1/1886/330.

13 Warland to Peterswald, 20 April 1886, SAPHS COP 001162, and SRSA GRG 5/2/1886/356.

14 Foelsche to Minister of Education, 14 July 1886, SAPHS 001162 and SRSA GRG 5/2/1886/356.

15 Willshire to Besley, 18 February 1887, SRSA GRG 5/2/1887/65.

16 Ibid.

17 Minister of Education, 1 March 1889, SRSA GRG 5/2/1888/822.

18 Alice Springs Police Journal, Officer in Charge, 1886–1889, 13 March 1887, NTAS F255.

19 Ibid., 18 March 1887.

20 Daer to Besley, 11 August 1887, SRSA GRG 5/2/1887/475.

21 Daer to Besley, 6 September 1887, SRSA GRG 5/2/1887/475.

22 Daer to Besley, 11 August and 6 September 1887, SRSA GRG 5/2/1887/475.

23 Robert Thornton quoted in Charles Chewings, SRSA GRG 5/2/1887/631.

24 Charles Chewings to the Commissioner of Police, 9 November 1887, SRSA GRG 5/2/1887/631.

25 Charles Chewings, Letter to the Editor (draft), 9 November 1887, SRSA GRG 5/2/1887/631.

26 Willshire to Besley, 21 November 1887, SRSA GRG 5/2/1887/631.

27 Charles Chewings to Commissioner of Police, SRSA GRG 5/2/1887/631.

28 Heidenreich to Peterswald, 8 March 1888; Willshire to Besley, 1 September 1888, SRSA GRG 5/2/1888/164.

29 Alice Springs Police Journal, Officer in Charge, 1886–1889, 27 April 1888, NTAS F255.

30 F H Brauer, 'The Coming of European Man', in Gillian Cook (ed.), *Man in the Centre*, Commonwealth Scientific and Industrial Research Organisation (CSIRO), Western Australia, Perth, 1983, p. 42.

31 South to Peterswald, 20 October 1888, SRSA GRG 5/2/1888/822.

32 D J Mulvaney, *Encounters in Place: Outsiders and Aboriginal Australians 1606–1985*, University of Queensland Press, St Lucia, Queensland, 1989, p. 126.

33 Finke River Mission Inquiry, opened 21 July 1890, SRSA GRG 1/2/1890/253, pp. 70–73.

34 William Henry Willshire, *A Thrilling Tale of Real Life in the Wilds of Australia*, Frearson & Brother, Printers, Adelaide, 1895, p. 13.

35 Willshire to Besley, 6 May 1890, SRSA GRS 1/2/1890/234.

4 Ethnography as Surveillance

1 J A Barnes, 'Anthropology in Britain Before and After Darwin', in *Mankind*, vol. V, no. 9, 1960, p. 1.

2 Peter J Bowler, *The Non-Darwinian Revolution: Reinterpreting a Historical Myth*, Johns Hopkins, Baltimore, 1988, p. 47.

3 C S Wake, 'The Mental Characteristics of Primitive Man, as Exemplified by
   the Australian Aborigines', in *Journal of the Anthropological Institute of Great
   Britain and Ireland*, 1872, pp. 83–84; E B Tylor, *Primitive Culture*, London,
   1871, p. 21.

4 *Adelaide Observer*, 27 May and 18 November 1876.

5 Ibid., 16 January 1875.

6 A P Elkin, 'The Development of Scientific Knowledge of the Aborigines',
   in H Shiels (ed.), *Australian Aboriginal Studies*, 1963, pp. 6–10; K Burridge,
   *Encountering Aborigines. A Case Study: Anthropology and the Australian
   Aboriginal*, London, 1973, p. 47.

7 *South Australian Register*, 30 May 1885.

8 *Adelaide Observer*, 24 July 1886.

9 Philip Jones, 'Preface' in J D Woods (ed.), *The Native Tribes of South
   Australia*, 1879; reprint, State Library, Adelaide, 1997.

10 Philip Jones, 'Objects of Mystery and Concealment: A History of Tjurunga
   Collection', in *Oceania Monograph* 45, 1995, p. 68.

11 *Adelaide Observer*, 18 May 1889.

12 Samuel Gason, *The Dieyerie Tribe of Australian Aborigines*, W C Cox,
   Government Printer, Adelaide, 1874; P Foelsche, 'Notes on the Aborigines
   of North Australia', in *Transactions of the Royal Society of South Australia*,
   vol. 5, 1882.

13 William Henry Willshire, *The Aborigines of Central Australia*, Drysdale
   Printer, Port Augusta, 1888, pp. 3–8.

14 Ibid., p. 8.

15 Ibid., pp. 17–18.

16 Ibid., p. 15.

17 Ibid.

18 Ibid., p. 10.

19 Ibid., p. 5.

20 Ibid., p. 12.

21 Deborah Bird Rose, 'Aboriginal Life and Death in Australian Settler
   Nationhood', in *Aboriginal History*, vol. 25, 2001, pp. 151–156.

22 Willshire, 1888, pp. 19–27.

23 Jones, 1995, p. 76.

24 Ibid.

25 Ibid.

26 Ibid., p. 83.

27 J G Frazer, 'Notes on the Aborigines of Australia. Answers to Questions on the Manners, Customs, Religions, Superstitions, &c, of Uncivilised or Semi-civilised Peoples', in *Royal Anthropological Institute Journal*, 1895, vol. 24, pp. 158–198.

28 Ibid., p. 180.

29 Louis Shulze, 'The Aborigines of the Upper and Middle Finke River', in *Transactions of the Royal Society of South Australia*, vol. 14, 1891; H Kempe, 'A Grammar and Vocabulary of the Language Spoken by the Aborigines of the Macdonnell Ranges', in *Transactions of the Royal Society of South Australia*, vol. 14, 1890.

30 Willshire, 1888, p. 4.

31 Willshire, 'Preface', 1891.

32 Ibid.

33 Ibid.

34 John Molony, *The Native-Born: The First White Australians*, Melbourne University Press, Melbourne, 2000, p. 23.

35 Ibid.

36 Nicholas Thomas, 'Home Décor and Dance: The Abstraction of Aboriginality' in Rebecca Coates and Howard Morphy (eds), *In Place (Out of Time): Contemporary Art in Australia*, Museum of Modern Art, Oxford, 1997, p. 28.

37 William Henry Willshire, *A Thrilling Tale of Real Life in the Wilds of Australia*, Freason & Brother, Printers, Adelaide, 1895, p. 43.

38 Russel Ward, *The Australian Legend*, Oxford University Press, Melbourne, 1987, p. 2.

39 Ibid., pp. 200–201.

40 Willshire, 1891, p. 26.

41 Ibid., pp. 27–29.

42 Ibid., p. 33.

43 Ibid., p. 34.

44 *Port Augusta Dispatch*, 10 January 1888.

45 Ibid., 24 January 1888. The photograph and its press commentary are discussed in detail by Nicolas Peterson, 'A Colonial Image: Penetrating the Reality of the Message', in *Australian Aboriginal Studies*, no. 2, 1989, pp. 59–62.

46 Peterson, p. 62.

47 Besley to Willshire, 5 December 1889, SRSA GRG 5/21890/359.

48 Willshire to Besley, 17 December 1889, SRSA GRG 5/2/1890/359.

49 Besley to Willshire, 4 January 1890, SRSA GRG 5/2/1890/359.

5 The Missionaries under Scrutiny

1 Minister of Education to Besley, 16 December 1889, SRSA GRS 1/1/1890/92.

2 Willshire to Besley, 14 January 1890, GRS 1/1/1890/93.

3 Willshire to Besley, 8 and 9 January 1890, GRS 1/1/1890/40.

4 T G H Strehlow, *Journey to Horseshoe Bend*, Angus & Robertson, Sydney, 1969, pp. 43–45.

5 Willshire, William Henry, *The Aborigines of Central Australia*, Drysdale Printer, Port Augusta, 1888; reprint, C E Bristow, Government Printer, Adelaide, 1891.

6 Ibid.

7 *South Australian Register*, 10 January 1890.

8 Ibid.

9 Willshire to Besley, 21 February 1890, SRSA GRG 5/2/1890/260.

10 Ibid.

11 Ibid.

12 Ibid.

13 Ibid.

14 *Advertiser*, 6 May 1890.

15 Ben Rogers, *South Australian Register*, 2 April 1890.

16 Ibid.

17 *Adelaide Observer*, 31 May 1890.

18 Alice Springs Police Journal, Officer in Charge, 1886–1889, 13 March 1887, NTAS F255.

19 1 June 1890, SRSA GRS 1/1/1890/395

20 *South Australian Register*, 1 April 1890.

21 14 January 1890, SRSA GRS 1/1/1890/93.

22 Willshire to Besley, 8 January 1890, GRS 1/1/1890/40.

23 *South Australian Register*, 1 April 1890.

24 *Advertiser*, 11 June 1890.

25 *South Australian Register*, 6 May 1890.

26 6 May 1890, SRSA GRS 1/1/1890/234.

27 *South Australian Register*, 17 May 1890 and 3 June 1890; *Adelaide Observer*, 24 May 1890.

28 *South Australian Register*, 10 June 1890; *Advertiser*, 26 July 1890.

29 J Harris, *One Blood. 200 Years of Aboriginal Encounter with Christianity: A Story of Hope*, Albatross Books, Sutherland, New South Wales, 1990, p. 396.

30 *South Australian Register*, 30 August and 24 September, 1890.

31 Finke River Mission Inquiry, opened 21 July 1890, SRSA GRG 1/2/1891/253.

32 Ibid., pp. 1–2

33 Ibid., pp. 3–5.

34 Ibid., pp. 7–8

35 Ibid., pp. 22–24.

36 Ibid., pp. 70–73.

37 Ibid., p. 65.

38 Ibid., p. 67.

39 Ibid., pp. 20–21.

40 Ibid., p. 28.

41 Ibid., p. 50.

42 Ibid., p. 38.

43 Ibid., p. 50.

44 'Report of Messrs. Swan and Taplin on their visit to Finke, &c., Mission Stations, 30 September 1890, *South Australian Parliamentary Papers*, no. 148. pp. 1–3.

45 Willshire, 1891, p. 34.

46 Ibid., p. 36.

47 Ibid.

48 Ibid., p. 40.

49 Ibid., p. 38.

6 The Police under Scrutiny

1 Willshire to Besley, 26 February 1891, SRSA GRS 1/1/1891/254.

2 Ibid.

3 Willshire to Besley, 4 March 1891, SRSA GRS 1/1/1891/253.

4 *Adelaide Observer*, 11 and 18 April, 2, 16, 23 and 30 May 1891.

5 Ibid., 11 April, 2 and 9 May 1891.

6 Ibid., 18 and 25 April, 2 May 1891.

7 Ibid., 11 April 1891.

8 Five pages of loose notes in the consolidated file pertaining to the Finke River Mission Inquiry, SRSA GRS 1/2/1891/253.

9 Homburg to South, 11 April 1891, SRSA GRS 1/2/1891/253.

10 Consolidated file of telegrams to and from Attorney-General 11–18 April 1891 in SRSA GRS 1/2/1891/253.

11 Caldwell and Holder's report after interviewing Willshire at Ooramina on 22 February 1891, dated 17 April 1891 in SRSA GRS 1/2/1891/253.

12 Depositions taken at the preliminary hearing before F J Gillen, GRG 52/92.

13 Ibid., pp. 1–3.

14 Ibid., pp. 4–5.

15 Ibid., pp. 6–8.

16 Ibid., pp. 8–9.

17 Ibid., p. 9.

18 Ibid., p. 13.

19 Ibid., pp. 11–12.

20 Willshire to Belsey, 6 June 1889, SRSA GRS 1/1/1890/38.

21 Gillen to Homburg, 27 April 1891 in a consolidated file of telegrams
    c. 22–27 April 1891, SRSA GRS 1/2/1891/253.

22 Homburg to Gillen, n.d., SRSA GRS 1/2/1891/253.

23 Depositions taken at the preliminary hearing before F J Gillen, GRG 52/92,
    p. 15.

24 Ibid., p. 16.

25 Ibid., p. 10.

26 Ibid., p. 22.

27 Ibid., p. 18.

28 Ibid., p. 25.

29 Ibid., p. 27.

30 Ibid., p. 83.

31 Ibid.

32 Gillen to the Attorney-General, 30 April 1891, SRSA GRG 1/2/1891/524.

33 South to Besley, 1 May 1891, SRSA GRG 5/2/1891/418.

34 G A Heidenreich to Attorney-General Homburg, 20 April 1891, SRSA
    GRG 1/1/1891/253.

35 Ibid.

36 'Report of the Pastoral Lands Commission, together with Minutes of
    Proceedings', *South Australian Parliamentary Papers*, no. 33 of 1891,
    pp. 112–113, 117, 125, 127, 131.

7 The Trial of William Willshire

1 File of telegrams, 24–30 April 1891, SAPHS COP 001385.

2 Peterswald to Besley, 29 April 1891; Besley to Peterswald, 30 April 1891,
   SAPHS COP 001385.

3 *Adelaide Observer*, 16 May 1891.

4 F H Brauer, 'The Coming of European Man', in Gillian Crook (ed.), *Man in
   the Centre*, Commonwealth Scientific and Industrial Research Organisation
   (CSIRO), Western Australia, Perth, 1983, p. 42.

5 William Henry Willshire, *A Thrilling Tale of Real Life in the Wilds of Australia*, Freason & Brother, Printers, Adelaide, 1895. p. 35.

6 Prisoners brought to Her Majesty's Gaol, Port Augusta, GRG 54/197.

7 James Willshire to Attorney-General Homburg, 11 May 1891, SRSA GRG 1/1/1891/499.

8 Peterswald to Besley, 15 May 1891, SAPHS COP 001385.

9 T G H Strehlow, *Journey to Horseshoe Bend*, Angus & Robertson, Sydney, 1969, p. 48; *Adelaide Observer*, 25 July 1891.

10 *Adelaide Observer*, 25 July 1891.

11 Ibid.

12 Ibid.

13 Ibid.

14 Ibid.

15 *Adelaide Observer*, 15 August 1891.

16 *The Port Augusta Dispatch*, 31 July 1891.

17 William Henry Willshire, *Land of the Dawning*, W K Thomas & Co., Printers, Adelaide, 1896. p. 20.

18 Besley to Daer and South, 12 August 1891, SRSA GRG 5/2/1892/255.

19 Mounted Constable Cowle to Besley, 1 September 1893; Corporal Humphries to Protector of Aborigines, 24 November 1893, SRSA GRS 1/1/1893/394.

20 Sub Protector Gillen's Annual Report for 1893, 29 January 1894, SRSA GRS 1/1/1894/101.

8 Thrilling Tales

1 South to Besley, 1 May 1891, SRSA GRG 5/2/1891/418.

2 South Australian Museum Register, Item no. 9621. The entry for the item indicates that it was donated to the museum by J H Johnson who obtained it from 'Mtd Const. Willshire; belonged to "Logic"'.

3 Robert Foster, 'Logic's Unexpected Celebrity', in J Simpson and L Hercus (eds), *History in Portraits: Biographies of Nineteenth Century South Australian*

Aboriginal People, Aboriginal History Monograph 6, Aboriginal History Inc., Canberra, 1998, p. 185.

4 Record of Conduct, vol. 2, SRSA GRG 5/18.

5 Besley to Parkhouse, 12 October 1892, SRSA GRG 52/1/1892/304.

6 Finke River Mission Inquiry, opened 21 July 1890, SRSA GRG 1/2/1891/253, pp. 22–24.

7 Norman B Tindale, Genealogies of Australian Aborigines, vol. 6, 1939–1939, SAM AA 346/5/3/6

8 Willshire to Field, 4 December 1895, SAPHS COP 304/1893.

9 Willshire to Besley, 22 February 1893, SAPHS COP 304/1893.

10 Peterswald to Besley, 24 February 1893, SAPHS COP 304/1893.

11 Besley to Peterswald, 6 March 1893, SAPHS COP 304/1893.

12 Peterswald to Saunders, 30 March 1893, SAPHS COP 304/1893.

13 Tom Griffiths, 'The Social and Intellectual Context of the 1890s' in S Morton and D Mulvaney (eds), *Exploring Central Australia: Society, the Environment and the 1894 Horn Expedition*, Surrey Beatty & Sons, Chipping Norton, 1996, p. 13.

14 Baldwin Spencer (ed.), *Report on the Work of the Horn Scientific Expedition to Central Australia*, Part IV, Melville, Mullen and Slade, Melbourne, 1896, p. 3.

15 F J Gillen, 'The Natives of Central Australia', in *Royal Anthropological Institute Journal*, vol. 24, 1898, p. 19.

16 William Henry Willshire, *A Thrilling Tale of Real Life in the Wilds of Australia*, Freason & Brother, Printers, Adelaide, 1895. p. 7.

17 Willshire, 1895, pp. 11–12.

18 Various letters to the Minister Controlling the Northern Territory, for instance, GRS 1/1/105, 283, 336, 448 of 1889, on 15 August 1890 he requested Plans for the country explored by Teitkins, who had accompanied Giles on his explorations through Central Australia in 1872 and 1875, see GRS 1/1/1890/610.

19 Ernest Giles, *Australia Twice Traversed: The Romance of Exploration, being a Narrative Complied from the Journals of Five Exploring Expeditions into and through Central South Australia, and Western Australia, From 1872 to 1876*,

2 vols, Sampson Low, Marston, Searle & Rivington, London, 1889. Giles
account of the 1872 expedition was originally published as 'Mr Ernest Giles's
Explorations, 1872', in *Proceedings of the Parliament of South Australia*, paper
no. 21 of 1875, vol. 2, pp. 1–32.

20 Willshire, 1895, pp. 13, 15, 17, 34 and 36.

21 Robert Dixon, *Writing the Colonial Adventure*, Cambridge University Press,
Melbourne, 1992, pp. 4–9.

22 Ibid.

23 Willshire, 1895, p. 12.

24 Ibid., p. 8.

25 Ibid., pp. 9–12.

26 Ethel Castilla, *The Australian Girl and Other Verses*, George Roberston & Co.,
Melbourne, 1900.

27 Willshire, 'Dedication', 1895.

28 Ibid., p. 23.

29 Ibid., p. 23.

30 Ibid., p. 16.

31 Ibid., p. 13.

32 Ibid., p. 23.

33 Ibid., p. 21.

34 Ibid., pp. 27–28.

35 Ibid.

36 William Henry Willshire, *The Aborigines of Central Australia*, Drysdale
Printer, Port Augusta, 1888, p. 4.

37 Willshire, 1895, p. 28.

38 Ibid., p. 21.

39 Ibid., p. 14.

40 Ibid., p. 15.

41 Ibid., p. 16.

42 M A Smith, *Peopling the Cleland Hills: Aboriginal History in Western Central
Australia 1850–1980*, Aboriginal History Monograph 12, Aboriginal History
Inc., Canberra, 2005, pp. 24–25. The Northern Territory historian Dick

Kimber has drawn the same conclusion about the 'fumigating machine' (Pers. Comm. 2005).

43 Ibid., p. 15.

44 Ibid., pp. 15–19.

45 Ibid., p. 26.

46 Ibid., pp. 26–27.

47 Ibid., p. 34.

48 Ibid., p. 35.

49 Ibid.

50 Ibid., p. 37.

51 Ibid., Willshire is given a 'wife' (12–13), the 'Native name "Oleara" (12), he is the 'hunter' (16), given a 'skin' group, (19), participates in a ceremony (31), settles a tribal dispute (36), and arranges a 'marriage' (38).

52 Ibid., p. 31.

53 Ibid., p. 24.

54 Ibid., pp. 40–41.

55 Ibid., p. 43.

56 Ibid., p. 42.

57 Ibid., p. 41.

58 Ibid., pp. 44–45.

59 Ibid., p. 45.

9 Land of the Dawning, End of an Era

1 Police Station Timber Creek and predecessor Agency: 1894–1898, Police Station Gordon Creek (henceforth 'Timber Creek Police Journal'), 26 June 1894, NTAS F 302.

2 Willshire to Besley, 18 February 1887, SRSA GRG 5/2/1887/65.

3 Timber Creek Police Journal, 15 August 1894, NTAS F 302.

4 Ibid., 30 August 1894.

5 Ibid., 3 December 1894.

6 Government Resident Dashwood to Minister Controlling the Northern Territory, 4 December 1894, SRSA GRS 1/1/1894/408.

7 Willshire to Foelsche, 26 January 1895, SRSA GRS 1/1/1895/121.

8 Timber Creek Police Journal, 18 March 1895, NTAS 302.

9 Timber Creek Police Journal, 19 March 1895, NTAS 302.

10 Timber Creek Police Journal, 20 March 1895, NTAS 302.

11 Timber Creek Police Journal, 21 March 1895, NTAS 302.

12 Jock Makin, *The Big Run: The Story of Victoria River Downs Station*, Lansdowne, Sydney, 1970, p. 82.

13 Deborah Bird Rose, 'Aboriginal Life and Death in Australian Settler Nationhood', in *Aboriginal History*, vol. 25, 2001. p. 149.

14 Makin, p. 82.

15 Peter Monteath (ed.), *Diary of Emily Caroline Creaghe, Explorer*, Corkwood Press, Adelaide, 2005, Thursday 8 February 1883.

16 Timber Creek Police Journal, 8 July 1895, NTAS 302.

17 Ibid.

18 Inspector Foelsche to Minister Controlling the Northern Territory, 12 June 1895, SRSA GRS 1/1/1895/211.

19 Ibid., 20 June 1895.

20 Timber Creek Police Journal, 30 May 1895.

21 Memo from the Minister Controlling the Northern Territory (Pro Tem) to Chief Secretary, 8 May 1895, SRSA GRS 1/1/1895/211.

22 Ibid.

23 Timber Creek Police Journal, 8 July and 22–23 July, 1895, NTAS 302.

24 Timber Creek Police Journal, 27 July 1895, NTAS 302.

25 William Henry Willshire, 'Preface' in *Land of the Dawning*, W K Thomas & Co., Printers, Adelaide, 1896.

26 Willshire, 1896, p. 35.

27 Ibid., p. 35.

28 Ibid., p. 7.

29 Ibid., p. 13.

30 Ibid., p. 26.

31 Rosslyn Haynes, *Seeking the Centre: The Australian Desert in Literature, Art and Film*, Cambridge University Press, Cambridge, 1998, p. 112.

32 Henry Kendall, 'Leichhardt', in William Maddock (ed.) *Songs From The Mountains*, Sydney, 1880.

33 Willshire, 1896, p. 18.

34 Ibid., p. 30

35 Ibid., p. 78–79.

36 Ibid., p. 81.

37 Ibid., p. 48.

38 Ibid., p. 21.

39 Ibid., p. 34.

40 Ibid., p. 43.

41 Ibid., p. 34.

42 Ibid., p. 52–53.

43 Ibid., p. 26.

44 Ibid., p. 50.

45 Ibid., p. 48.

46 Ibid., p. 57.

47 Ibid., p. 66.

48 Ibid., pp. 66–67.

49 Ibid., p. 71.

50 Ibid., p. 20.

51 Minutes by Peterswald, 7 May 1895, SRSA GRS 1/1/1895/121.

52 Letterhead on letter dated 10 February 1896, SRSA GRS 1/1/1895/121.

10 Race and Nationalism in the Shadow of the Frontier

1 Besley to Saunders, 4 December 1895, SRSA GRG 5/2/1893/304.

2 Marriage of William Henry Willshire and Ellen Sarah Howell, 13 September 1896, Births, Deaths and Marriages Registration Office, Adelaide, no. 877.

3 Willshire to Reid, 4 December 1896, GRG 5/2/1896/203, SAM AA 309.

4 Cowell Police Station Journal, SRSA GRG 5/341, 1896–1904.

5 Austin Stapleton, *Willshire of Alice Springs*, Hesperian Press, Victoria Park, 1992, p. 42

6 H J Schmiechen, The Hermannsburg Missions Society in Australia
   1866–1895: Changing Missionary Attitudes and their Effects on the
   Aboriginal Inhabitants (BA Honours thesis), University of Adelaide, 1971,
   pp. 87–88.

7 Ibid., pp. 80–81.

8 Baldwin Spencer (ed.), *Report of the Work of the Horn Scientific Expedition
   to Central Australia*, Melville, Mullen and Slade, Melbourne, 1896,
   pp. 40–41.

9 Ibid., p. 111.

10 Ibid.

11 *Adelaide Observer*, 1 October 1898.

12 For instance, *Adelaide Observer*, 2 April, 17 September and
   1 October 1898.

13 *Adelaide Observer*, 2 April 1898.

14 D J Mulvaney and J H Calaby, *'So Much That Is New': A Biography
   1860–1929*, Melbourne University Press, Melbourne, 1985, pp. 167–173.

15 Ibid., p. 180.

16 *Adelaide Observer*, 8 September 1900.

17 Ibid.

18 Ibid., 15 September 1900.

19 Ibid., 6 October 1900.

20 Ibid., 13 October 1900, 2 and 23 March 1901.

21 *Adelaide Observer*, 1, 22, 27 and 29 June, 27 July, 3 August, 7 December 1901,
   8, 22 and 29 March 1902.

22 Ibid., 17 September 1898.

23 Willshire to Clode, n.d., SRSA GRG 5/2/1905/407.

24 Robert Foster, An Imaginary Dominion: The Representation and Treatment
   of Aborigines in South Australia, 1834–1911 (PhD thesis), University of
   Adelaide, 1993, pp. 325–326.

25 Ibid., pp. 326–332.

26 SRSA GRG 5/2/1907/287.

27 SRSA GRG 5/23, vol. 11.

28 An Act to make better provision for the better Protection and Control of the Aboriginal and Half-cast Inhabitants of the State of South Australia, no. 1048 of 1911, paras 12–23.

29 Ibid., para. 34.

30 *South Australian Parliamentary Debates*, 6 October 1910, p. 969.

31 *Report of the Protector of Aborigines for the Year Ending June 20, 1912*, p. 6.

32 Ibid., p. 7.

33 SRSA GRG 52/1/1911/21.

34 Robert Foster, '"endless trouble and agitation", Aboriginal Activism in the Protectionist Era', in *Journal of the Historical Society of South Australia*, no. 28, 2000, pp. 17–19.

35 Mark Horgon and Michael Sharkey, 'Vision Spendid or Sandy Blight?' in Ken Stewart (ed.), *1890s: Australian Literature and Literacy Culture*, University of Queensland Press, St Lucia, 1996, p. 69.

36 See for instance Kay Schaffer, *Women And The Bush: Forces Of Desire In The Australian Cultural Tradition*, Cambridge University Press, Melbourne, 1988; Susan Sheridan, *Along The Faultlines: Sex, Race And Nation In Australian Women's Writing 1880s–1930s*, Allen & Unwin, St Leonards, New South Wales, 1995.

37 Banjo Paterson, 'In Defence of the Bush', in *The Bulletin*, 23 July 1892.

38 William Henry Willshire, *Land of the Dawning*, W K Thomas & Co., Printers, Adelaide, 1896. p 72.

39 Willshire, 'Appendix'. 1896.

40 Willshire, 1896, p. 20.

41 *Adelaide Observer*, 11 April 1891.

42 Sir Henry Parkes, 'The Australian Flag', *Australian Readers*, Book IV, Macmillan, London, 1899.

43 Alan Powell, *Far Country: A Short History of the Northern Territory*, Melbourne University Press, Melbourne, 1982, pp. 179–180.

44 Andrew Marcus, *Governing Savages*, Allen & Unwin, Sydney, 1990, p. 136.

45 Ibid., p. 58.

46 Cited in Marcus, 1990, p. 47.

11 Epilogue

1 T G H Strehlow, *Journey to Horseshoe Bend*, Angus & Robertson, Sydney, 1969, p. 49.

2 'Pleasure Central' in *4X4 Australia*, March 2004, pp. 94–99.

3 *Adelaide Observer*, 5 September 1925, p. 45.

4 Some examples are Tony Austin, *Simply the Survival of the Fittest: Aboriginal Administration in South Australia's Northern Territory 1863–1910*, Historical Society of the Northern Territory, Darwin, 1992, p. 22; D J Mulvaney, *Encounters in Place: Outsiders and Aboriginal Australians 1606–1985*, University of Queensland Press, St Lucia, Queensland, 1989, p. 128; Richard Kimber, 'Genocide or Not? The Situation in Central Australia 1860–1895' in Colin Tatz (ed.), *Genocide Perspectives I: Essays in Comparative Genocide*, Centre for Comparative Genocide Studies, Sydney, 1997, pp. 41–64; Deborah Bird Rose, *Hidden Histories: Black Stories from Victoria River Downs, Humbert River and Wave Hill Stations*, Aboriginal Studies Press, Canberra, 1991; Deborah Bird Rose, 'Oral Histories and Knowledge' in B Attwood and S G Foster (eds), *Frontier Conflict: The Australian Experience*, National Museum of Australia, Canberra, 2003, p. 121; Nicolas Peterson, 'A Colonial Image: Penetrating the Reality of the Message', in *Australian Aboriginal Studies*, no. 2, 1989, pp. 59–62; Francesca Merlan, '"Making People Quiet" in the Pastoral North', in *Aboriginal History*, vol. 12, 1978, p. 83.

5 As one piece puts it, 'William Willshire is not much read today because the exultation with which he gloated over the slaughter of Aborigines would scarcely appeal to late 20th century readers' ('Territory Trooper Gloated over Butchery of Blacks', *Daily Mirror*, 20 June 1985, p. 32).

6 'Rebel Mountie Tried to Tame Frontier', *The Sydney Sun*, 5 February 1980, p. 38.

7 Austin Stapleton, *Willshire of Alice Springs*, Hesperion Press, Victoria Park, 1992, p. v.

8 Bill Wilson, 'The Establishment and Operations of the NT Native Police', in *Journal of Northern Territory History* 7, 1996, p. 71.

9 Ibid.

10 Note dated 1 October 1972, pasted inside the cover of the Far Northern Division Police Journal (Correspondence Files 1884–1890), SAPHS 000319.

11 James Warden, 'Making Peace with the Past: Remembering the Coniston Massacre 1928–2003', in *Aboriginal History*, vol. 27, 2003, pp. v–vi.

BIBLIOGRAPHY

Primary records
Northern Territory Archive Office (NTAS)

Police Station, Timber Creek (Commonwealth) and predecessor Agency:
1894–1898, Police Station, Gordon Creek, F 302.

Alice Springs police station, Police Journals, Officer in Charge,
1886–1889, F 255.

State Records of South Australia (SRSA)

Aborigines Department, Protector's Letter Book, State Records,
GRG 52/7.

Attorney-General's Office, Correspondence Files, GRG 1/2.

Chief Secretary's Office, Letters Received, GRG 24/6.

Depositions taken at the preliminary hearing before F J Gillen.
GRG 52/92.

Minister of Education and Minister Controlling the Northern Territory,
Correspondence Files, GRS 1/1.

Minister of Education and Minister Controlling the Northern Territory,
Index to Correspondence, GRS 1/3.

Police Commissioner's Office, Correspondence Files, GRG 5/2.

Police Commissioner's Office, Record of Conduct, vol. 2. GRG 5/18.

Police Commissioner's Office, Register of ex-members of the SA Police
Force, 1838–1920, GRG 5/23.

South Australian Police Gazette, GRG 5/50/1891.

Register of Prisoners, Port Augusta Gaol, vol. 1, GRG 54/197.

South Australian Police Historical Society (SAPHS)

Far Northern Police Division Journal (Correspondence Files 1884–1890),
000319.

Papers 00319 Loc 2-2/43 (Cool 87).

Police Commissioner's Office, Correspondence Files, filed as
COP 001385 and COP 304/1893.

South Australian Museum (SAM)

4 December 1896. SAM AA 309.

Library of the Supreme Court of South Australia

Mr Justice Bundey, Circuit Court Notebook, no. 3, 16 July 1889–
24 July 1891.

Births Deaths and Marriages, Registration Office, Adelaide.

William Henry Willshire's certificates of Birth, Death and Marriage.

Parliamentary records

South Australian Parliamentary Papers (SAPP)

Report of Messrs. Swan and Taplin on their visit to Finke, &c., Mission
Stations, 30 September 1890, *SAPP*, no. 148. pp. 1–3.

Parsons, Report for the Quarter ending December 1884, *SAPP* no. 53
of 1885.

Report of the Pastoral Lands Commission together with Minutes of
Proceedings, Evidence, and Appendices, no. 33 of 1891.

Report of the Protector of Aborigines for the Year Ending June 20, 1912, p. 6.

Acts of Parliament

An Act to make better provision for the better Protection and Control of the Aboriginal and Half-cast Inhabitants of the State of South Australia, no. 1048 of 1911.

Newspapers and magazines

Adelaide *Advertiser*

Adelaide Observer

Port Augusta Dispatch

South Australian Register

Sydney Sun

Adelaide *Bulletin and Lantern*

Lantern

Melbourne *Age*

NT Times & Gazette

4X4 Australia

Quiz

Books and articles

Austin, Tony, *Simply the Survival of the Fittest: Aboriginal Administration in South Australia's Northern Territory 1863–1910*, Historical Society of the Northern Territory, Darwin, 1992.

Barnes, J A, 'Anthropology in Britain Before and After Darwin', in *Mankind*, vol. V, no. 9, 1960.

Benstead, William, Short Stories of my Life and Travels (typescript), private collection, n.d.

Bowler, Peter J, *The Non-Darwinian Revolution: Reinterpreting a Historical Myth*, John Hopkins, Baltimore, 1988.

Brauer, F H, 'The Coming of European Man', in Gillian Cook (ed.), *Man in the Centre*, Commonwealth Scientific and Industrial Research Organisation (CSIRO), Western Australia, Perth, 1983.

Burridge, K, *Encountering Aborigines. A Case Study: Anthropology and the Australian Aboriginal*, London, 1973.

Castilla, Ethel, *The Australian Girl and Other Verses*, George Robertson & Co., Melbourne, 1900.

Clyne, R, *Colonial Blue: A History of the South Australian Police Force 1836–1916*, Wakefield Press, Netley, South Australia, 1987.

Connor, John, *The Australian Frontier Wars*, University of New South Wales Press, Sydney, 2002.

Dixon, Robert, *Writing the Colonial Adventure*, Cambridge University Press, Melbourne, 1992.

Elkin, A P, 'The Development of Scientific Knowledge of the Aborigines', in H Shiels (ed.), *Australian Aboriginal Studies*, 1963.

Foelsche, P, 'Notes on the Aborigines of North Australia', in *Transactions of the Royal Society of South Australia*, vol. 5, 1882.

Foster, Robert, An Imaginary Dominion: The Representation and Treatment of Aborigines in South Australia, 1834–1911 (PhD thesis), University of Adelaide, 1993.

Foster, Robert, 'Logic's Unexpected Celebrity', in J Simpson and L Hercus (eds), *History in Portraits: Biographies of Nineteenth Century South Australian Aboriginal People*, Aboriginal History Monograph 6, Aboriginal History Inc., Canberra, 1998.

Foster, Robert, '"endless trouble and agitation": Aboriginal Activism in the Protectionist Era', in *Journal of the Historical Society of South Australia*, no. 28, 2000.

Frazer, J G, 'Notes on the Aborigines of Australia. Answers to Questions on the Manners, Customs, Religions, Superstitions, &c, of Uncivilised or Semi-civilised Peoples', in *Royal Anthropological Institute Journal*, 1895, vol. 24.

Gason, Samuel, *The Dieyerie Tribe of Australian Aborigines*, W C Cox, Government Printer, Adelaide, 1874.

Gason, Samuel, 'The Manners and Customs of the Dieyerie Tribe of Australian Aborigines', reproduced in J D Woods (ed.) *The Native Tribes of South Australia*, E S Wigg & Son, Adelaide, 1879, facsimile edition produced by the Friends of the State Library of South Australia, Adelaide, 1997.

Giles, Ernest, *Australia Twice Traversed: The Romance of Exploration, being a Narrative Complied from the Journals of Five Exploring Expeditions into and through Central South Australia, and Western Australia, From 1872 to 1876*, 2 vols, Sampson Low, Marston, Searle & Rivington, London, 1889.

Gill, Sam D, *Storytracking: Texts, Stories, and Histories in Central Australia*, Oxford University Press, New York, 1998.

Gillen, F J, 'The Natives of Central Australia', in *Royal Anthropological Institute Journal*, vol. 24, 1898.

Gillen, R S (ed.), *F. J. Gillen's First Diary 1875*, Wakefield Press, Netley, 1995.

Grey, Jeffrey, *A Military History of Australia*, Cambridge University Press, Melbourne, 1999.

Griffiths, Tom, 'The Social and Intellectual Context of the 1890s' in S Morton and D Mulvaney (eds), *Exploring Central Australia: Society, the Environment and the 1894 Horn Expedition*, Surrey Beatty & Sons, Chipping Norton, 1996.

Harris, J, *One Blood. 200 Years of Aboriginal Encounter with Christianity: A Story of Hope*, Albatross Books, Sutherland, New South Wales, 1990.

Hartwig, M C, 'The Progress of White Settlement in the Alice Springs District and its Effects upon the Aboriginal Inhabitants 1860–1894 (PhD dissertation), University of Adelaide, 1965.

Haynes, Rosslyn, *Seeking the Centre: The Australian Desert in Literature, Art and Film*, Cambridge University Press, Cambridge, 1998.

Headrick, Daniel, *The Tools of Empire: Technology and European Imperialism in the Nineteenth Century*, Oxford University Press, New York and Oxford, 1981.

Hirst, John, *The Sentimental Nation: The Making of the Australian Commonwealth*, Oxford University Press, Melbourne, 2000.

Horgon, Mark and Sharkey, Michael, 'Vision Spendid or Sandy Blight?' in Ken Stewart (ed.), *1890s: Australian Literature and Literacy Culture*, University of Queensland Press, St Lucia, 1996.

Jones, Philip, 'Objects of Mystery and Concealment: A History of Tjurunga Collection', in *Oceania Monograph* 45, 1995.

Jones, Philip, 'Preface' in J D Woods (ed.), *The Native Tribes of South Australia*, 1879; reprint, State Library, Adelaide, 1997.

Kempe, H, 'A Grammar and Vocabulary of the Language Spoken by the Aborigines of the Macdonnell Ranges', in *Transactions of the Royal Society of South Australia*, vol. 14, 1891.

Kendall, Henry, 'Leichhardt', in William Maddock (ed.), *Songs From The Mountains*, Sydney, 1880.

Kimber, Richard, 'Genocide or Not? The Situation in Central Australia 1860–1895' in Colin Tatz (ed.), *Genocide Perspectives I: Essays in Comparative Genocide*, Centre for Comparative Genocide Studies, Sydney, 1997.

Koch, Grace, *Kaytetye Country: An Aboriginal History of the Barrow Creek Area*, Institute of Aboriginal Development, Alice Springs, 1993.

Makin, Jock, *The Big Run: The Story of Victoria River Downs Station*, Lansdowne, Sydney, 1970.

Marcus, Andrew, *Governing Savages*, Allen & Unwin, Sydney, 1990.

Merlan, Francesca, '"Making People Quiet" in the Pastoral North', in *Aboriginal History*, vol. 12, 1978.

Molony, John, *The Native-Born: The First White Australians*, Melbourne University Press, Melbourne, 2000.

Monteath, Peter (ed.), *Diary of Emily Caroline Creaghe, Explore*, Corkwood Press, Adelaide, 2005.

Morris, Barry, 'Frontier Colonialism as a Culture of Terror', in B Attwood and J Arnold (eds), *Power, Knowledge and Aborigines*, La Trobe University Press and National Centre for Australian Studies, Bundoora, Victoria, 1992.

Mulvaney, D J and Calaby, J H, *'So Much That Is New': A Biography 1860–1929*, Melbourne University Press, Melbourne, 1985.

Mulvaney, D J, *Encounters in Place: Outsiders and Aboriginal Australians 1606–1985*, University of Queensland Press, St Lucia, 1989.

Mulvaney, D J, Morphy, H and A Petch, *'My Dear Spencer': The Letters of F J Gillen to Baldwin Spencer*, Hyland House, Melbourne, 1997.

Palmer, Alison, *Colonial Genocide*, Crawford House Publishing, Adelaide, 2000.

Parkes, Sir Henry, 'The Australian Flag', in *Australian Readers*, Book IV, Macmillan, London, 1899.

Paterson, Banjo, 'In Defence of the Bush', in *The Bulletin*, 23 July 1892.

Peterson, Nicolas, 'A Colonial Image: Penetrating the Reality of the Message', in *Australian Aboriginal Studies*, no. 2, 1989.

Powell, Alan, *Far Country: A Short History of the Northern Territory*, Melbourne University Press, Melbourne, 1982.

Reid, Gordon, *A Picnic with the Natives: Aboriginal-European Relations in the Northern Territory to 1910*, Melbourne University Press, Melbourne, 1990.

Rose, Deborah Bird, *Hidden Histories: Black Stories from Victoria River Downs, Humbert River and Wave Hill Stations*, Aboriginal Studies Press, Canberra, 1991.

Rose, Deborah Bird, 'Oral Histories and Knowledge' in B Attwood and S G Foster (eds), *Frontier Conflict: The Australian Experience*, National Museum of Australia, Canberra, 2003.

Rose, Deborah Bird, 'Aboriginal Life and Death in Australian Settler Nationhood', in *Aboriginal History*, vol. 25, 2001.

Rose, Deborah Bird, 'Hard Times: An Australian Story' in Klaus
    Newmann et al (eds), *Quicksands: Foundational Histories in Australia
    and Aotearoa New Zealand*, University of New South Wales Press,
    Sydney, 1999.

Schaffer, Kay, *Women And The Bush: Forces Of Desire In The Australian
    Cultural Tradition*, Cambridge University Press, Melbourne, 1988.

Schmiechen, H J, The Hermannsburg Missions Society in Australia
    1866–1895: Changing Missionary Attitudes and their Effects on the
    Aboriginal Inhabitants, (BA Honours thesis), University of Adelaide,
    1971.

Shepherd, Shirley, 'The Significance of the Overland Telegraph Line', in
    Journal of Northern Territory History, vol. 7, 1996.

Sheridan, Susan, *Along The Faultlines: Sex, Race And Nation In Australian
    Women's Writing 1880s–1930s*, Allen & Unwin, St Leonards, New
    South Wales, 1995.

Shulze, Louis, 'The Aborigines of the Upper and Middle Finke River',
    in *Transactions of the Royal Society of South Australia*, vol. 14, 1891.

Smith, M A, *Peopling the Cleland Hills: Aboriginal History in Western
    Central Australia 1850–1890*, Aboriginal History Monograph 12,
    Aboriginal History Inc., Canberra, 2005.

Spencer, Baldwin (ed.), *Report of the Work of the Horn Scientific
    Expedition to Central Australia*, Melville, Mullen and Slade, Melbourne,
    1896.

Stapleton, Austin, *Willshire of Alice Springs*, Hesperian Press, Victoria
    Park, 1992.

Strehlow, T G H, *Journey to Horseshoe Bend*, Angus & Robertson,
    Sydney, 1969.

Stuart, John McDouall, *Explorations in Australia: The Journals of John
    McDouall Stuart*, Saunders, Otley & Co., London, 1865.

Thomas, Nicholas, 'Home Décor and Dance: The Abstraction of Aboriginality' in Rebecca Coates and Howard Morphy (eds), *In Place (Out of Time): Contemporary Art in Australia*, Museum of Modern Art, Oxford, 1997.

Tylor, E B, *Primitive Culture*, London, 1871.

Wake, C S, 'The Mental Characteristics of Primitive Man, as Exemplified by the Australian Aborigines', in *Journal of the Anthropological Institute of Great Britain and Ireland*, 1872.

Ward, Russel, *The Australian Legend*, Oxford University Press, Melbourne, 1987.

Warden, James, 'Making Peace with the Past: Remembering the Coniston Massacre 1928–2003', in *Aboriginal History*, vol. 27, 2003.

White, R, *Inventing Australia: Images and Identity 1688–1980*, Allen & Unwin, Sydney, 1981.

Willshire, William Henry, *The Aborigines of Central Australia*, Drysdale Printer, Port Augusta, 1888; reprint, C E Bristow, Government Printer, Adelaide, 1891.

Willshire, William Henry, *A Thrilling Tale of Real Life in the Wilds of Australia*, Freason & Brother, Printers, Adelaide, 1895.

Willshire, William Henry, *Land of the Dawning*, W K Thomas & Co., Printers, Adelaide, 1896.

Wilson, Bill, 'The Establishment and Operations of the NT Native Police', in *Journal of Northern Territory History* 7, 1996.

Woods J D (ed.), *The Native Tribes of South Australia*, 1879; reprint, State Library, Adelaide, 1997.

ACKNOWLEDGEMENTS

This is a project that has been in gestation for a very long time and the authors would like to express their appreciation to the many people and organisations who helped along the way. Firstly we would like to thank Mandy Paul for assistance with research on the project, and we much appreciate the University Research Grant that funded that research. We are also indebted to the Faculty of Humanities and Social Sciences at the University of Adelaide for awarding us the Fred Johns Scholarship for biography that funded an invaluable field-trip to Central Australia and a research trip to Canberra. The staff at the Australian Institute of Aboriginal and Torres Strait Islander Studies in Canberra were extraordinarily generous with their time and support. We would like to thank Daryl Lewis for providing us with his transcription of Willshire's 'Timber Creek Police Journal', and to Françoise Barr, of the Northern Territory Archives Service, for answering our inquiries about this volume and for expeditiously providing us with digital copies of selected sections. Thanks to Simon Whiley for providing us with some of his Willshire files. Many thanks to the staff at State Records of South Australia who, late in the process, patiently answered our requests and slaved tirelessly over the photocopier. We also appreciate the assistance of the Museum of Victoria and the South Australian Museum. Thanks also to the volunteers at the South

Australian Police Historical Society who provided generous assistance. Important thanks go to our colleagues in the Disciplines of English and History who in various seminars and corridors heard us thinking aloud and offered us generous and substantial feedback. Finally, we would like to thank Dick Kimber for his generous suggestions and for reading the final draft of the manuscript, and Michael Bollen of Wakefield Press for his support of the project and editorial advice.

INDEX

www.ingramcontent.com/pod-product-compliance
Lightning Source LLC
Chambersburg PA
CBHW032347280326
41935CB00008B/480